THE UNITED STATES SINCE 1980

This book describes the sharp right turn the United States has taken following the election of Ronald Reagan as president in 1980. It details how the policies pursued by the Reagan administration were a break from the policies pursued by prior administrations and the policies pursued in other wealthy countries. The Reagan administration policies had the effect of redistributing both before- and after-tax income upward, creating a situation in which the bulk of the economic gains over the last quarter century were directed to a small segment of the population. The analysis explains how both political parties have come largely to accept the main tenets of Reaganism, putting the United States on a path that is at odds with most of the rest of the world and furthermore is not sustainable. The book also describes the major developments in U.S. foreign policy, politics, and society over the last quarter century.

Dean Baker is the cofounder of the Center for Economic and Policy Research in Washington, DC. Before founding the center, he was a senior economist at Washington's Economic Policy Institute. He has authored or edited several books, including *The Conservative Nanny State: How the Wealthy Use the Government to Stay Rich and Get Richer* (2006); *Social Security: The Phony Crisis* (1999, with Mark Weisbrot); *Getting Prices Right: The Debate over the Consumer Price Index*, which won a Choice book award as one of the outstanding academic books of 1998; and *Globalization and Progressive Economic Policy* (Cambridge University Press, 1998, coedited with Jerry Epstein and Bob Pollin). Dr. Baker has also written for a variety of professional and general audience publications. His work on economic policy issues is often cited in the media, and he is frequently interviewed on television and radio. Dr. Baker has also testified a number of times before congressional committees. He received his PhD in economics from the University of Michigan.

THE WORLD SINCE 1980

This new series is designed to examine politics, economics, and social change in important countries and regions over the past two and a half decades. No prior background knowledge of a given country will be required by readers. The books are written by leading social scientists.

Volumes published

Brazil Since 1980; Francisco Vidal Luna and Herbert S. Klein
The United States Since 1980; Dean Baker

Volumes in preparation

Britain Since 1980; Roger Middleton
France Since 1980; Timothy Smith
India Since 1980; Sumit Ganguly
Israel Since 1980; Guy Ben-Porat, Schlomo Mizrachi, Ayre Naor, and
    Erez Tzfadia
Japan Since 1980; Thomas Cargill and Takayuki Sakamoto
Mexico Since 1980; Stephen Haber, Herbert S. Klein, Noel Maurer, and
    Kevin J. Middlebrook
Russia Since 1980; Steven Rosefielde and Stefan Hedlund

THE UNITED STATES
SINCE 1980

Dean Baker

Center for Economic and Policy Research, Washington, DC

CAMBRIDGE
UNIVERSITY PRESS

CAMBRIDGE UNIVERSITY PRESS
Cambridge, New York, Melbourne, Madrid, Cape Town, Singapore, São Paulo

Cambridge University Press
32 Avenue of the Americas, New York, NY 10013-2473, USA

www.cambridge.org
Information on this title: www.cambridge.org/9780521860178

First published 2007

Printed in the United States of America

A catalog record for this publication is available from the British Library.

Library of Congress Cataloging in Publication Data

Baker, Dean, 1958–
The United States since 1980 / Dean Baker.
  p.   cm. – (The world since 1980)
Includes bibliographical references and index.
ISBN-13: 978-0-521-86017-8 (hardback)
ISBN-10: 0-521-86017-2 (hardback)
ISBN-13: 978-0-521-67755-4 (pbk.)
ISBN-10: 0-521-67755-6 (pbk.)
1. United States – Politics and government – 1981–1989.   2. United States – Politics and
government – 1989–   3. Reagan, Ronald – Influence.   4. Reagan, Ronald – Political and
social views.   5. Conservatism – United States.   6. United States – Economic policy.
7. United States – Social conditions – 1980–   I. Title.   II. Series.
E876.B35   2007
973.92 – dc22   2006026344

ISBN   978-0-521-86017-8 hardback

ISBN   978-0-521-67755-4 paperback

Contents

List of Figures and Tables

Preface

Writing a history inevitably involves a long sequence of judgments by the author. From an infinite series of events, the author must decide which ones are important and how they should be tied together. The author must also decide how the events actually transpired, based on his or her assessment of which accounts are accurate and which ones should be largely dismissed.

Needless to say, I have made many such decisions in writing this book. The introduction should leave little doubt as to what I consider the key thread running through the history of the United States over the last quarter century. Beginning with the Reagan administration, the United States took a sharp turn away from a path that it had followed in the post–World War II era. Prior to the election of Ronald Reagan, the United States could be seen as following the welfare states of Western Europe in building up a set of institutional supports that ensured most of the population a decent standard of living. These supports included government programs that guaranteed families minimum levels of income, health care, and other basic needs. However, even more important was the shaping of the market in ways that ensured that most of the workforce would benefit from economy-wide increases in productivity.

This pattern was reversed following the election of Ronald Reagan in 1980. The Reagan administration weakened or eliminated government programs intended to provide income security. More important, the Reagan administration also changed the structure of the market in ways that disadvantaged the bulk of the country's workforce. The result was that most workers have seen very little benefit from the huge gains in productivity in the United States over the last quarter century.

This is a sharp departure from the path followed in Europe and indeed by almost every other wealthy country. While the structure of the welfare state continues to be hotly contested across the industrialized world, the institutional structure that ensured that the gains from productivity growth would be broadly shared remains largely intact outside of the United States.

The fact that this theme does not completely permeate every chapter is the result of a conscious decision. The basic thesis has been placed on the table at the beginning. Many readers may opt to take a different perspective on the events of the last quarter century. If the book does not rule out that option, I will not consider it to be a failure.

Acknowledgments

Many people helped in the writing of this book by suggesting source material, discussing aspects of the period covered, or commenting on earlier drafts. In particular, my colleagues at the Center for Economic and Policy Research, Mark Weisbrot, Heather Boushey, John Schmitt, David Rosnick, Diane Schwartz, and Lynn Erskine, were extremely helpful. Helene Jorgensen gave me very detailed feedback on the entire manuscript. Nihar Bhatt and Kathryn Bogel did helpful copyediting in addition to assisting with some of the research. Most important, I thank Helene, Walnut, and Fulton for being so tolerant of my neglect as I took the time necessary to write this book.

1

Turning Away: The United States Breaks Ranks

In November 2001, the representatives of more than 140 countries signed the Kyoto Protocol to the United Nations Framework Convention on Climate Change. The pact was intended to be a first step in combating global warming, a phenomenon that scientists were nearly universal in regarding as a major environmental threat.

The set of countries signing the agreement included every country in the European Union, Japan, Russia, China, and Canada, and almost every country in Latin America. The United States was not among this group. President Bush had earlier announced that he viewed the Kyoto process as fundamentally flawed and that the United States would not participate in further negotiations toward an agreement, except as an observer. In other words, as the rest of the world felt the need to confront a major environmental threat, the United States was sitting on the sidelines watching.

This sort of split could not have taken place in 1980. At that time, the United States was tightly intertwined in its cold war alliance. This meant both that the other countries within this alliance deferred to the leadership of the United States on major international issues and that the United States was committed to addressing important concerns that arose within this alliance. It would have been difficult to imagine an issue taking on the same importance across the industrialized world in the seventies, as global warming did in the nineties, only to be largely ignored by the U.S. government. The split on the Kyoto agreement and global warming was emblematic of how far the United States had moved from the other Western democracies in the years since 1980.

By 2005, global warming was not the only issue on which the United States found itself at odds with its traditional allies. The 2003 invasion of Iraq involved a break with many post–World War II allies, most importantly France, Germany, and Canada. In trying to push a hemisphere-wide trade agreement, the Bush administration finds itself confronting a brick wall of opposition in Argentina and Brazil, the two biggest economic powers in South America. In addition, there are a large number of international pacts regarding issues from the punishment of war crimes to restrictions on tax havens that are moving forward without the participation of the United States. Although the United States remained the world's preeminent military and economic power in 2005, it was increasingly isolated in international affairs, taking positions that many of its traditional allies found unacceptable.

Part of this divergence between the United States and the other wealthy countries undoubtedly reflects increasing assertiveness on the part of the other industrialized nations, especially the European countries that operate in an increasingly powerful European Union and no longer have any fears of the Soviet Union. But part of the divergence also reflects a lack of concern on the part of the United States. In 2005, the U.S. government did not feel the need to achieve some degree of consensus among its allies on major international issues. It was content to act unilaterally in ways that would have been hard to envision a quarter century earlier.

The changing international position of the United States reflects a changed domestic situation. The United States had a very different process of development and growth that always set it somewhat apart from Japan and Europe. However, the differences between the United States and the rest of the industrialized world in 1980 were far smaller than they are today by a wide variety of measures. In the period since the Great Depression, the United States had developed a welfare state that was less generous than the average across Europe but not qualitatively different. Like the European welfare states, the United States had a nearly universal system of retirement benefits. It had a national system of unemployment insurance for workers who had lost their jobs and a system of income support (welfare) that provided the basic necessities for the poorest families.

Furthermore, the United States still appeared to be moving in the direction of further expansion of the welfare state at the time. The Medicare program, which extended health care insurance to the elderly, and the Medicaid program, which provided health care to the poor of all ages, were important new welfare state protections added in the sixties – still the relatively recent past in 1980. For many, it seemed only a matter of time before the United States followed the path of the other wealthy countries in providing health care insurance to its entire population. Similarly, the Head Start program, established in the sixties, was a major extension of the state's obligation to provide child care and early childhood education, although only for a segment of lower-income children. Still, it was reasonable to believe in 1980 that this benefit would be extended to larger segments of the population in the years ahead.

This was not the course the country followed over the next quarter century. While there were still extensions of the welfare state in some areas, an explicit goal of much public policy in this period was to limit the expansion of the welfare state and in many cases to roll back prior gains. And this policy shift did not apply only to government social welfare programs. There was a larger agenda to tilt the playing field in ways that favored those at the top end of the income distribution.

During this quarter century, there were several successful national political campaigns around the themes of reducing tax rates for high-income families and cutting government benefits for low-income families. While these changes received the most attention, they were actually just a subset of a larger shift in government policies that had the effect of benefiting those at the top of the income distribution at the expense of those in the middle and at the bottom. This larger policy shift included areas such as trade policy, rules governing labor-management relations, and the deregulation of several key industries. The change in the ground rules affecting the market distribution of income has had a much greater impact on the country than the change in tax and transfer policy. It is essential to have a clear understanding of the change in these ground rules in order to appreciate the ways in which the United States was a different country in 2005 than in 1980.

Changing the Ground Rules and Tilting the Field

The years following 1980 saw changes in a whole set of economic policies, all of which had the effect of redistributing before-tax income upward. The policy areas include trade policy, immigration policy, rules governing labor-management relations, macroeconomic policy, deregulation of major industries, and the minimum wage. In each of these areas, the government adopted policies during this period that had the effect of weakening the bargaining power of workers in the middle and at the bottom of the wage distribution, thereby improving the relative situation of those at the top. The cumulative effect of the new policies was a massive upward redistribution of income. The share of national income that went to the richest 5 percent of families rose by more than one-third over this period.[1] The share of income going to the poorest 20 percent of the population fell by more than 25 percent.

Although the stated rationale for these policies was to increase economic efficiency (not to redistribute income upward), whether in fact they accomplished this outcome is in many cases debatable. It is worth noting that the economy did not perform exceptionally well during this period. The overall growth in gross domestic product (GDP) averaged 3.1 percent annually, compared to 3.7 percent in the period following World War II prior to 1980.[2] Productivity growth – the increase in output per hour of work, which is arguably the more meaningful measure – was also slower in the years from 1980 to 2005, rising at an average annual rate of 2.1 percent, compared to a 2.4 percent annual rate in the years from the end of World War II up to 1980.[3] While it can be argued that the economy would have done even more poorly without the shift in economic policy over this period, clearly this was not a period of exceptional economic growth overall.

It is also important to note that some policies that would have fostered growth but redistributed income downward were not pursued. This is most clearly the case with trade and immigration policy, where workers in higher-paying occupations, such as doctors and lawyers, were largely protected from international competition, but there are

[1] L. Mishel, J. Bernstein, and S. Allegretto, *The State of Working America 2004/2005* (Ithaca, NY: Cornell University Press, 2005), table 1.12.

[2] Bureau of Economic Analysis, *2005 Annual Revision of the National Income and Product Accounts* (Washington, DC: U.S. Government Printing Office, 2005), table 1.1.6 (Real Gross Domestic Product, Chained Dollars).

[3] These numbers are taken from the Bureau of Labor Statistics (BLS) measure of productivity in the nonfarm business sector. It understates the falloff in productivity growth in one important dimension. In the last quarter century, unlike the years from 1947 to 1980, a growing share of GDP has been used to replace obsolete equipment as an increasing portion of investment is devoted to short-lived computers and software. While the replacement of obsolete capital is essential for the economy, it provides no direct benefit in the form of increased living standards. The share of depreciation in output has increased at the rate of approximately 0.3 percentage points annually, which means that a net measure of productivity growth over the last quarter century would be approximately 0.3 percentage points lower than the 2.1 percent figure indicated by the BLS data. This means that there has been, on a net basis, a 0.6 percentage point decline in annual productivity growth, which has gone from 2.4 percent to 1.8 percent in the years since 1980.

other examples as well. (The mechanisms put in place during this period to redistribute income upward are discussed in more detail in the appendix to this chapter.)

In short, the government implemented a series of policies during this period that had the effect of shifting wage income upward. This was a predictable result of policies that placed downward pressure on the wages of a large segment of the labor force. These polices removed protections of various types for workers in the bottom three-quarters of the labor force and subjected these workers to increased international competition. While these policies were generally justified as increasing economic efficiency, no comparable drives for economic efficiency were directed toward the protections that benefited higher-income workers. This one-sided application of market forces had the effect of redistributing income from those who lost protection to those who were able to maintain it.

As a result, for most of the population of the United States, the quarter century from 1980 to 2005 was an era in which they became far less secure economically,[4] and the decrease in security affected their lives and their political attitudes. It is important to realize that this decrease was the result of conscious policy, not the accidental workings of the market.

The United States and the Other Rich Countries: 1980 and 2005

The combination of the upward redistribution of market income and the curtailing of government redistribution policies had the effect of making the United States look increasing different from the rest of the industrialized world by a wide variety of measures. Of course, the United States was not entirely alone in pursuing policies that redistributed income upward over this period. The political leadership in many other countries, most notably the United Kingdom under Prime Minister Margaret Thatcher, also sought to pursue policies that redistributed income upward. However, the opposition to such policies

---

[4] See J. Hacker, *The Great Risk Shift: The New Economic Insecurity and What Can Be Done About It* (Oxford: Oxford University Press, 2005), for a fuller analysis of the mechanisms that have increased economic insecurity for large segments of the U.S. population.

Table 1–1. *Trends in wage inequality (ratio of 90th percentile wage to 10th percentile wage)*

	1980–4	1995–9
Australia	2.9	3.1**
Austria	3.5	3.6***
Belgium	2.4*	2.3***
Denmark	2.2	2.2
Finland	2.5	2.4
France	3.2	3.1
Germany	2.9	2.9
Italy	2.3*	2.4
Japan	3.1	3.0
Netherlands	2.5	2.9
New Zealand	2.9	3.3
Sweden	2.0	2.3**
United Kingdom	3.1	3.4**
United States	3.9	4.6**
All non-U.S.	2.7	2.8

* Data from 1985–9.
** Data from 2000–1.
*** Data from 1990–4.
Source: Organisation for Economic Co-operation and Development, *OECD Employment Outlook 2004*, table 3.2.

was generally more effective elsewhere than in the United States. As a result, the upward redistribution of income in the United States was sharper and the associated effects more deeply felt than was the case with most other countries.

Trends in Wage Inequality

Table 1–1 presents a simple measure of wage inequality for the United States and several other wealthy countries over the last quarter century. The table shows the ratios of weekly earnings (pretax) of full-time workers at the 90th percentile of wage earners to the earnings of workers at the 10th percentile. A worker at the 90th percentile is near the top of the wage distribution, with 90 percent of all workers earning less and only 10 percent of all workers earning a higher wage. By contrast, a worker at the 10th percentile is near the bottom of the wage distribution, earning less than 90 percent of all workers and more than just 10 percent. Therefore, this ratio is a good summary measure of the extent of wage inequality in an economy.

As can be seen, at the start of the period the United States had the most unequal wage distribution of any of the countries listed. The ratio of 3.9 to 1 means that a worker at the 90th percentile of the wage distribution earned 3.9 times more than a worker at the 10th percentile of the wage distribution. In other words, if a worker at the 10th percentile of the wage distribution earned $7.00 an hour in 1980 (which was approximately the wage for such a worker in 1980, measured in 2005 dollars), then a worker at the 90th percentile would have earned 3.9 times more, or $27.30. The next highest ratio is 3.5 to 1 (the ratio for Austria). Most of the countries in the table had a ratio of less than 3 to 1, with the non-U.S. average being 2.7 to 1.[5]

Although the United States started this period with a much more unequal distribution of wage income than other wealthy countries, its wage distribution became far more unequal in this period, whereas there was little change in the degree of inequality in other countries. By 2001, the ratio of the wage income for workers at the 90th percentile to the wage income of workers at the 10th percentile had risen to 4.6 to 1. This means that if a worker at the 10th percentile of the wage distribution earned $10,000 a year in 2001, then a worker at the 90th percentile earned $46,000.

This rise in wage inequality in the United States over this period pulled it further away from other wealthy countries. There was no consistent pattern in the trends for wage inequality in other countries, with the ratio for other countries rising by an average of just 0.1 percent. Some countries, like New Zealand and the United Kingdom, did experience a noticeable rise in wage inequality, but in other countries there was little change. Some countries, such as France and Japan, even had a small decline in wage inequality. No country had an increase in wage inequality as large as that in the United States.

In fact, Table 1–1 probably understates the extent of the divergence in wage inequality between the United States and other wealthy countries, since the income of workers even further up the wage distribution

---

[5] This is an unweighted average for the non-U.S. countries. This means that the number for a small country such as Denmark or Austria has the same importance as the number for a large country such as Italy or Germany.

rose more rapidly than it did for workers at the 90th percentile. From 1979 to 2003, the real average hourly wage for a worker at the 95th percentile rose by 31.1 percent, compared to an increase of 27.2 percent for a worker at the 90th percentile.[6] While there are no comparable data available for workers higher up the wage distribution in other countries, these data imply that a fuller measure of wage inequality may show even more of a divergence between the Unites States and other countries during this period.

Unionization Rates

Unions have always been much weaker in the United States than in the rest of the industrialized world, but the gap in union power increased substantially in the quarter century from 1980 to 2005. In other wealthy countries, unions continued to be central actors in the economy, representing a majority of the workforce in most countries. Other governments did try to diminish the power of unions over this period, but few were anywhere near as successful in this effort as the United States.

Table 1–2 shows the percentage of employees in several wealthy countries who were covered by collective bargaining agreements in 1980 and 2000.[7] The table shows that the United States ranked near the bottom in the percentage of workers covered by a union contract in 1980, edging out Japan by a percentage point. In the twenty years from 1980 to 2000, the percentage of workers covered by a collective bargaining agreement was nearly halved, falling from 26 percent in 1980 to just 14 percent in 2000. Most of other wealthy countries saw little change, with several European countries actually seeing some increase in coverage rates. (The big exceptions to this trend were New Zealand and the United Kingdom, both of which experienced sharp declines in their coverage rates.) By 2000, the United States had fallen

---

[6]   Mishel et al., *State of Working America 2004/2005*, table 1.6.
[7]   In the United States, there are very few workers who are not union members but who are covered by a collective bargaining agreement. However, in other wealthy countries, a very large segment of the workforce may fall in this category. This is due to the fact that in many countries a union contract can apply to a whole industry, even firms whose workers are not actually members of the union that negotiated the agreement. For this reason, it is more accurate to use the percentage of workers covered by a collective bargaining agreement rather than the percentage who are members of a union as a measure of union power.

Table 1–2. *Trends in collective bargaining coverage: percentage of workers covered by a collective bargaining agreement*

	1980	2000
Australia	80	80
Austria	95	95
Belgium	90	90
Canada	37	32
Denmark	70	80
Finland	90	90
France	80	90
Germany	80	68
Italy	80	80
Japan	25	15
Netherlands	70	80
New Zealand	60	25
Norway	70	70
Sweden	80	90
United Kingdom	70	30
United States	26	14
All non-U.S.	71.8	67.7

Source: Organisation for Economic Co-operation and Development, *OECD Employment Outlook 2004*, table 3.3.

below Japan in its union coverage rate and was even further below the average coverage rate for the other wealthy countries, which had changed little over this twenty-year period.

There is an important aspect to union coverage in the United States that is worth noting in the context of the sharp decline in coverage rates shown in the table. Unlike in most countries, in the United States most workers have "employment at will" contracts, meaning that they can be fired at any time by their employer without any cause.[8] The major exceptions are public sector workers, who generally only can be fired for cause, and workers in the private sector who are covered by union contracts. Because the decline in unionization rates was even

[8] It is illegal for an employer to fire a worker based on race, sex, and several other legally protected characteristics.

larger in the private sector than in the workforce as a whole, the share of the workforce subject to employment at will increased by even more than the decline in unionization rates.

In 1980, the union coverage rates in the public and private sectors were roughly equal, so that close to one-quarter of the private sector workforce was covered by a union contract. However, by 2004, the share of the private sector workforce covered by a union contract had fallen to less than 9 percent.[9] The portion of the workforce employed in the public sector remained roughly constant, at just over 18 percent throughout this period, which means that the percentage of the workforce that was protected from being fired at will fell over this period from approximately 39 percent in 1980 to just 25 percent by 2005.

Most employers will not fire a worker arbitrarily, especially if the worker has special skills that are difficult to replace. However, the fact that most workers risk being fired if they do anything that sufficiently angers their employer does place a substantial element of insecurity in their life. This is especially the case in a country such as the United States in which health care insurance is usually provided by the employer. A worker in the private sector who is not protected by a union contract knows that she may suddenly be without both an income and health insurance for her family if she gets her boss sufficiently angry. Very few workers in other wealthy countries ever experience this degree of insecurity.

Noneconomic Measures of Well-Being

It is not only by strictly economic measures that the United States moved apart from the industrialized world over the last quarter century. There are a wide variety of social indicators that show the United States moving further away in this period. This section deals with some key noneconomic measures of well-being.

Crime and Incarceration Rates. The United States already had a far higher incarceration rate than other industrialized countries in 1980. However, this gap widened dramatically as the number of people

---

[9] These data can be found in the Bureau of Labor Statistics, *Union Members in 2004* (Washington, DC: U.S. Government Printing Office, 2005), table 3, ftp://ftp.bls.gov/pub/news.release/union2.txt.

incarcerated in the United States more than quadrupled between 1980 and 2003, rising from 502,000 in 1980 to 2,086,000 in 2003, the most recent year for which data are available.[10] There were many causes for the increase in the prison population in this period, but the most important factor was a turn to harsher sentences, especially for drug-related crimes.[11] It is important to note that there was a sharp drop in the incidence of violent crime in this period, although the drop did not begin until the mid-nineties, when both changing demographics and an improving economy became important factors affecting crime rates.[12] Even after this drop, violent crime rates in the United States remained much higher than in most other wealthy countries.

Table 1–3 shows the incarceration rate in the United States and other industrialized countries. The rate of incarceration in the United States is more than four times higher than in New Zealand, which has the second highest rate among industrialized countries. The gap is even more dramatic when the U.S. rate is compared with the rates in continental Europe. The incarceration rate in the United States is more than seven times the rate in Germany, nearly eight times the rate in France, and more than ten times the rate in Denmark, Finland, and Norway.

This gap in incarceration rates implies that the prison system plays a qualitatively different role in the United States than it does in other wealthy countries. More than 1 percent of the country's adult population is incarcerated at any point in time in the United States. Since there is rapid turnover in this population, a large percentage of citizens can expect to spend a portion of their life either in prison or on probation. This is especially the case for African Americans, who make up more than 40 percent of the prison population. Young African American men are more likely to spend time in prison or jail than in college.

---

[10] P. M. Harrison and A. J. Beck, *Prisoners in 2003*, Bureau of Justice Statistics Bulletin NCJ 205335 (Washington, DC: U.S. Department of Justice, Office of Justice Programs, 2004).

[11] See E. Bertram, *Drug War Politics* (Berkeley, CA: University of California Press, 1996).

[12] The trend in violent crime rates over this period can be found at the Bureau of Justice Statistics website http://www.ojp.usdoj.gov/bjs/glance/viort.htm. For a discussion of the factors behind this trend, see E. Currie, *Crime and Punishment in America* (New York: Owl Books, 1998), and J. Chambliss, *Power, Politics, and Crime* (Boulder, CO: Westview Press, 2000).

Table 1–3. *Rates of incarceration: United States and
other wealthy countries (2003–4)*

	Prisoners per 100,000 population
United States	726
New Zealand	166
United Kingdom	145
Spain	142
Portugal	124
Netherlands	123
Australia	121
Canada	116
Austria	106
Italy	97
Germany	96
France	91
Belgium	88
Ireland	85
Greece	82
Sweden	81
Denmark	70
Finland	66
Norway	65
Japan	60

Source: International Centre for Prison Studies, Kings
College, London. *Entire World, Prison Population Rates
per 100,000 of the National Population.*
http://www.kcl.ac.uk/depsta/rel/icps/worldbrief/
highest_to_lowest_rates.php.

The number of people who are under the court's control through
probation or parole is more than twice as large as the number who
are incarcerated at any point in time. The cost of the corrections
system in the United States is already more than 1 percent of GDP, an
amount that is larger than the defense budget in most other wealthy
countries. While the criminal justice system is a relatively minor part
of the government in most other wealthy societies, it is an important
and rapidly growing component of the economy and society in the
United States.

There is another aspect of the U.S. criminal justice system that sets the United States apart from most other wealthy countries: capital punishment. Capital punishment is prohibited in the European Union's charter, which means that all members of the European Union must outlaw capital punishment as a condition of membership. By contrast, more than three-quarters of the states in the United States have the death penalty, as does the federal government. In 2004, the states executed a total of fifty-nine people.

This divergence between the United States and Europe largely arose in the quarter century from 1980 to 2005. Several countries in Europe, most notably France, still had the death penalty in 1980. The abolition of the death penalty across Europe is a relatively new development. In 1980, it was also not clear how common the death penalty would become in the United States. The U.S. Supreme Court had overturned all existing death penalty statutes in 1973 on the grounds that the death penalty had been applied in too haphazard a manner. It first approved a new death penalty statute in 1976, which allowed for executions to resume after a nine-year moratorium. Still, only three executions in the United States had taken place by the end of 1980.

As more states passed laws that met the Supreme Court's standards and more prisoners completed their appeals, the rate of executions increased. In 1999, there were ninety-eight executions in the United States, the largest number in almost half a century.[13]

Health Care Spending and Outcomes. In 1980, the U.S. health care system did not look very different from the health care systems of other wealthy countries, measured by either outcomes or cost. Ranked by life expectancy at birth, the United States was somewhat below the average for other wealthy countries but still in the middle of the pack. The United States devoted a larger share of its GDP to health care than the average in 1980, but its expenditures were not hugely out of line with other countries and not even enough to put it at the top of the list.

The standing of the United States in both categories had changed hugely by the end of this period. The United States ranked last (tied with Denmark) in life expectancy at birth, and it was by far the most

---

[13] Bureau of Justice Statistics, *Key Facts at a Glance: Executions* (Washington, DC: Bureau of Justice Statistics, 2005), http://www.ojp.usdoj.gov/bjs/glance/tables/exetab.htm.

Table 1–4. *Life expectancy for total population at birth (in years): United States and other wealthy countries*

	1980	2003
Australia	74.6	80.3
Austria	72.6	78.6
Belgium	73.4	78.1
Canada	75.3	79.7
Denmark	74.3	77.2
Finland	73.4	78.5
France	74.3	79.4
Germany	72.9	78.4
Greece	74.5	78.1
Ireland	72.9	77.8
Italy	74.0	79.9
Japan	76.1	81.8
Netherlands	75.9	78.6
New Zealand	73.2	78.7
Norway	75.8	79.5
Portugal	71.5	77.3
Spain	75.6	80.5
Sweden	75.8	80.2
United Kingdom	73.2	78.5
United States	73.7	77.2
All non-U.S.	74.2	79.0

Source: Organisation for Economic Co-operation and Development, *OECD Health Data 2005*, June 2005.

profligate spender on health care. Table 1–4 shows life expectancy at birth for the United States and other wealthy countries in 1980 and 2003. Table 1–5 shows the share of GDP devoted to health care spending in these years.

In 1980, life expectancy at birth in the United States was 73.7 years, somewhat below the average of 74.2 years for other wealthy countries. However, the United States still ranked ahead of countries such as the United Kingdom and New Zealand, which had a life expectancy of 73.2 years, or former West Germany, which had a life expectancy of 72.9 years. By 2003, the United States ranked last, with a life expectancy of 77.2 years, compared with an average of 79 years for other wealthy countries. Life expectancy in France was more than

Table 1–5. *Total health expenditures as percentage of*
GDP: United States and other wealthy countries

	1980	2003
Australia	7.0	9.3
Austria	7.4	7.6
Belgium	6.4	9.6
Canada	7.1	9.9
Denmark	9.1	9.0
Finland	6.4	7.4
France	7.1	10.1
Germany	8.7	11.1
Greece	6.6	9.9
Ireland	8.4	7.3
Italy		8.4
Japan	6.5	7.9
Luxembourg	5.9	6.1
Netherlands	7.5	9.8
New Zealand	5.9	8.1
Norway	7.0	10.3
Portugal	5.6	9.6
Spain	5.4	7.7
Sweden	9.1	9.2
United Kingdom	5.6	7.7
United States	**8.7**	**15.0**
All non-U.S.	**7.0**	**8.8**

Definition: www.irdes.fr/ecosante/OCDE/411010.html.
Sources and methods per country: www.irdes.fr/ecosante/
OCDE/500.html.
Source: Organisation for Economic Co-operation and
Development, *OECD Health Data 2005*, June 2005.

2 full years longer, at 79.4 years. Sweden had a life expectancy that
was 3 full years longer, at 80.2. In Japan, with a life expectancy of
81.8 years, people could expect to live 4.6 years longer than people
in the United States. Using life expectancy as a yardstick, the health
care system in the United States was performing considerably more
poorly than those of other wealthy countries by the end of this
period.

Of course, not everyone in the United States gets bad health care.
The life expectancy for people near the top of the income distribution

in the United States is comparable to the life expectancies in other wealthy countries. Most of the differences are further down the income ladder, with people in the bottom 20 percent of the income distribution in the United States doing especially poorly.[14]

In addition, the cost of health care in the United States has soared far beyond the range in other wealthy countries. While the share of GDP devoted to health care spending in the United States was more than the average in 1980, Sweden and Denmark devoted a larger share of their GDP to health care, and former West Germany spent the same share as the United States. However, by 2003, health care spending in the United States was hugely out of line with spending in other wealthy countries. The 15 percent of GDP that the United States spent on health care in 2003 was nearly 4 full percentage points more than in Germany, the next biggest spender. It was 6.2 percentage points more than the average spending share for other countries.

This additional spending in the United States has a substantial economic impact. The 6.2 percentage point gap in spending between the United States and the average among other wealthy countries is equal to $775 billion ($2,700 per person) at the 2005 level of GDP. This is equivalent to approximately 1.5 times the annual defense budget. In short, the United States went from having a health care system that was near the middle in terms of outcomes and costs at the beginning of the period to one that ranked at the bottom in outcomes and at the top in costs at the end.

Educational Attainment and Outcomes. It is not easy to find good data for international comparisons at the beginning of this period, but clearly by its end the United States stood behind most other wealthy countries in many measures of educational attainment. While the United States still ranked near the top in the percentage of the college-age population who complete college, the level of educational attainment by the bulk of its students ranked near the bottom among wealthy countries.

Table 1–6 shows the performance of students in the United States on standardized tests in math and science compared with students in other countries. The first column in Table 1–7 shows the ranking among

---

[14] D. Keating and C. Hertzman, eds., *Developmental Health and the Wealth of Nations: Social, Biological, and Educational Dynamics* (New York: Guilford Press, 1999).

Table 1–6. *International comparisons of math and science literacy (1999)*

Math literacy		Science literacy	
Finland	544	Hungary	552
Korea	542	Japan	550
Netherlands	538	Korea	549
Japan	534	Netherlands	545
Canada	532	Australia	540
Belgium	529	Czech Republic	539
		England	538
New Zealand	525	Finland	535
Australia	524	Belgium	535
Czech Republic	516	Slovak Republic	535
		Canada	533
Denmark	514	Russian Federation	529
France	511	Bulgaria	518
Sweden	509	**United States**	**515**
Austria	506	New Zealand	510
Germany	503	Italy	493
Slovak Republic	498		
Norway	495		
Poland	490		
Hungary	490		
Spain	485		
United States	**483**		
Russian Federation	468		
Italy	466		

Source: Program for International Student Assessment. These data can be found in the National Center for Education Statistics, Program for International Student Assessment.
http://nces.ed.gov/surveys/international/IntlIndicators/index.asp?SectionNumber=3&SubSectionNumber=4&IndicatorNumber=40.

wealthy countries of fifteen-year-old students in overall mathematical literacy. The second column shows the ranking of eighth-graders on a science achievement test. Both tests were administered in 1999. As can be seen, the performance of students in the United States ranks well below the performance of students in most other wealthy countries in both areas. It even ranks below the performance of some of the former Soviet bloc countries, such as the Slovak Republic,

Table 1–7. *Ratio of science and engineering PhDs granted by foreign universities to science and engineering PhDs granted by U.S. universities*

	1975	1989	2001	2003	2010
Major Asian countries	0.22	0.48	0.96		
China	NA	0.05	0.32	0.49	1.26
Japan	0.11	0.16	0.29		
European Union*	0.93	1.22	1.54	1.62	1.92

* The fifteen members states prior to the 2005 expansion.
Source: R. B. Freeman, "Does Globalization of the Scientific/Engineering Workforce Threaten U.S. Economic Leadership?" in *Innovation Policy and the Economy*, vol. 6, ed. A. Jaffe, J. Lerner, and S. Stern. Cambridge, MA: MIT Press, 2006.

Poland, and Hungary, all of which are far poorer than the United States. If students in the United States consistently perform worse than students in other developed countries and even developing countries, it will impede their ability to compete for higher-paying jobs in the future.

It is not clear to what extent these rankings display a relative deterioration in the position of the United States since 1980, because comparable data do not exist for earlier years. However, it does seem clear that other countries have placed more emphasis on the educational performance of their students in recent years, as they have managed to achieve much better outcomes than the United States.

It is possible to show a relative deterioration in the number of postgraduate degrees in science and technical fields granted to students in the United States. Table 1–7 shows the ratio of PhDs in science and engineering conferred by universities in the European Union as well as China and Japan to the number conferred by universities in the United States. By this measure, there has been a sharp deterioration in the relative position of the United States, as the number of PhDs conferred by universities in other countries has increased sharply over this period in comparison to the number conferred in the United States.

Although the United States was the world leader, in both absolute and per capita terms, in the number of PhDs conferred in these fields at the start of the period, this was no longer true by its end. The European Union had far surpassed the United States in both the absolute number of degrees conferred and the number conferred relative to its population. China is also likely to soon pass the United States in the absolute number of degrees conferred, but with more than four times the population, it will still be far behind the United States in degrees per capita.

Productivity, Employment, and Output

In 1980, the United States stood first among the industrialized nations in per capita income. It had retained its lead from the end of World War II, with other rich countries still in a process of catching up. By 2005, the United States had actually increased its lead in per capita income over other wealthy countries, having experienced considerably more rapid income growth (and GDP growth) than the average among other rich countries.

Table 1–8 shows per capita GDP in the United States and several other wealthy countries in 1980 and 2004. At the beginning of the period, the United States ranked at the top of this list, with a per capita GDP that was 35.6 percent higher than the weighted average for the fifteen countries that composed the European Union at the time. Rather than having this gap close, the United States actually increased its lead over the EU 15, so that by the end of the period, its per capita GDP was nearly 40 percent higher than the average for the EU 15.

While to some extent this more rapid growth indicates greater economic success, the growing income gap is also in part the result of policy choices, with the United States having opted for a different path than most other wealthy countries.

The size of a country's economy depends on two things. The first factor is its level of productivity. This is the amount of output for each hour that a worker works. The second factor is the number of hours worked. The total hours of work depends on both the number of people working and the number of hours that each worker works. It turns our that the gap in the growth rate between the United States and other wealthy countries over this quarter century is attributable to differences in hours of work, not differences in productivity. There was little difference between the average rate of productivity growth in the United States and other wealthy countries in this period. In fact, at the end of the period, the United States actually ranked below

Table 1–8. *Per capita GDP in 1980 and 2004*
(in 2004 dollars)

	1980	2004
Australia	$19,716	$30,751*
Austria	$20,675	$31,944
Belgium	$19,860	$30,851
Canada	$22,025	$31,395
Denmark	$20,949	$31,627
Finland	$18,540	$36,597
France	$19,387	$29,554
Germany	$19,329	$28,605
Greece	$14,532	$21,689
Ireland	$12,417	$35,767
Italy	$18,612	$27,236*
Japan	$17,929	$28,618*
Netherlands	$20,110	$31,082*
New Zealand	$17,204	$24,498
Norway	$19,161	$30,765
Portugal	$10,506	$19,197*
Spain	$13,781	$25,583
Sweden	$20,615	$30,362
Switzerland	$25,484	$33,678
United Kingdom	$17,066	$31,437
United States	$24,354	$39,732
EU 15	$17,961	$28,258*

* GDP data for 2003.
Note: Per capita GDP at purchasing power parity (adjusted using U.S. GDP deflator).
Source: Organisation for Economic Co-operation and Development Statistical Databases, Annual National Accounts, http://cs4hq.oecd.org/oecd/eng/TableViewer/wdsview/dispviewp.asp.

several other countries in its level of output per worker, as shown in Table 1–9.

Table 1–9 shows that the United States ranked behind many other wealthy countries in productivity by 2000, including France, Germany, and Italy. While the data show the United States to have a somewhat higher level of productivity than the average among other wealthy countries, the difference is not very large. The OECD estimated that

Table 1–9. *Hourly labor productivity in 1980 and 2000*

	1980*	2000*
Australia	81.5	83.2
Austria	94.0	103.8
Belgium	105.4	121.0
Canada	87.5	83.1
Denmark	84.5	100.5
Finland	72.1	93.0
France	102.2	121.5
Germany		103.9
West Germany	97.9	
Ireland	61.4	102.7
Italy	95.5	101.6
Japan	63.2	76.8
Netherlands	113.6	112.1
New Zealand	78.3	66.7
Norway	106.1	130.7
Portugal	47.4	56.6
Spain	72.6	81.5
Sweden	88.6	89.7
Switzerland	110.4	93.3
United Kingdom	79.4	92.3
United States	100.0	100.0

* United States equals 100 in each year.
Source: Analysis of Groningen Growth and Development Centre and the Conference Board, Total Economy Database, January 2005. Accessed July 5, 2005, from http://www.ggdc.net.

the level of productivity for the EU 15 in 2003 was 91.8 percent of the level of productivity in the United States in that year.[15] In many ways,

[15] OECD Productivity Database, February 14, 2005. Even this modest gap in productivity is attributable in part to explicit policy decisions. Laws in most European countries make it far more difficult to set up large-scale retailers such as Wal-Mart. These retailers are far more efficient than traditional retailers, since they can sell far more goods for each hour of work by their employees. However, European countries have to a large extent made a conscious decision to try to preserve their traditional retail industry. This means that they have less output per hour of work in retail but manage to preserve the sort of small shops that many view as central to the character of Paris, Copenhagen, and other European cities. See S. Basu,

productivity can be seen as the best basic measure of wealth, and most economists view it as the primary determinant of living standards over the long term. By this measure, there is not a large gap between the United States and other wealthy countries.

The main reason for the differences between the United States and other countries in per capita GDP at the end of the period, as well as differences in growth during the period, is that the United States averages more hours a year of work per person than other wealthy countries. This is attributable in part to the fact that the United States was more successful in maintaining a low rate of unemployment than most other wealthy countries and in part to the fact that workers in other countries managed to win shorter workweeks and longer vacations whereas there was little change in workers' hours in the United States.

Table 1–10 shows the unemployment rates in 1980 and 2005 for the United States and other wealthy countries. In 1980, the unemployment rate in the United States was considerably higher than in most other rich countries. For example, the unemployment rates in France and former West Germany were 6.3 percent and 3.2 percent, respectively. This compared to a 7.2 percent unemployment rate in the United States. By 2005, the situation had been reversed, with the unemployment rate in the United States at 5.1 percent, while the unemployment rates in France and Germany were both 9.5 percent. Although several European countries still have comparable or lower unemployment rates, the United States has clearly outperformed Europe as a whole by this measure. The average unemployment rate for the EU 15 in 2005 was 7.9 percent, nearly 3 full percentage points more than the rate in the United States.

There is an ongoing debate among economists as to why the United States has been relatively successful in maintaining a low unemployment rate. The predominant view within the economics profession is that weak unions, low unemployment benefits, and a relatively unregulated labor market have supported rapid job growth, since firms can

J. Fernald, N. Oulton, and S. Srinivasan, "The Case of the Missing Productivity Growth, or Does Information Technology Explain Why Productivity Accelerated in the United States but Not in the United Kingdom?" in *NBER Macroeconomics Annual 2003*, ed. M. Getler and K. Rogoff, 9–63 (Cambridge, MA: MIT Press, 2003).

Table 1–10. *Unemployment rates in 1980 and 2005*

	1980	2005*
Australia	6.0	5.1
Austria	1.4	5.1
Belgium	6.7	8.4
Canada	7.5	6.8
Denmark	6.0	5.0
Finland	4.6	8.4
France	6.3	9.5
Germany		9.5
West Germany	3.2	
Ireland	7.3	4.3
Italy	7.7	7.7**
Japan	2.0	4.4
Netherlands	4.0	4.7
New Zealand	2.5	5.1
Norway	1.7	4.7***
Portugal	8.4	7.3
Spain	9.3	9.7
Sweden	2.0	6.3****
United Kingdom	6.2	4.7***
United States	7.2	5.1
EU 15		7.9

* Data for 2005 are through September unless indicated otherwise.
** Data run through June.
*** Data run through July.
**** Data run through March.
Source: International Monetary Fund and Organisation for Economic Co-operation and Development. OECD data accessed November 14, 2005, at http://www.oecd.org/dataoecd/41/13/18595359.pdf.

easily hire and fire workers and move them around on the job so as to maximize their flexibility.[16]

---

[16] The evidence for this view is questioned in D. Howell, ed., *Fighting Unemployment: The Limits of Free Market Orthodoxy* (New York: Oxford University Press, 2004), and L. Kenworthy, *Egalitarian Capitalism: Jobs, Incomes, and Growth in Affluent Countries* (New York: Russell Sage Foundation, 2004).

An alternative explanation for this success focuses on the pursuit by the Federal Reserve Board of more expansionary policies than those chosen by the central banks of European countries and the European Central Bank (established in 1998). The Federal Reserve Board has maintained a policy of using low interest rates to combat unemployment. For example, it lowered the short-term interest rate it controls to just 1 percent in 2002 and held this rate for two years in order to boost the economy out of the 2001 recession. By contrast, the European Central Bank focuses only on keeping inflation under control. It never allowed its short-term interest to fall below 2 percent even though Europe's economy had considerably more unemployment and idle capacity than the U.S. economy. But regardless of the causes, much of the rest of the developed world – and, in particular, continental Europe – has experienced a problem of chronically high unemployment in the last fifteen years. The United States has managed to avoid this problem.

For those who do have jobs, the decline in hours worked in other developed countries clearly reflects a divergence in policy between these countries and the United States. In most other developed countries, there has been a conscious policy decision to have workers take part of the benefits of higher productivity in the form of more leisure. Most European countries require employers to give workers four to six weeks of paid vacation each year. (In fact, the social charter of the European Union requires member states to have enacted legislation granting workers at least twenty days of paid time off each year.) In addition, several countries, most notably France, have taken steps to shorten the standard workweek to less than forty hours.[17]

By contrast, in the United States, there are no federal or state requirements for any paid time off whatsoever. Millions of full-time, full-year workers have no paid vacation days, and some workers do not even get holidays such as Christmas and Independence Day as paid days off. The result of this divergence in policies has been a growing gap in average hours worked for full-time workers. Table 1–11 shows the average number of hours worked in 2004 in the United States and other wealthy countries.

---

[17] A 1998 OECD analysis of working hours found sharp reductions in average hours since 1980 in nearly every OECD country except the United States. In most countries, the decline was at least partially attributable to government regulations (OECD, *Employment Outlook* [Paris: OECD, 1998], Chapter 5, http://www.oecd.org/dataoecd/8/51/2080270.pdf).

Table 1–11. *Average annual hours per worker in 2004*

Norway	1,336
Netherlands	1,338
France	1,398
Germany	1,446
Denmark	1,481
Austria	1,498
Switzerland	1,510
Sweden	1,562
Belgium	1,565
Finland	1,588
Italy	1,590
Ireland	1,612
United Kingdom	1,619
Portugal	1,698
New Zealand	1,752
Australia	1,757
Canada	1,757
Japan	1,760
Spain	1,799
United States	1,817

Source: Analysis of Groningen Growth and Development Centre and the Conference Board, Total Economy Database, January 2005. Accessed on July 5, 2005, from http://www.ggdc.net.

The table shows that workers in the United States average more hours of work in a year than do workers in any other wealthy country. In many cases, the differences are quite large. For example, workers in the United States work an average of 25.7 percent more hours annually than do workers in Germany and nearly 30 percent more hours than workers in France. This difference in hours worked per worker each year is by far the most important explanation for the difference between the United States and EU 15 in per capita GDP. While GDP per capita would still be somewhat higher in the United States than in the EU 15 even if workers in Europe and the United States put in the same number of hours, this gap would not be large. The main reason that the United States is wealthier than Europe is that workers in Europe have opted to take more of the benefits of productivity growth in the form of leisure time whereas workers in the United States have on average received the benefits in the form of higher income.

Labor, Leisure, and the Environment

The trade-off between more leisure and higher incomes depends on individual preferences and social values; from an economic perspective, both are equally good ways for individuals to benefit from the greater wealth associated with higher levels of productivity. However, there are important environmental implications to this choice. The decision to take the benefits of higher productivity growth in the form of more income can be expected to exact a greater toll on the environment, since the use of most resources and the emission of many pollutants (most importantly greenhouse gases) are highly correlated with GDP. The fact that the United States has a substantially higher per capita income than the average European country causes it to use more resources and emit more pollutants on a per capita basis than European countries.

Table 1–12 shows energy use per person in the United States and other wealthy countries 2001. The United States ranks behind only Luxembourg and Canada in energy use per capita, using nearly twice as much energy per person as Germany and France. Of course, Canada's high ranking is attributable in large part to its cold climate.

While there are many factors that explain the differences in per capita energy use, the fact that people in the United States own relatively more and bigger cars would rank high on the list. Similarly, homes in the United States are bigger on average than in most European countries. People in the United States are also likely to heat or air condition their houses to more moderate temperatures than would be the case in most other countries.[18] More and bigger cars, larger houses, and more comfortable indoor temperatures are all items that can be purchased with higher incomes. In other words, these differences in lifestyles are part of the dividend that people in the United States enjoy as a result of working more hours on average than their European counterparts.

---

[18] The more severe climate endured by a large portion of the country is also a factor that increases energy use in the United States relative to Europe.

Turning Away: The United States Breaks Ranks

Table 1–12. *Per capita energy use in 2003*
(kg of oil equivalence)

Australia	5,668
Austria	4,086
Belgium	5,701
Canada	8,240
Denmark	3,853
Finland	7,204
France	4,519
Germany	4,205
Greece	2,709
Ireland	3,777
Italy	3,140
Japan	4,053
Luxembourg	9,472
Netherlands	4,983
New Zealand	4,333
Norway	5,100
Portugal	2,469
Spain	3,240
Sweden	5,754
Switzerland	3,689
United Kingdom	3,893
United States	7,843

Source: World Bank, *World Development Indicators 2005.*

However one views the trade-off between more income and less leisure at a personal level, the decision to opt for higher income does typically have an environmental cost. The greater per capita use of energy in the United States leads to more rapid depletion of fossil fuels, which are ultimately in fixed supply. The United States also ranks near the top in per capita emissions of greenhouse gases. The same would likely be the case for most forms of pollutants, with the United States at or near the top of per capita emissions in most cases.

In the category of energy use and greenhouse gas emissions, the United States may not have gotten any more out of line with its European counterparts over the last quarter century, but it clearly did little to promote convergence in an area where it was already substantially out of line. The number of cars per person increased, as did their size. Average commuting distances grew longer, and roads became more congested. House sizes increased. In a world where it is ever clearer that environmental problems such as global warming do not respect national boundaries, the discrepancy between U.S. and European consumption patterns can take on considerably greater significance.

The United States Goes Its Own Way

The history of the United States differs in many important respects from the history of other wealthy countries. In 1980 there were already important ways in which the social and institutional structures in the United States set it apart. However, at that time, there were reasons to believe that these differences were getting smaller, with the United States adopting institutions that were more like those that existed in other wealthy countries, most notably by strengthening its welfare state.

Instead of converging over the next quarter century, the gaps between other wealthy countries and the United States grew larger. The political leadership in the United States repeatedly took steps to roll back the size of the U.S. welfare state in this period, reducing the level of benefits and economic security that the government guarantees its citizens. While there have been similar efforts to roll back the welfare state in all of the wealthy countries, for the most part the governments that have attempted to move in this direction have been blocked by public pressure. As a result, the United States looks less like the other wealthy countries today by a wide variety of measures than it did in 1980.

Whether the United States took the right path is certainly debatable. The United States has enjoyed considerably more rapid economic growth in this period than most other wealthy countries. It has also enjoyed a lower unemployment rate than most of these countries. These gains have been offset by much greater levels of inequality and much less security for the bulk of the population. In addition, lower levels of educational attainment and much higher rates of incarceration raise questions about the sustainability of the U.S. path. There are still many questions to be answered about the benefits and costs from this unexpected divergence in policies.

APPENDIX
Redistributing Income Upward: Freeing Some Trade, Protecting Some Workers

There is a long list of policy changes over the last quarter century that have had the effect of redistributing income upward. This appendix describes some of the most important changes in economic policy during this period. It treats economic policy in more detail than other parts of the book, but it does not require extensive knowledge of economics.

Freeing Some Trade, Protecting Some Workers

The best place to start a discussion of the policy changes that redistributed income upward during the quarter century from 1980 to 2005 is the direction of trade policy in this period. This provides a clear example of an area in which policy was implemented in a way that helped those at the top at the expense of workers in the middle and at the bottom of the income distribution. Ostensibly, the main goal of trade policy in this period was to spread "free trade." This was generally taken to mean the removal of obstacles to international trade in goods and services – most immediately through the reduction or elimination of tariffs and quotas.

However, this free trade agenda also involved reducing or eliminating many nontariff barriers, such as quality and safety regulations that arguably did more to protect domestic industry from competition than to protect consumers. This free trade agenda also required new rules governing foreign investment in the developing world so that U.S. corporations could have confidence that their factories would not be confiscated or their control over their foreign profits restricted. To advance this free trade agenda, the United States signed dozens of regional and bilateral trade agreements over this quarter century in addition to being the driving force behind the Uruguay Round of international trade talks that led to the creation of the World Trade Organization (WTO) in 1995.

U.S. trade policy did remove many of the obstacles to trade in manufactured goods. As a result, the share of the demand that was met by imports soared from 10.5 percent in 1980 to 16.2 percent in

2005.[19] This increase in imports clearly benefited consumers, who opted to buy foreign-produced goods and services that were cheaper or better than comparable domestic products.

However, the availability of these imports created new and intense competition for workers in the affected industries. In effect, manufacturing workers in the United States suddenly had to compete with workers in the developing world, who frequently were paid less than one-tenth as much. This led to substantial job losses in the manufacturing sector. In 1980, 20.7 percent of the workforce was employed in manufacturing. The manufacturing share of total employment had fallen to 10.7 percent by 2005.[20] Even manufacturing workers who kept their jobs were often forced to accept substantial reductions in wages and benefits in order to be able to compete with workers in the developing world.

Manufacturing employment has historically been important for workers who do not have a degree from a four-year college (still more than 70 percent of the workforce) because it is a source of relatively high-paying jobs for this group. However, the pressure of international competition led to both a substantial reduction in manufacturing employment and a decline in relative wages for the remaining workers in this sector. As a result, there was downward pressure not only on the wages of manufacturing workers but on the wages of all workers without college degrees.[21]

---

[19] The rise in the value of the dollar over this period was also an important factor behind the increase in imports. This issue is addressed in later chapters.

[20] Not all of this decline in employment can be attributed to trade. Productivity growth in the manufacturing sector consistently outpaces overall productivity growth. This means that if the share of real output devoted to manufactured goods remained constant, there would be a decline in the manufacturing share of total employment. A simple approximation of the impact of the trade deficit on manufacturing employment can be obtained by taking the size of the deficit in traded goods relative to total manufacturing output in 2005. In the third quarter of 2005, the deficit in traded goods was $813.8 billion (Bureau of Economic Analysis, *2005 Annual Revision of the National Income and Product Accounts* [Washington, DC: U.S. Government Printing Office, 2005], table 4.2.5, line 25 minus line 2), and the net value added in manufacturing output was $1,343.1 billion (table 6.1D, line 8), implying that the trade deficit in 2005 was equal to 60 percent of the value added in manufacturing. This implies that manufacturing employment would increase by approximately 60 percent if the trade deficit was eliminated through increased domestic production of manufactured goods.

[21] This basic argument, along with some preliminary estimates of the size of this effect, is laid out in R. Freeman, L. Katz, and G. Borjas, "How Much Do Immigration

It is important to recognize that the negative impact of trade on the wages of less-educated workers was not a natural outcome of free trade policies but rather the result of trade policies that subjected certain groups of workers to international competition while leaving others protected. Although trade agreements negotiated in this era sought to make it as easy as possible to produce manufactured goods in the developing world and export them back to the United States, they were not designed to remove all barriers to trade.

In particular, these agreements did little or nothing to remove the professional and licensing barriers that protect highly paid professional workers, such as doctors, dentists, and lawyers. If trade negotiators had applied the same principles to these professions as were used in the manufacturing sector, they would have sought to standardize international professional and licensing requirements. Following the criteria applied to government restrictions on trade in goods, it would then have been necessary to prove in the case of any professional restriction that it served a clearly defined and accepted purpose, such as promoting consumer safety.

There were enormous potential economic gains from removing restrictions on foreign workers in the highly paid professions practiced in the United States. For example, doctors in other wealthy countries earn on average less than half as much as doctors in the United States. If the salaries of doctors in the United States could just be brought in line with their counterparts in rich countries, this would result in savings to consumers and taxpayers of more than $70 billion a year.[22] If U.S. doctors also had to face the full brunt of competition with qualified doctors in the developing world (like manufacturing workers), the savings might be even greater.

---

and Trade Affect Labor Market Outcomes?" *Brookings Papers on Economic Activity*, no. 1 (1997): 1–90. See also the estimates in W. Cline, *Trade and Income Distribution* (Washington, DC: Institute for International Economics, 1997).

[22] According to the OECD, the average annual pretax income of doctors in the United States in 1995 was $196,000. By comparison, it reports that doctors in Switzerland earned on average $82,000, in Japan $57,300, and in Denmark $52,600 (Organisation for Economic Co-operation and Development, *OECD Health Data 1998* [Paris: OECD, 1998]). While these figures are now somewhat dated, there is no reason to believe that the relative wages have changed. This suggests that the average earnings of doctors in Europe total at least $100,000 less than in the United States. There are approximately 800,000 physicians in the United States, which implies that the savings from paying doctors at European wage rates would be close to $80 billion a year.

However, U.S. trade policy was not aimed at making U.S. doctors face international competition. In fact, the opposite happened. In 1997, several national physician organizations complained to Congress that an influx of foreign doctors was driving down their wages. (They did not focus their complaints on the quality of the foreign doctors.) Congress responded by reducing the quotas for the number of foreign medical residents who could enter the country and by imposing new restrictions on foreign-trained physicians that were intended to make it more difficult for foreign doctors to practice in the United States. These restrictions had their desired effect – the number of foreign doctors entering the United States fell sharply.[23]

The story in the other highly paid professions is similar, if less dramatic. While trade policy during this period was quite consciously designed to put manufacturing workers in direct competition with low-paid workers in the developing world, barriers that protected highly paid professionals from foreign competition remained largely untouched, or were in some cases even increased. The result was that trade placed substantial downward pressure on the wages of less-educated workers but not on the salaries of the most highly paid workers in the country.

In addressing the issue of foreign competition in professional services, trade policy can run over into immigration policy, although it is important to make some clear distinctions. Foreign professionals face no particular obstacles to entering the United States and even working – if they are prepared to work in a menial job, such as driving a cab or busing tables. They only face serious restrictions if they try to practice their profession in United States, in which case U.S. licensing requirements and work restrictions on immigrants act as protectionist barriers to entry.[24]

---

[23] For a discussion of the debate over the impact of foreign doctors on the wages of U.S. physicians, see "Caught in the Middle," *Washington Post*, March 19, 1996, H10; "A.M.A. and Colleges Assert There Is a Surfeit of Doctors," *New York Times*, March 1, 1997, A7; and "U.S. to Pay Hospitals Not to Train Doctors, Easing Glut," *New York Times*, February 15, 1997, A1. The success of this policy change in restricting the inflow of foreign doctors was noted five years later. See "Fewer Foreign Doctors Seek U.S. Training," *Washington Post*, September 4, 2002, A7, and "Test Tied to Slip in Foreign Applicants for Medical Residences," *New York Times*, September 4, 2002, A19.

[24] Since the absolute number of people in highly paid professions is small, the conditions in the labor market for these professions could be substantially altered if just a

Immigration and the Supply of Labor

Immigration has likely been an important factor affecting wages in some sectors of the economy.[25] There was a substantial increase in the size of immigration flows in the period from 1980 to 2005 compared with prior decades. From 1970 to 1980, legal immigrants averaged fewer than 300,000 annually. From 1990 to 2004, legal immigrants averaged more than 600,000 a year, and as many as 400,000 more immigrants entered the country each year without legal authorization.[26] This more rapid flow of immigrants has had a significant effect on the labor market for less educated workers, since immigrants were disproportionately concentrated in this segment of the labor market. Immigrant workers from developing countries are often willing to take jobs at wages and with working conditions that most native-born workers would find unacceptable, thereby depressing wages in the areas in which they are concentrated.

It is important to realize that the fact that immigrant workers are disproportionately less educated is a function of policy and not of the potential immigrant workforce. Although a substantial number of immigrants are working in the country legally, in the last quarter century a comparable number have entered the country – primarily in search of work – without proper documentation. While it is illegal for employers to hire these immigrants, there is very little enforcement of prohibitions against hiring workers without proper work permits. As a result, undocumented workers make up a large percentage of workers in many occupations in large parts of the country.

This pattern of enforcement of immigration laws works to the benefit of relatively more educated workers, since they do not experience the same sort of competition from immigrant workers. This can been seen by comparing hospitals, which generally do not hire immigrant

---

fraction of the less-educated workers currently entering the country were replaced by more highly educated workers.

[25] See G. Borjas, *Heaven's Door* (Princeton, NJ: Princeton University Press, 1997), for a discussion of the impact of immigration on the economy and wage inequality. For an assessment arguing that immigration had a much smaller impact on wage distribution, see D. Card, "Is the New Immigration Really So Bad?" (unpublished manuscript, University of California, 2005).

[26] Social Security Administration, *2005 Annual Report of the Board of Trustees of the Federal Old-Age and Survivors Insurance and Disability Insurance Trust Funds* (Washington, DC: U.S. Government Printing Office, 2005), table V.A1.

doctors in violation of labor laws and licensing rules, and restaurants, which frequently do. If hospitals operated like restaurants, they would offer doctors salaries that would be very attractive to doctors in developing countries but equal only a fraction of the standard pay for doctors in the United States.

This practice would allow them to attract a very large pool of applicants from developing countries, and most hospitals could easily fill all of their staff positions with well-qualified foreign physicians – even if they excluded those who were not fluent in English. If a significant number of hospitals adopted this practice, they would be able to charge much lower fees and thereby undercut the hospitals that restricted themselves to complying with labor laws regarding immigrant doctors. In time, most hospitals would be forced to adopt the wage scales set by those who relied primarily on immigrant doctors, leading to a permanent lowering of wages for doctors in the United States.

This pattern of hiring is a violation of immigration law for both restaurants and hospitals, but restaurant workers are far less powerful than the American Medical Association and other physician organizations. This means that restaurants can routinely ignore immigration laws with impunity. However, a hospital that openly hired undocumented workers as doctors at salaries far lower than those prevailing for native-born physicians and legal immigrants would almost certainly face serious fines and possibly criminal sanctions if it continued to violate immigration laws. Furthermore, established physicians in developing countries are less likely than relatively unskilled workers to be willing to take the risk of working illegally in the United States.

The same principles apply to most areas in which more-educated workers are employed. It is far more difficult for firms that rely on relatively well educated workers to ignore the legal restrictions on hiring immigrant workers. If an accounting firm, an insurance company, or a software producer openly hired large numbers of undocumented workers at a fraction of the standard wage in the field, it would almost certainly face legal consequences. The same principles do not apply, however, to meatpacking or apparel factories or firms supplying janitorial services. Consequently, current immigration policies force less-educated workers in the United States to compete against immigrant workers while still largely protecting more-educated workers.[27] It is

---

[27] In recent years, there has been a growing practice of bringing in more skilled immigrant workers through visas such as the H-1 and L-1 visa classifications.

worth noting that if immigration policy had been applied equally, so that there were the same opportunities for highly skilled and less-skilled immigrants to enter the country, the sharp upward redistribution of wage income over this period would probably have led to a substantial increase in the proportion of highly skilled immigrants entering the United States.

Labor-Management Policies

A third important factor leading to an upward redistribution of wages over this period was a change in the nature of labor-management relations. This was also brought about by a deliberate shift in policy. Prior to 1980, unions were an accepted part of the economic landscape. Workers were able to petition to form unions, and the National Labor Relations Board (NLRB) acted as a reasonably neutral arbiter of elections and voting procedures. It was also generally accepted that when workers went on strike, firms temporarily shut down for the duration of the strike, or at least did not fire striking workers. Both practices changed in the eighties.

Under President Reagan, the NLRB became substantially more tilted toward management. Far more cases were decided in management's favor than under prior boards appointed by either Democratic or Republican administrations.[28] Perhaps even more serious was the fact that the board developed long backlogs so that cases were often not decided for years after they were brought. Since the sanctions for losing a case are generally minor, such backlogs meant that management could break the law with virtual impunity.[29] Beginning in

While this does force some groups of more skilled workers to face downward wage pressure from foreign workers, the effects are still limited by the relatively small number of work visas and by the fact that employers are still obligated to make some pretense of hiring domestic workers at the prevailing wage. For example, it would be unlikely that any firm would seek to hire large numbers of foreign workers under these visa classifications at one-third the wage paid to U.S. workers in the same occupation even though this may still prove to be an attractive salary to many skilled workers in developing countries.

[28] D. Vogel, *Fluctuating Fortunes: The Political Power of Business in America* (New York: Basic Books, 1989), 270.

[29] It is a violation of the National Labor Relations Act to fire a worker for trying to form a union. However, the penalty, if a firm is found guilty of such illegal firing, is the difference between the pay that the worker had at the job from which he

the Reagan years, it became a standard management practice to simply fire workers involved in union organizing drives.[30] This made it
considerably more difficult to successfully organize unions in the private sector. (By contrast, most public sector employees enjoy some
job protection through civil service laws. Therefore, they cannot simply be fired without cause if they are involved in a union organizing
drive.)

The other major change in labor-management relations was the
use of replacement workers during strikes. While there were always
employers who would try to bring in new workers during a strike,
prior to 1980 this was an exceptional practice. Most major companies
would not engage in such confrontational tactics, both because it was
assumed that they would have to deal with their union employees on
a long-term basis and because it would be considered a bad public
relations move.

This changed in 1981, when President Reagan responded to a strike
by the Professional Association of Air Traffic Controllers by firing the
striking air controllers and replacing them with air traffic controllers
from the military.[31] This move was soon followed by several high-
profile cases where major companies responded to strikes by replacing
striking workers.[32] The possibility that strikes would result in job loss
reduced their value as a bargaining chip for unions and therefore substantially reduced union power in collective bargaining.

---

was fired and the pay at whatever job he held since the date of firing. Since most
workers have to quickly find new jobs after being fired, this lost pay is usually
small. As a result, it became standard practice to fire workers engaged in organizing
unions. Many of the tactics employers have used in recent years to obstruct union
organizing are documented in a book by a former management consultant, M. J.
Levitt, with T. Conroy, *Confessions of a Union Buster* (New York: Crown Publishers,
1993).

[30] R. LaLonde, B. Meltzer, and P. Weiler, "Hard Times for Unions: Another Look
at the Significance of Employer Illegalities," *University of Chicago Law Review* 58,
no. 3 (1991): 953–1014; see also K. Bronfenbrenner, "Employer Behavior in Certification Elections and First Contract Campaigns: Implications for Labor Law
Reform," in *Restoring the Promise of American Labor Law*, ed. S. Friedman, 75–89
(Ithaca, NY: ILR Press, 1994).

[31] This strike was a violation of government laws that prohibited strikes by federal
employees. In prior years, employees at all levels of government often struck in
spite of such laws. In the vast majority of cases, the strikes did not lead to firing or
criminal actions being taken against strike organizers.

[32] The strikes against the Greyhound Bus Company and Eastern Airlines in 1982 were
two important instances in which striking workers lost their jobs to replacement
workers.

The change in NLRB enforcement and management practices had the predictable effect. The percentage of private sector employees who were represented by unions plummeted during this period. In 1980, close to 20 percent of private sector employees were unionized, but the figure had fallen to just 8 percent by 2004.[33] The fact that this decline was largely attributable to changing power relations and not the result of more negative attitudes toward unions among workers is demonstrated by the fact that during this period there was relatively little change in unionization rates in the public sector. In 2004, more than 36 percent of public sector workers still belonged to unions.

If the decline in private sector unionization rates was primarily a consequence of changes in workers' attitudes, it would be expected that there would be comparable declines in both the public and private sectors. However, the evidence suggests that in the public sector, where employers could not pursue aggressive antiunion tactics, many workers continued to value collective bargaining arrangements. By contrast, such tactics effectively denied many workers in the private sector the option of union representation.

Federal Reserve Board Policy

A fourth important factor placing downward pressure on the wages of less-educated workers over this quarter century was the relatively restrictive monetary policy implemented by the Federal Reserve Board. In the wake of the spiraling inflation of the seventies, the Federal Reserve Board sharply shifted the focus of its monetary policy. With the appointment of Paul Volcker as the chairman of the Federal Reserve Board in 1979, combating inflation became the dominant concern of Fed monetary policy. While the Fed was legally committed to the pursuit of dual goals, full employment (defined as 4 percent unemployment) and price stability, it was clear during this period that the commitment to price stability, or low rates of inflation, was preeminent.

The Fed proved willing to tolerate unemployment rates that would have been viewed as politically unacceptable ten years earlier. In the

---

[33] Economy-wide unionization rates for the whole period are taken from Mishel et al., *State of Working America 2004/2005*, Figure 2V. Recent data on unionization rates in the public and private sectors are available in the Bureau of Labor Statistics annual release on unionization rates (http://www.bls.gov/news.release/pdf/union2.pdf).

recession of 1980–2, the unemployment rate eventually peaked at 10.8 percent, a level that would have been unimaginable in the sixties. The unemployment rate did come down quickly from its 1982 peak, and the economy actually achieved the full-employment target in 2000, when the year-round average unemployment rate was just 4 percent; however, the unemployment rate for the quarter century as a whole was far higher than it had been in the period from the end of World War II until 1980. Unemployment averaged 6.4 percent from 1980 to 2004, 1.4 percentage points higher than the 5 percent average in the period from 1948 to 1979.

High unemployment does not hit everyone equally. People who lose their job in periods of high unemployment are disproportionately less-educated workers and members of minority groups.[34] The unemployment rate for African Americans is on average approximately twice as high as the overall unemployment rate, and the unemployment rate for African American teens averages approximately six times the overall unemployment rate. Similarly, the unemployment rate for workers with a high school degree is typically two times higher than the unemployment rate for workers with a college degree, and the unemployment rate for workers who have not completed high school is close to three times higher.

This means that if the Fed uses higher unemployment as a tool to combat inflation, less-educated workers and minorities will disproportionately bear the cost of this policy.

This cost shows up not just in higher unemployment but also in lower wages. Since high unemployment disproportionately reduces the demand for less-educated workers, these workers are less likely to see healthy wage gains during periods of high unemployment. The low unemployment at the end of the nineties provides a simple test of the impact of unemployment on different segments of the workforce.

---

[34] The relatively greater rise in unemployment among less-educated workers can be explained if firms are more likely to lay off production and nonsupervisory workers during a downturn than managers and professional staff, who tend to be more highly educated. The pattern of higher unemployment among minorities during periods of slack employment can be explained if employers discriminate against minorities. In periods of low unemployment, they may not have the option to discriminate and may be forced to hire minorities even if they would prefer not to; however, in periods of high unemployment, they would be able to hire only white workers. See R. Blank, M. Dabady, and C. Citro, eds., *Measuring Racial Discrimination* (Washington, DC: National Academies Press, 2004).

When unemployment reached the lowest levels since the late sixties, workers at all points along the wage distribution experienced real wage growth, with many of the largest gains going to those at the bottom.[35]

But the late nineties were the exception, as for most of this period unemployment was much higher than the average of the fifties and sixties. This meant that for most workers there was considerable slack in the labor market and therefore considerable downward pressure on wages.

Industry Deregulation and the Minimum Wage

There were other important policy shifts that also put downward pressure on the wages of less-skilled workers. Several major sectors of the economy that had provided relatively well paying jobs to less-educated workers were deregulated in this period. Beginning in the late seventies, the federal government weakened or eliminated regulation in the airline, electricity, telecommunication, and trucking industries. There were clearly efficiency gains from deregulating important sectors that had long been protected from competition. Also, in the case of the telecommunication industry in particular, some deregulation was probably necessary to allow for the gains from the rapid development of information technology.

Nonetheless, deregulation also had the effect of putting substantial downward pressure on the wages of many of the workers in these sectors. It also put pressure on firms to reduce their workforce, which is how deregulation increases efficiency. The net result from the standpoint of the workforce is that these sectors, which had provided relatively well paying jobs for workers without college degrees, became smaller and the wages they offered became less generous.[36] This in turn was another source of downward pressure on the wages of the less educated in the economy as a whole.

One last important change in the regulatory environment that had a large impact on the labor market was the erosion in the value of the

---

[35] The impact of low unemployment on wage growth for less-educated workers is documented in J. Bernstein and D. Baker, *The Benefits of Full Employment* (Washington, DC: Economic Policy Institute, 2004). See also J. Galbraith, *Created Unequal: The Crisis in American Pay* (Chicago: University of Chicago Press, 2000).

[36] See J. Peoples, "Deregulation and the Labor Market," *Journal of Economic Perspectives* (Summer 1998): 111–30.

minimum wage. In prior decades, the standard practice had been to raise the minimum wage to more or less keep pace with economy-wide productivity growth. However, this changed with the election of Ronald Reagan in 1980. He declared his opposition to the minimum wage and obstructed any legislated increases during his term in office, allowing the real value of the minimum wage to be eroded by inflation. Although there were two increases in the minimum wage in the years after Reagan left office, in 2005 the real value of the minimum wage was 40 percent lower than in 1980.

In 1980, the minimum wage was equal to 45 percent of the average hourly wage for production and nonsupervisory workers. By 2005, it was equal to just 32 percent of the average hourly wage. By 2005, more than 10 percent of the workforce, or more than 14 million people, were working at wages below the 1980 value of the minimum wage. Had the minimum wage moved in step with average wage growth over this period, it would have been $7.30 in 2005, $2.15 higher than its actual level of $5.15.[37]

The combined effect of these measures was to redistribute wages upward from workers in the middle and at the bottom of the wage distribution to those at the top. For example, a worker at the 90th percentile in wage income did relatively well in this period. (This is a worker who earns more money than 90 percent of all workers and less money than 10 percent.) In 2003, the ratio of the wage of workers at the 90th percentile to the wage of workers at the 50th percentile was 2.3.[38] (A worker at the 50th percentile earned just more than $15 an hour in 2003, while a worker at the 90th percentile earned $34 an hour.) The ratio of the wage of workers at the 90th percentile to the wage of workers at the 10th percentile was 4.6. By comparison, these two ratios in 1979 had been 1.8 and 3.7, respectively.

The shift to very high end workers, those in the top 5 percent of the wage distribution, was even larger, as workers at the 95th percentile of the wage distribution experienced substantially more rapid wage growth in this period than did workers at the 90th percentile, with a rate of wage increase roughly 10 percentage points greater. It is

[37] These numbers are based on the data in Mishel et al., *State of Working America 2004/2005*, table 1.6.

[38] These data are taken from Mishel et al., *State of Working America 2004/2005*, table 1.7.

likely that the small groups of workers even higher up the wage ladder, primarily higher-level business executives and highly paid professionals such as doctors and lawyers, gained even more over this quarter century.

In short, the government implemented a series of policies during this period that had the effect of shifting wage income upward. This was a predictable result of policies that placed downward pressure on the wages of a large segment of the labor force. These polices involved removing protections of various types for workers in the bottom three-quarters of the labor force and subjecting these workers to increased international competition. While these policies were generally justified as increasing economic efficiency, no comparable drives for economic efficiency were directed toward the protections that benefited higher-income workers. This one-sided application of market forces had the effect of redistributing income from those who lost protection to those who were able to maintain it.

Tax and Transfer Policy

On top of this upward redistribution of market income, there was also an effort to change tax policy in this period so that wealthier taxpayers faced lower tax bills. This effort at reducing the tax bill for higher-income families started with the Reagan tax cuts in the years 1981 to 1983. These tax cuts reduced the top marginal income tax rate from 70 percent when Reagan took office in 1981 to 50 percent in 1983. The top tax rate was reduced further to just 28 percent with the tax reform of 1986. (The actual reduction in the tax burden on the wealthy was considerably less than indicated by the reduction in tax rates, because many loopholes were also eliminated, most importantly the special treatment of capital gains.)

These tax cuts for high-income taxpayers were partially reversed by tax increases backed by the first President Bush in 1990 and President Clinton in 1993, which raised the top marginal tax rate back to 39.6 percent.[39] However, tax cuts put in place by the second President

---

[39] The 1993 tax bill also removed the cap on the Medicare tax, thereby applying a 2.95 percent tax on all wage income. Previously, this tax did not apply to wage income greater than the equivalent of $90,000 in 2005 dollars.

Bush lowered the top tax rate back to 35 percent in 2002. More important, they reduced the tax rate paid on dividends and capital gains, the main sources of income for the wealthiest taxpayers, to just 15 percent – far below the marginal tax rate paid by many middle-income families.

The cumulative effect of these changes was to reduce the share of income paid in federal taxes by the richest 1 percent of taxpayers from 37 percent in 1979 to 32.7 percent in 2002, a decline of 4.3 percentage points. By comparison, the net federal tax burden for those in the bottom quintile fell by 3.4 percentage points, from 8 to 4.6 percent of their income.[40] (Data for later years, which would incorporate the full effects of the Bush tax cuts, are likely to show an even sharper decline in tax rates for high-income taxpayers.)

If the government was taking less from those at the top by the end of the period, it was also redistributing less to those at the bottom. A range of government programs providing various forms of assistance to low-income families were substantially cut back over this quarter century. Most notably, the main federal welfare program, Aid to Families with Dependent Children (AFDC), was transformed and cut back, providing benefits to far fewer people and imposing much more stringent qualification rules. The beneficiaries of the new Temporary Aid to Needy Families program in 2003 totaled roughly half of the number of people who benefited from AFDC in the late seventies (5 million versus 10 million).[41] This decline occurred in spite of the fact that the unemployment rate was comparable during these two periods and that the population was approximately one-third greater in 2003 than in the late seventies.

There are many other areas in which there were substantial cutbacks in government programs intended to assist lower-income families in this period. To a large extent, these cutbacks were part of an explicit government policy of requiring families to be less dependent on government assistance and more reliant on the market. These cutbacks, along with the tax cuts of this era, were the focus of many of the

[40] Congressional Budget Office, *Historical Effective Federal Tax Rates: 1979 to 2002* (Washington, DC: Congressional Budget Office, 2005), Supplemental Tables, table 1A, http://www.cbo.gov/Spreadsheet/6133_Tables.xls.

[41] Congressional Budget Office, *Changes in Participation in Means-Tested Programs* (Washington, DC: Congressional Budget Office, 2005), http://www.cbo.gov/showdoc.cfm?index=6302&sequence=0.

political debates that dominated elections in the last quarter century. Although the impact of these cutbacks was important, the shift in policies affecting the market distribution of income was certainly more important in the lives of most families. Yet this shift, which resulted in a large upward redistribution of market income, has received far less attention in public debates.

2

Setting the Scene: The United States in 1980

In the summer of 1979, President Jimmy Carter gave the country what came to be known as his "malaise" speech, in which he decried the self-ishness of the American people. He warned that the country faced tough times ahead, most immediately from the energy crisis that had sent oil prices soaring and led to long lines at gas stations. He implored the country to be prepared to share in sacrifice as he set forth an agenda for energy conservation and the development of alternative sources of energy.

These were not the words the country wanted to hear. President Carter's approval rating sank to new lows, rivaling those of President Nixon just before he was forced to resign after being implicated in the Watergate scandal. Things did not get much better for President Carter in the year and a half leading up to the 1980 election. A close U.S. ally in Nicaragua was overthrown by a popular uprising. The U.S. embassy was seized in Iran and the staff taken hostage. A carefully planned rescue mission ended with a helicopter crash in the Iranian desert the following year.

Domestically, oil prices continued to rise, pushing inflation to lev-els not seen since data had been kept. The Federal Reserve Board responded by raising interest rates to unprecedented levels. The rise is interest rates had a mitigating effect on inflation, but it also sent the economy into a recession in the spring of 1980. This was not a good backdrop for a president running for reelection.

The End of the Postwar Golden Age

From an economic standpoint, the seventies, or more precisely the years after 1973, marked the end of a golden age. The years from the end of World War II up to that point had been a period of a largely unbroken prosperity. The economy had grown rapidly through most of the period, with low rates of both unemployment and inflation. The periods of recession were relatively short and mild, with the economy bouncing back quickly in the aftermath. Also, the economic gains from this period were evenly shared, with workers at all points along the wage distribution enjoying the gains of rapid productivity growth.

Although there is still considerable dispute among economists about the factors that led to the end of the economic golden age following World War II, the basic facts are clear enough. First and foremost, there was a sharp slowing of productivity growth. Productivity growth is a key measure of economic progress because it measures the increase in economic output per hour of work. For example, if productivity grows 2 percent in a year, then on average, the economy has 2 percent more output for every hour worked. This means that workers can all receive 2 percent higher wages and 2 percent more in pension and health care benefits, the government can offer 2 percent more services, and corporate profits can also increase by 2 percent. Of course, one of these components can grow more rapidly – for example, wages can grow by 3 percent if there is some redistribution from profits or elsewhere – but 2 percent productivity growth means that the base growth rate for all parts of the economy is 2 percent, changes in distribution aside.

Productivity had grown at a 2.8 percent annual rate from 1947 until 1973. From 1973 to 1980, it grew at just a 1 percent rate.[1] A variety of theories have been put forward to explain this slowdown in productivity growth, including growing international competition, the stultifying effects of powerful labor unions, and higher energy prices. Most economists accept that energy prices played a role in the productivity slowdown, but there is little agreement beyond this point.[2] However, the fact that productivity was growing more slowly meant that things could not continue as they had before.

---

[1] These data refer to productivity in the nonfarm business sector. The data can be found in the *2005 Economic Report of the President*, table B-49.

[2] For a discussion of the productivity slowdown, see E. Denison, *Accounting for Slower Economic Growth* (Washington, DC: Brookings Institution, 1979); N. Baily and R. Gordon, "The Productivity Slowdown, Measurement Issues, and the Explosion of Computer Power," *Brookings Papers on Economic Activity*, no. 2 (1998): 465–521; and T. Weisskopf, S. Bowles, and D. Gordon, "Hearts and Minds: A Social Model of U.S. Productivity Growth," *Brookings Papers on Economic Activity*, no. 2 (1983): 381–441.

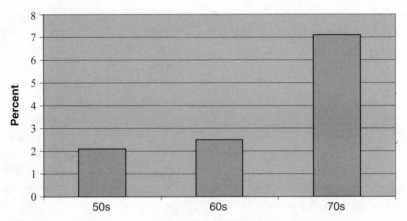

Figure 2–1. Inflation rates in the seventies.

Most important, it was no longer possible for real wages to rise at the same rate as they had in the golden age. During the period from 1947 to 1973, real wages had been rising at a rate of approximately 2 percent a year. If firms maintained this same rate of wage growth in a period of 1 percent productivity growth, it would lead to either an acceleration in the rate of inflation, as firms passed higher wages on in the form of higher prices, or a squeeze in corporate profits. The seventies saw both occur. The inflation rate for the decade as a whole averaged 7.1 percent annually (Figure 2-1). This compared to 2.1 percent in the fifties and 2.5 percent in the sixties.[3] At the same time, the profit share of corporate income was squeezed to its lowest level in the postwar era, falling to 17.1 percent in 1979 from an average of 20.7 percent in the sixties, a decline in profit share of almost 20 percent.[4]

This mix of events led to considerable economic anxiety in all corners. Workers could no longer count on continually rising real wages; the wages of many workers did not keep pace with inflation after 1973. The real average hourly wage for production and nonsupervisory workers (more than 80 percent of the workforce) fell by 11 percent between 1973 and 1980. In addition, workers were made far more

[3] This is based on the CPI-U-RS for 1978–80 and the CPI-UX1 for 1950–78; these data are available in the "Get Detailed Statistics" section of the Bureau of Labor Statistics website (bls.gov).

[4] Profit data are taken from the Commerce Department's National Income and Product Accounts, table 1.1.4, line 8 divided by line 3 (bea.gov).

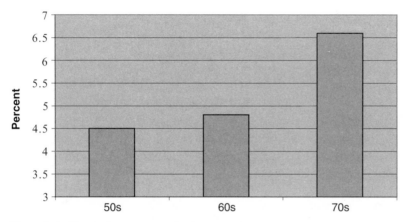

Figure 2–2. Unemployment rates in the seventies.

insecure by the relatively high unemployment in the period, with the unemployment rate averaging 6.6 percent between 1973 and 1980, compared with an average of 4.5 percent in the fifties and 4.8 percent in the sixties (Figure 2-2).

The profit squeeze was not good news for the stock market, which fell by 44.9 percent between its 1968 peak and 1980, after adjusting for inflation.[5] Higher inflation also led to higher interest rates. The interest rate on ten-year treasury bonds had averaged 3.2 percent in the fifties and 4.9 percent in the sixties. This jumped to 8.3 percent for the years from 1973 to 1980. High interest rates were an especially important political issue, because they meant high mortgage interest rates. With the huge baby boom cohort first beginning to form their own households in these years, the prospect of double-digit mortgage interest rates threatened to make homeownership unaffordable for tens of millions of families.[6]

The squeeze on wages and family incomes also translated into a squeeze on public budgets, as workers became less willing to acquiesce to higher taxes. Although government at all levels had expanded rapidly

---

[5] This refers to the S&P 500 Index.

[6] In economic theory, the real interest – the difference between the market interest rate and the rate of inflation – should be the factor affecting home buying and other economic activity, not the market interest rate. The real interest rate was in fact quite low throughout most of the decade of the seventies. However, it is likely that many people do not have a clear understanding of the real interest rate and make their decisions based largely on the market interest rate, without fully recognizing the importance of inflation.

in the fifties and sixties, the public became increasingly resistant to further tax increases in the seventies.[7] The incident that typified this resistance was Proposition 13, a property tax limitation initiative in California that was placed on the ballot without the backing of the established leadership of either political party. The measure passed in June 1978 by a margin of 65 percent to 35 percent. It appeared as a ballot initiative in a primary election that pulled out 70 percent of registered voters. In the wake of the passage of Proposition 13, there was a nationwide wave of tax limitation measures at the state and local level. Some of these measures were Proposition 13–type initiatives, while others were implemented through the legislative process, but over the next few years numerous states and local governments had implemented tax or spending restrictions modeled after Proposition 13.

There was an important racial dimension to these tax and spending measures. Proponents of these restrictions would often portray the beneficiaries of government programs as a distinct population from those who paid taxes. Howard Jarvis, the coauthor of Proposition 13, often described the measure as part of the battle of "us against them," where "us" referred to hardworking taxpayers and "them" to government bureaucrats and welfare recipients. The fact that many voters saw themselves as benefiting little from government programs and did not identify with the people they viewed as beneficiaries played an important role in advancing the antitax movement of this era.[8]

The United States and the World in the Post-Vietnam Era

By 1980, the United States had still not come to grips with the meaning of its defeat in the Vietnam War. The fall of Vietnam as well as Laos

---

[7] The tax share (at all levels of government) of GDP rose from 24.1 percent in 1950 to 28.6 percent in 1980. Since 1980, it has fallen back slightly, to 27.6 percent of GDP in 2003.

[8] There is an extensive literature on the economic stagnation of the seventies and its political implications. For example, see A. Blinder, *Economic Policy and the Great Stagflation* (New York: Academic Press, 1981); S. Bowles, D. Gordon, D. Bell, and I. Kristol, eds., *The Crisis in Economic Theory* (New York: Basic Books, 1981); and T. Weisskopf, *Beyond the Wasteland: A Democratic Alternative to Economic Decline* (New York: Anchor Press/Doubleday, 1983). For a discussion of the tax revolts of the late seventies and their legacy, see A. Sullivan, T. Sexton, and F. Sheffrin, *Property Taxes and Tax Revolts: The Legacy of Proposition 13* (Cambridge: Cambridge University Press, 1995), and D. A. Smith, *Tax Crusaders and the Politics of Direct Democracy* (London: Routledge, 1998).

and Cambodia to the movements that the United States had been fighting was a military defeat without precedent in U.S. history. The final chapter in the spring of 1975 was particularly humiliating to the image of the United States as an unchallenged superpower, with embassies evacuated by helicopter as the victorious forces allowed the United States to remove the last elements of a once massive presence in the region. While many of those who had cooperated with the United States during the war were evacuated as well, a much larger number were left an uncertain fate.

The Vietnam War had been incredibly divisive within the United States, leading to the downfall of two presidents. There had been massive protests across the country, with some turning violent or prompting violent responses from the police or National Guard. As various leaks and investigations of the seventies exposed, the federal government, along with local police forces, had engaged in illegal spying and sabotage efforts aimed at disrupting the antiwar movement. The contention surrounding the war in Southeast Asia persisted after the war ended. Supporters of the war maintained that the military had been betrayed and held back from using the force that would have allowed it to achieve victory. Opponents of the war viewed the Vietnam War as demonstrating that the government could not be trusted, especially with the use of military power.[9]

In the aftermath of the war, there was a clear reluctance on the part of the public to see U.S. troops deployed in combat – a reluctance that became known as the "Vietnam Syndrome." This became a problem for U.S. administrations as client regimes were challenged by internal opposition throughout the developing world. The inability of the United States to use military force openly to keep friendly regimes in power, as it had done, for example, in the Dominican Republic in 1965, was a serious restriction on U.S. power.

---

[9] In 1975, a Senate committee headed by Idaho Senator Frank Church conducted extensive investigations into U.S. covert operations over the prior three decades. It uncovered many instances in which the United States appeared to be acting to subvert democracy in foreign countries, in many cases supporting military coups and the killing of political opponents. For a discussion of this and other investigations, see K. Olmstead, *Challenging the Secret Government: The Post-Watergate Investigations of the CIA and FBI* (Chapel Hill, NC: University of North Carolina Press, 1996). For a discussion of some of the domestic spying directed against antiwar groups during the sixties and seventies, see F. Donner, *Protectors of Privilege: Red Squads and Police Repression in Urban America* (Berkeley, CA: University of California Press, 1992).

This was especially important in the context of the cold war. At the time, the Soviet Union appeared to be the ascendant power. Its economy was still growing at healthy pace, whereas the U.S. economy seemed mired in stagnation. According to publicly available assessments, the overall military strength of the Soviet Union was comparable to that of the United States, and it was reported to have clear superiority in certain areas. In particular, it was widely reported that the Soviet Union's military forces in Europe were far superior to those of the United States and its NATO allies, creating the possibility that the Soviet Union's ground forces could easily overwhelm NATO defenses.[10] In fact, the Defense Department planned to introduce a set of short-range nuclear missiles and battlefield nuclear weapons into Europe in order to address this perceived military imbalance.

However, the diminishing ability of the United States to protect its allies in the developing world was probably the most immediate concern in policy circles. The clearest example of the loss of U.S. influence in the world was the overthrow of the shah of Iran in February 1979. The shah had been a close U.S. ally for a quarter century. He was put in power on the back of a U.S.-organized military coup that overthrew a popular nationalist government. At the time, Iran was important both because it was the second largest oil exporter in the world (after Saudi Arabia) and because it had a large population and a relatively powerful military. The United States had actually sought to build up Iran as a regional power under the Nixon and Ford administrations in order to help it project power in the Middle East.

There was a long lead-up to the Iranian revolution in the form of ever larger street demonstrations against the shah's rule.[11] The support for these demonstrations came from all segments of society. The shah's repression and corruption had united the country in opposition. Although the Islamic clerics provided an institutional basis of support for the opposition (most other forms of institutional opposition had been banned by the shah), the opposition included many secular

[10] The most noteworthy group in raising the alarm about growing Soviet power was the Committee on the Present Danger, which was formed in 1976. The group took the name of an earlier group formed in 1950 to warn about the Soviet threat in the immediate aftermath of World War II. The reformed Committee on the Present Danger included many prominent academics and former government officials. Many of its members came to hold top foreign policy positions in the Reagan administration.

[11] On the Iranian revolution see M. Parsa, *Social Origins of the Iranian Revolution* (New Brunswick, NJ: Rutgers University Press, 1989), and N. Keddie, *Modern Iran: Roots and Results of Revolution* (New Haven, CT: Yale University Press, 1993).

nationalists, including many highly educated professionals who had studied in Western Europe and the United States. As the wave of strikes and protests grew throughout 1978, the Carter administration appeared to have been completely caught off guard by the depth of the hostility to the shah.

Furthermore, it was completely powerless to do anything to stem the tide. The opposition to the shah was so widespread that nothing short of a massive U.S. military presence could keep him in power. And even then a U.S. military force would have almost certainly faced years of guerilla resistance, with no guarantee of eventual success. In the wake of Vietnam, it was inconceivable that a U.S. administration would send hundreds of thousands of troops to Iran to keep the shah in power.

The last days of the shah's regime gave a clear demonstration of the limited ability of the Carter administration to steer events in Iran. The shah was persuaded to leave the country and turn over power to a former political opponent, Shapour Bakhtiar, who was considered a pro-U.S. moderate. However, this change only further fueled the opposition movement. On February 1, 1979, Ayatollah Ruhollah Khomeini, the symbolic leader of the opposition, returned from a fifteen-year exile. Several million people marched in the streets of Teheran in a show of support for Khomeini and the revolution. The massive demonstrations continued for the next several days. Against this enormous mass of humanity, the shah's powerful army proved helpless. They would not fire on their friends and relatives. On February 11, 1979, a provisional government supported by Khomeini took power after Bahktiar had resigned and left the country.

This set of events would have been humiliating enough for the United States in its status as a superpower. However, there was more yet to come. In September 1979, at the urging of former Secretary of State Henry Kissinger, arrangements were made to have the shah come to the United States from his exile in Panama. The ostensible reason was that he needed to come to the United States to receive appropriate treatment for the cancer that he was suffering from at the time. The actual reason was to show the world that the United States would stand behind its allies, at least to the extent of ensuring them a safe place of refuge.[12]

---

[12] The efforts of Henry Kissinger to engineer the shah's entrance into the United States are discussed in D. Harris, *The Crisis: The President, the Prophet, and the Shah – 1979 and the Coming of Militant Islam* (New York: Little, Brown and Co., 2004), 185–94.

This step provoked outrage in Iran. It led to large and angry street protests against the United States. Finally, in November, a group of radicals used the shah's admission to the United States as a pretext to seize the U.S. embassy and hold its staff hostage. While the seizure of the embassy and the taking of hostages was a central event in the ongoing power struggle in Iran, in the United States it was widely seen as yet another humiliation. Embassy staffers were photographed being led around blindfolded by their captors. And there seemed to be nothing that the United States could do about it.

Things did not appear to be going much better for the United States elsewhere in the world. In July 1979, the president of Nicaragua, Anastasio Somoza, was overthrown by a left-wing nationalist guerilla movement. Somoza was a corrupt dictator whose father had been installed by the U.S. military in the 1930s. The Sandinistas, the movement that overthrew Somoza, took their name from the nationalist leader Augusto Cesar Sandino, who had been a leader of the opposition to the U.S. occupation of Nicaragua in the thirties. Sandino had been killed by the senior Somoza in 1934.[13]

As in Iran, the United States appeared relatively powerless to influence the course of events in Nicaragua. The Somoza dynasty had been closely allied with the United States since it was installed in power in the thirties. The members could be counted on to give unwavering support not only to domestic policies favorable to U.S. multinationals but also to policies helpful to U.S. interests internationally. For example, they allowed Nicaragua to be used as a staging ground for the Bay of Pigs invasion of Cuba in 1961. In return, the United States had been willing to tolerate the Somoza dynasty's repressive measures and its corruption.

Somoza had never been very popular. Nicaragua was among the poorest countries in the Western Hemisphere, with low levels of literacy and a high infant mortality rate, but the event that really fed the disaffection with Somoza was the corruption surrounding the rebuilding efforts following a major earthquake in Nicaragua in 1972. The public

---

[13] Accounts of the background events leading up to the Nicaraguan revolution and the unrest in Central America at the time can be found in H. Vanden and G. Prevost, *Democracy and Socialism in Sandinista Nicaragua* (Boulder, CO: Lynne Rienner Publishers, 1992); W. LaFeber, *Inevitable Revolutions: The United States in Central America* (New York: W. W. Norton and Co., 1993); and R. Woodward, *Central America: A Nation Divided* (New York: Oxford University Press, 1999).

saw very little benefit from the international relief aid that poured in following the disaster, as Somoza and his allies pocketed much of this money.

The level of discontent was demonstrated to the world after a dramatic hostage-taking by the Sandinistas in the summer of 1978, in which they managed to seize many of the top political figures in the country and some of Somoza's closest associates. The Sandinistas negotiated a release of the hostages in exchange for the freeing of several political prisoners and a substantial sum of money. When the hostage takers were being escorted from Managua to the city airport, tens of thousands of people lined the road waving Nicaraguan flags in a gesture of support for the Sandinistas.

One year later, the Sandinistas had seized power, overwhelming Somoza's small but loyal National Guard. The Carter administration had worked vigorously to the end to keep the National Guard intact as a military unit. However, the Sandinistas refused to budge on this point. Carter's last effort was to try to persuade the Organization of American States to sponsor an intervention that would keep the Sandinistas from taking power. When this too failed, the only thing left for the Carter administration to do was to organize an orderly transfer of power to the new government.

As with Iran, the new government had support from all segments of the population. Although there were many disputes and subsequent divisions within its leadership, it was clear that the Sandinistas would not maintain the same sort of relationship with the United States as Somoza. At the top of their agenda was promoting literacy and extending access to health care. Among their allies were Cuba and the Soviet Union.

Making matters even worse from the standpoint of the Carter administration, the Sandinista revolution served as an inspiration to insurgencies elsewhere in Central America. In particular, armed opposition groups in El Salvador and Guatemala, who were also confronting repressive dictatorships, received a substantial morale boost from seeing the first successful insurrection in Latin America in more than twenty years. In the wake of the Sandinista revolution, the ability of the governments in both countries to hold onto power was open to question.

The forces allied with the United States were also not faring well in Africa. By the mid-seventies, Africa was in the last phase of its decolonization process. Portugal, the last European country with substantial colonies in Africa, granted independence to Angola,

Mozambique, and Guinea-Bissau in 1974 and 1975. In each country, parties that were at least loosely allied with the Soviet Union came to power, although civil wars continued to rage well into the eighties in both Angola and Mozambique.

The United States was also at least implicitly allied with Africa's two white settler states, Zimbabwe (Rhodesia at the time) and South Africa. This alliance with governments that were openly racist was difficult to justify given official commitments to democracy and equality. Zimbabwe presented the more urgent problem. A white settler government had seized power against the wishes of Great Britain in 1965 and declared Rhodesia's independence. Whites made up just 5 percent of the population in Zimbabwe, compared with 20 percent in South Africa, and could only maintain their privileged existence by denying the rights of the black majority. From its creation, the white government was subject to international sanctions, which were supported by the United States.

By the mid-seventies, substantial guerilla opposition to white rule had developed. The Carter administration worked actively to try to install a moderate black government, hoping to keep the two guerilla movements that had been fighting for democratic rule from reaching power. Both movements claimed to be socialist, one being allied with the Soviet Union, the other being allied with China. The Carter administration's efforts fell apart when the guerilla groups won a commitment from the Rhodesian government to a United Nations–supervised election in February 1980. The two guerilla groups together won almost 90 percent of the vote, while the moderate candidate backed by the Carter administration barely received 5 percent.[14]

There is one final point on the map worth mentioning in painting the global picture at the beginning at the eighties. The Soviet Union invaded Afghanistan in December 1979.[15] A year earlier, a pro-Soviet government had come to power, promising to reform the

---

[14] For an account of the U.S. role in Rhodesia/Zimbabwe, see G. Horne, *From the Barrel of a Gun: The United States and the War Against Zimbabwe, 1965–1980* (Chapel Hill, NC: University of North Carolina Press, 2001).

[15] On the situation in Afghanistan prior to the invasion, see R. Magnus, E. Naby, and D. Rather, *Afghanistan: Mullah, Marx, and Mujahid* (Boulder, CO: Westview Press, 2002). On the invasion itself, see M. Kakar, *Afghanistan: The Soviet Invasion and the Afghan Response 1979–82* (Berkeley, CA: University of California Press, 1997).

still largely feudal country. Afghanistan was one of the poorest countries in the world at the time. The central government had limited control in Afghanistan. Much of the power rested with tribal chiefs in this mountainous country possessed of a poorly developed transportation system. The new government made a commitment to modernizing Afghanistan, which included moving toward secular rule (a difficult goal in a conservative Islamic country) and promoting the rights of women.

It was not long before the government ran into substantial opposition. In September 1979, there was a violent change of leadership within the government as Hafizullah Amin, the defense minister, seized control. The change in leadership did not help the government in establishing control. In response to the failures of the Amin government and Amin's resistance to advice from the Soviet Union, the Soviet leadership decided to take matters directly in its own hands. It arranged for the overthrow of Amin and moved its own troops into Afghanistan, just before the end of the year.

This advance of the Soviet Union beyond its borders prompted fear and outrage in the United States. President Carter described the invasion as the greatest threat to peace since World War II. He proposed increases to the defense budget and took the first step toward reinstituting the military draft, requiring universal registration by eighteen- and nineteen-year-old men. He also cancelled U.S. participation in the Olympics, which were scheduled to be held in Moscow in the summer of 1980, making obvious the comparison with the 1936 Olympics, held in Berlin as Hitler was laying the groundwork for World War II.

Much of the news coverage of the invasion portrayed it as part of a much grander scheme of conquest. For example, it was alleged that this invasion was partly intended to realize the long-standing Russian dream of obtaining a warm-water port, even though the southern border of Afghanistan is more than 200 miles from the Indian Ocean.[16] It became standard practice to refer to this poor, mountainous, landlocked country as "strategically located." Following in the wake of the Iranian revolution and the seizure of the U.S. embassy, as well as

---

[16] This assertion can be found, for example, in J. Kirkpatrick, *Legitimacy and Force: National and International Dimensions* (Somerset, NJ: Transactions Publishers, 1988), 284. Kirkpatrick served as ambassador to the United Nations in the Reagan administration.

events elsewhere in the world, there was a widely held view that the Soviet Union was gaining the upper hand in the cold war and that the United States was in retreat.

The Economic Crisis of 1979–1980

The economic problems of the post-1973 era were coming to a head in the years 1979–80. The 1974–5 recession had been much more severe than any prior postwar slump, with the unemployment rate peaking at 9 percent in May 1975. Although the economy bounced back and grew at a healthy pace from 1976 through 1978, the pre-1973 prosperity had not returned. The unemployment rate never got below 5.6 percent and was already back up to 6 percent by August 1979.

At least as important was the fact that wages were not keeping pace with prices. Although real wages had advanced by close to 2 percent a year in the fifties and sixties, the average real hourly wage for production and nonsupervisory workers was virtually unchanged from the end of 1976 to 1978.[17] Real wages began to plummet in 1979 as prices rose much faster than wages. The most important factors pushing up inflation were soaring gas and home heating oil prices, an outgrowth of the Iranian revolution. Strikes and other disruptions slowed the flow of oil from Iran to a trickle. As a result, the price of oil went from under $13 a barrel at the beginning of 1978 to more than $30 a barrel by the end of 1979. This led to a decline in real average hourly wages of almost 5 percent from December 1978 to December 1979. The real wage fell another 3 percent between the end of 1979 and the election in November 1980.

---

[17] This discussion uses the consumer price index that was in place at the time (CPI-W) as the basis for adjusting wages. It is widely accepted that this index substantially overstated the true rate of consumer inflation in these years, primarily because of its treatment of owner-occupied housing. However, most actors in the economy would have likely viewed the published CPI as the benchmark against which to assess their standard of living. At the time, many wage contracts were explicitly indexed to the CPI, so it is reasonable to believe that a substantial segment of the population had some knowledge of the published data. Recent research suggests that erroneous data can affect economic behavior and outcomes (see D. Baker, *The Effect of Mis-measured Inflation on Wage Growth* (Washington, DC: Economic Policy Institute, 1998), and A. Blinder and J. Yellen, "The Fabulous Decade: Macroeconomic Lessons from the 1990s," in *The Roaring Nineties*, ed. A. Krueger and R. Solow, 91–156 (New York: Russell Sage Foundation and Century Foundation, 2002).

The dollar was also plummeting in international financial markets, as strong currencies such as the German mark and the Japanese yen were reaching new highs against the dollar. The United States had run modest trade surpluses throughout most of the postwar era, but the run-up in oil prices had reversed this pattern, and by the late seventies the country was running trade deficits equal to approximately 1 percent of GDP. While trade deficits of this size are trivial compared to the trade deficits of the mid-eighties or the first decade of the current century (in 2005, the trade deficit was almost 6 percent of GDP), at the time they were viewed with alarm. For the first time in the postwar era, the United States was in a situation where it had to borrow money from abroad to pay for its imports. In fact, in the fall of 1978 the U.S. government was in the awkward position of having to arrange for a loan package from other central banks to support the dollar.

There was also concern over the size of the federal budget deficit. While the budget deficits of the era would be viewed as very modest by current standards, many people believed that they were growing out of control.[18] (The 1980 budget deficit was 2.7 percent of GDP, and the 1979 deficit was equal to just 1.6 percent of GDP. By comparison, in 1983 the deficit was 6 percent of GDP, and it was 3.6 percent of GDP in 2004.) The need to curtail budget deficits and balance the budget was a common theme among politicians at the time.

But the most immediate concern of economic policy makers was the acceleration of the inflation rate. While inflation was running at more than a 7 percent annual rate through the second half of 1978, it was running at more than a 13 percent pace through most of 1979. The Federal Reserve Board felt the need to slow the economy in the hope of bringing the rate of inflation down to acceptable levels. Its method was to slow the growth of the money supply and thereby push up interest rates. The federal funds rate, the short-term interest rate that is most directly under the Federal Reserve Board's control, jumped from 10 percent at the end of 1978 to almost 14 percent by the

[18] Part of the exaggerated concern over the budget deficits of the era was attributable to the failure to understand the impact of inflation. Although the budget deficit was hitting new highs in nominal terms, it was not especially large relative to the size of the economy. Furthermore, because inflation was eroding the real value of the government debt, the ratio of debt to GDP was actually falling throughout this period. The size of the gross federal debt fell from 35.2 percent at the end of fiscal year 1976 to 33.3 percent at the end of the fiscal year 1980.

end of 1979.[19] The Federal Reserve Board continued to push interest rates higher in the first four months of 1980, with federal funds rate eventually peaking at 17.6 percent in April 1980.[20]

The run-up in short-term interest rates had the desired effect of pushing up long-term interests, which have the most effect on the economy. Interest rates on corporate bonds and home mortgages soared, with the thirty-year mortgage rate peaking at 13.7 percent in May 1980, more than 4 full percentage points higher than its 9.6 percent average for 1978. This spike in mortgage rates sent construction plummeting. Just to ensure that its actions brought the desired economic slowdown, the Federal Reserve Board also took advantage of its power to limit credit card debt in March 1980, sharply slowing the growth of consumer borrowing.

Taken together, these steps did have the desired effect of slowing the economy. In the first half of 1980, the economy shrank at a 3.4 percent annual rate. The unemployment rate spiked in this period, reaching 7.8 percent in July 1980, more than 2 full percentage points above its level a year earlier. This slowdown helped to dampen inflation, even if the underlying rate still remained very high. The overall annual inflation rate peaked in the first quarter of 1980, reaching more than 18 percent. By the third quarter, the inflation rate had slowed to 12.3 percent.

In sum, the economic situation leading up to the election in 1980 could hardly have been worse for an incumbent president. The economy had just been through a short but deep recession. Although the data showed the economy recovering, it is unlikely that many workers saw much tangible evidence of improvement by election day in November. Real wages had been stagnant for several years but had fallen sharply in the two years just preceding the election. High mortgage interest rates were badly depressing the housing market, making a new house unaffordable for those looking to buy for the first time and keeping prices lower than expected for those hoping to sell. All

---

[19] The federal funds rate is the interest rate that banks charge each other to lend the reserves needed to meet regulatory standards. The Federal Reserve Board effectively sets this rate by increasing or decreasing the supply of funds available in this market. By raising or lowering this interest rate, it tries to raise or lower other interest rates, which will in turn slow or speed the pace of economic growth.

[20] These data can be found on the Federal Reserve Board's website at http://www.federalreserve.gov/releases/h15/data/m/fedfund.txt.

of this occurred against a backdrop of concerns about running out of oil, a weak dollar, and soaring trade and budget deficits.

This domestic situation was coupled with an international picture in which the United States appeared to be in retreat almost everywhere. Most important, or at least most visible in the media, fifty-two U.S. citizens were being held hostage in Iran and there was nothing that President Carter could do about it.

3

The Reagan Revolution: Running to the Right

There were two large headlines across the top of the *New York Times* on January 20, 1981. One reported that Ronald Wilson Reagan had been inaugurated the prior day as the fortieth president of the United States. The second reported that the fifty-two U.S. citizens, held hostage for 444 days after the seizure of the U.S. embassy in Iran, had finally been released. The announcement that the plane carrying them out of Iran had taken off came just minutes after President Reagan took the oath of office.

The freeing of the hostages was the best backdrop that President Reagan could have asked for. He had used the phrase "It's morning in America" as his campaign theme, implying that a Reagan presidency would be a period of resurgence in the nation, which would show its strength both domestically and internationally. The image of the mullahs in Iran rushing to turn over the hostages rather than confronting a new and powerful president was exactly the one that the Reagan team hoped to convey as the new president took office. Unlike Jimmy Carter, this was not a president who could be pushed around.

Of course, the reality was quite different. There is little reason to believe that the Iranians turned over the hostages because they had any special fears of the new administration. The deal had been struck months earlier. The fact that the transfer of the hostages was delayed until Reagan took office was most likely an act of spite against President Carter. In fact, the Reagan administration allowed U.S. arms to be sold to Iran through Israel during Reagan's first months in office, suggesting that the Iranian government might have actually welcomed the new administration.[1] But the reality of the situation was not especially important on January 20, 1981. President Reagan had gotten the story he wanted – in his first hours after taking office, the enemies of the United States were already backing down under the pressure.

The 1980 Election

The 1980 election presented voters with a much clearer choice between the presidential candidates of the major parties than is typically the case. Usually the more extreme candidates are weeded out during the party's nomination process. In 1980, Ronald Reagan was clearly running as the candidate of the right wing of the Republican Party.[2] He had managed to defeat the more centrist candidates, most notably George H. W. Bush, who had standing at the time as a former CIA director and head of the Republican National Committee, and Senator Robert Dole, who had been the Republican vice-presidential candidate in 1976.

Reagan had entered the 1980 Republican presidential race as the favorite, but his nomination was hardly a foregone conclusion. A two-term governor of California, he had established his national electoral credentials in 1976, when he had challenged the incumbent president, Gerald Ford, for the Republican nomination. He managed to take the race right down to the wire at the convention that year, but the party insiders stayed with Ford and held Reagan just short of the delegates needed to get the nomination. This experience as a national candidate, coupled with Ford's subsequent defeat by Carter, left Reagan as the front-runner for the Republican nomination.

At the same time, there was a clear recognition that Reagan was coming from the right wing of the Republican Party and that this

---

[1] An account of the arms flows from Israel to Iran can be found in M. Brzoska and F. Pearson, *Arms and Warfare: Escalation, De-escalation, and Negotiation* (Columbia, SC: University of South Carolina Press, 1994).

[2] For a largely sympathetic account of the Reagan presidency, see L. Canon, *President Reagan: The Role of a Lifetime* (New York: Public Affairs Press, 2000). For a somewhat less positive assessment, see M. Schaller, *Reckoning with Reagan: America and Its President in the 1980s* (Oxford: Oxford University Press, 1994), and also H. Johnson, *Sleepwalking Through History: America in the Reagan Years* (New York: W. W. Norton and Co., 2003).

could make him vulnerable in the general election. In 1964, Arizona Senator Barry Goldwater won the Republican nomination with the support of the right wing of the party and went on to lose in a landslide to President Lyndon Johnson in the fall election. This memory was still fresh enough to be a cause of major concern for many party leaders. A main difference was that Reagan was a former actor and an extremely talented politician who was able to smooth over his conservative views and make them palatable to many who did not share them.

There were several key issues on which Reagan staked out positions that were not only markedly different from those of President Carter but also those of the more mainstream members of his own party. At the top of this list was his proposal for tax cuts. He proposed cutting federal income taxes by a third, insisting that high tax rates were strangling the economy. He also promised to balance the budget. (In addition, he had plans for a substantial increase in the defense budget.) When Reagan was questioned about the consistency of these plans, he argued that his tax cuts would provide such a boost to growth that revenues would actually increase in spite of the lower tax rates.

Reagan described his plan of promoting growth through tax cuts as "supply-side" economics – the idea that increasing the incentives to work and invest would cause the country's potential economic output to grow more rapidly. Tax and spending policy in prior years had largely been focused on the demand side, and the main strategies were to raise aggregate demand in times of recession and high unemployment and to lower aggregate demand in periods in which inflation was getting to be a problem. While economic policies in areas such as trade, regulation, and education were designed with an eye toward increasing potential economic output, the main effect of tax and spending policies was thought to be on aggregate demand, not the supply side of the economy.[3] Needless to say, Reagan's view of the economy was not widely accepted. His principle challenger in the Republican primaries, George H. W. Bush, dubbed it "voodoo economics."

Reagan also argued for a more confrontational approach toward the Soviet Union. He claimed that Carter had allowed U.S. military strength to sag and that there had been a loss of respect for the United States in the world. He pledged to rebuild U.S. military strength. He

---

[3] For a brief explanation of supply-side economics by one of its leading proponents, see J. Wanniski, *The Way the World Works* (Parsippany, NJ: Polyconomics, Inc., 1989).

also called for rejecting arms limitation agreements with the Soviet Union that were nearing completion at the time. The United States had first signed a strategic arms limitation treaty (SALT I) with the Soviets during the Nixon administration. Negotiations on its successor, SALT II, had begun during the Nixon and Ford administrations and had continued under Carter. Reagan essentially rejected the basic framework and insisted on going back to the drawing board.

Reagan was also more conservative than the Republican mainstream on a number of social issues, most notably abortion. While Democrats were more likely to be pro-choice prior to Reagan, there were many prominent Republicans (including George H. W. Bush) who identified with this position before 1980. A key element of the coalition that carried Reagan to victory in the Republican primaries was the Christian Right, and abortion was an issue that was very important to it. Reagan took a strong anti-abortion position into the election and made it the mainstream position within the Republican Party.

Regardless of the concerns the party leaders may have had over Reagan's conservatism (or his age; at sixty-nine he was the oldest person to ever run for a first term on a major party ticket), he managed to tie up the Republican nomination quickly. His competitors withdrew from the race after he scored decisive victories in the early primaries.

Jimmy Carter had a somewhat more difficult time winning his party's nomination, even though he was running as an incumbent president. There was considerable dissatisfaction with Carter among many of the party's core constituencies, including labor unions and African Americans, as well as many liberals who were concerned about an arms buildup that was already under way in the last year of the Carter administration.

Labor unions were angry over the declining real wages of their members and the Carter administration's efforts to control inflation, which relied to a considerable extent on slowing the pace of wage growth. They were also upset over the failure of the Carter administration, in spite of Democratic control of Congress, to amend labor laws to make them more union friendly. The discontent among African Americans stemmed largely from the limited gains that they were experiencing during the Carter years. As a rule of thumb, the African American unemployment rate is generally twice the overall unemployment rate, which meant that the 7.1 percent unemployment rate for the country as a whole in Carter's last year in office meant an unemployment rate of more than 14 percent for African Americans. The country had also just seen the first major court decision rolling back affirmative action, the Bakke case, and some African American groups did not trust Carter to prevent further reverses.

Senator Edward Kennedy, the last surviving brother of President John Kennedy, saw the 1980 election as an opportunity to launch a long-awaited presidential campaign. While his stature ensured that he would be a serious candidate, Kennedy could not muster the support needed to deprive an incumbent president of his party's nomination. Kennedy won several major primaries and a substantial minority of the delegates at the convention, but he did not come close to actually winning the nomination. Although the Democrats eventually rallied around Carter, Kennedy's candidacy demonstrated considerable discontent within the party and a lack of confidence in Carter.

The General Election

In spite of the weakness of the economy and the ongoing embarrassment of the hostages being held in Iran, the outcome of the election was very much up for grabs until the final weeks. Reagan was clearly associated with the right wing of the Republican Party, including fundamentalist Christian groups. His economic agenda, and in particular his plan for large tax cuts, was outside of the broad consensus that had been shared by both major parties since World War II. His stance on foreign policy was also intended to be a break with the positions pursued not only by Carter but also by Nixon and Ford. This concern over Reagan's perceived extremism kept Carter strongly in contention, and often even ahead in the polls, right up to the last week before the election.

Concerns over Reagan's extremism also provided the base for a third major candidate in the race. John Anderson, a Republican congressman who had run unsuccessfully in his party's presidential primaries, broke with the party and ran as an independent. He appealed to many Republicans who felt that Reagan was too conservative as well as many Democrats and independents who questioned Jimmy Carter's competence as a leader. Through much of the summer, Anderson polled well into the double digits, at times approaching the support levels for the major party candidates. Although Anderson's support eventually faded (he received less than 7 percent of the vote), the fact that he was a major factor in the campaign is an important reminder of the extent to which Reagan was viewed as being outside of the political mainstream at the time of the 1980 election.

In the last weeks, driven in part by solid performances in the presidential debates, Reagan pulled clearly ahead of Carter and went on to win by a margin of more than 7 percentage points in the popular vote. This translated into a landslide victory in the electoral college, with Reagan winning 489 votes to Carter's 49. While this victory was predictable given the final preelection polls, a more surprising result was that the Republicans took control of the Senate, picking up twelve seats. This was the largest pickup of Senate seats in a single election since 1958. It also meant that the Republicans would control a chamber of Congress for the first time in twenty-six years. The Republican takeover of the Senate, together with many victories in state offices and state legislatures, ensured that Reagan would have considerable momentum as he assumed office.

Reagan's electoral majority had built on the southern base established by Nixon but added many disaffected working-class Democrats in the North. In the last weeks of the campaign, Reagan effectively posed the question, "Are you better off today than you were four years ago?" Millions of workers in northern states who would ordinarily have voted Democratic had to answer this question with a no. Even if most of them were not ardent believers in Reagan's "supply-side" economics, at least Reagan held out the hope of a more prosperous future. This was a much more promising picture than Carter's calls for further sacrifice.

The Reagan Economic Agenda in Action

The centerpiece of the Reagan economic agenda was his plan for across-the-board tax cuts. During the campaign, he pledged to cut income taxes by a third. Once in office this cut was watered down slightly, with the targeted reduction being 25 percent phased in over a three-year period. As a practical matter, this meant cutting a set of tax brackets so that income at each level would be taxed at a lower rate.

The income tax is a marginal tax, which means that income above each tax threshold is taxed at a different tax rate than the income below that threshold. For example, suppose that workers pay zero tax on income up to $10,000 a year, a 10 percent tax on income from

$10,001 to $30,000, and a 20 percent tax on income of more than $30,000. If a worker earning $50,000 a year faced this tax structure, his tax bill would be calculated as follows:

Income	Tax liability
$0–$10,000	$0
$10,001–$30,000	$2,000
$30,001–$50,000	$4,000
Total $50,000	Total $6,000
Average tax rate = 12% ($6,000/$50,000)	

At the time that Reagan took office, the top marginal tax rate was 70 percent. Reagan's tax cuts lowered this tax rate to 50 percent. Since this is a marginal (not an average) tax rate, it means high-income families pay this tax rate of 70 percent only on income *over* the top tax threshold – which was approximately $490,000 in 1980 (in 2005 dollars). Income under $490,000 was taxed at a considerably lower rate, even for the richest families, so no one was paying 70 percent of his whole income in taxes even before the Reagan tax cuts.

It is also important to recognize that income from capital gains, such as selling shares of stock or a business at a profit, was taxed at a considerably lower rate. In 1980, even before Reagan's tax cuts, only 40 percent of capital gains income was subject to tax. This meant that the top marginal tax rate on capital gains income before Reagan's tax cuts took effect was just 28 percent (70 percent of 40 percent), which was reduced to 20 percent by his tax cuts (50 percent of 40 percent). The treatment of capital gains income is important to keep in mind in assessing the distributional effects of the income tax, since much of the income of the richest families is in the form of capital gains.

The income tax is highly progressive – higher-income people pay a larger share of their income in taxes than do lower-income people. Since higher-income people pay a disproportionate amount of the tax, they will benefit disproportionately from an across-the-board cut in income taxes. This was certainly the case with the Reagan tax cuts. According to a study by the Congressional Budget Office, the Reagan tax cuts saved families in the top 1 percent of the income distribution an average of more than $25,000 a year in taxes, as their average tax

rate fell from 29.8 percent in 1980 to 24.8 percent in 1983.[4] Families
with more moderate income also benefited from the tax cut, but their
gains were not nearly as large, either in dollar amounts or as a share of
their income.

The Reagan tax cuts had the predictable effect on tax revenue and
the budget deficit. Individual income tax collection fell 1.5 percentage
points as a share of GDP, from 9.3 percent of GDP in 1981, the last
year before the Reagan tax cuts took effect, to 7.8 percent of GDP
in 1984, the first year they were fully implemented. A separate set of
cuts in corporate income taxes reduced revenue from the corporate
income tax by more than a third (measured as a share of GDP), from
2.4 percent of GDP in 1980, the year before the recession sent profits
plummeting, to 1.5 percent of GDP in 1984.

This loss of tax revenues led to the largest budget deficits (relative
to the size of the economy) of the postwar period. In 1983, the deficit
peaked at 6 percent of GDP; given the size of the economy in 2006,
this would be equivalent to a budget deficit of $750 billion. The deficit
did edge down to around 5 percent of GDP in 1984 and 1985 as the
economy continued its recovery from the 1981–2 recessions, but large
budget deficits remained a serious problem throughout the decade.

The increase in the deficit due to the tax cuts did help boost demand,
as most economists had predicted, helping to lift the economy out of
the recession. But this was the standard demand-side economic story.
For the last two decades, presidents had been using combinations of
tax cuts and spending increases to help boost the economy out of
recessions. The effect of the Reagan tax cut seemed to fit this mode,
except that the Reagan tax cut was larger than prior demand-side tax
cuts and was intended to be permanent rather than just providing a
temporary stimulus to the economy in bad times.

There is little, if any, evidence that the Reagan tax cuts had the
promised supply-side effects. Overall, average growth for the 1980s
business cycle (measured from the 1979 peak to the 1990 peak) was
2.9 percent, slightly lower than the 3.2 percent average growth rate
over the two 1970s cycles and far below the 4 percent average growth
rate during the economic golden age from 1947 to 1969. The 1980s'

---

[4] Congressional Budget Office, "Effects of the 1981 Tax Act on the Distribution
of Income and Taxes Paid" (staff working paper, Congressional Budget Office,
Washington, DC, 1986), table II.7, http://www.cbo.gov/ftpdocs/61xx/doc6173/
doc20a-Entire.pdf.

growth record is especially bad given that it got a lift from a sharp plunge in oil prices after 1982, following the quadrupling in real oil prices over the course of the 1970s.[5] Private sector savings fell in the 1980s, and labor force growth was no faster than in the 1970s among people in their prime working years.[6] This means that if the tax cuts gave people more incentive to work, save, and invest, the effects did not show up in any obvious way in the data.

Reagan and the Unions

The tax cuts may have been the most widely publicized part of the Reagan economic agenda, but arguably his policies toward unions had an even greater impact. Early in his administration, President Reagan steered himself into a conflict with the Professional Association of Air Traffic Controllers (PATCO), one of the unions representing federal employees.[7] PATCO had demanded a large pay increase as well as more control over working hours in what was universally recognized as a highly stressful job. Reagan insisted on limiting the pay increase to air controllers out of a stated desire to restrict spending. While the money involved in the dispute with the air controllers was relatively small, there would be considerably more at stake if large wage gains set a pattern for other federal employees.

The negotiations came to an impasse, and PATCO threatened to go on strike. Reagan countered by saying that striking workers would be fired and replaced. The law did in fact prohibit strikes by federal employees, just as many states had laws prohibiting strikes by state and local employees. However, there had been a large number of strikes in

---

[5] Oil prices fell from $70 per barrel in 1981 to a low of $20 per barrel in 1986, before rising gradually to $28 per barrel by the end of the decade (all measured in 2005 dollars). This price decline was an inevitable reaction to the sharp run-up in prices at the end of the seventies. In response to higher oil prices, oil producers increased investment and brought new sources of supply to the market. Energy consumers adopted technologies that were more energy efficient (especially outside of the United States, where high energy taxes in many rich countries provided an additional incentive to conserve), limiting the growth in demand.

[6] See B. Bosworth and G. Burtless, "Effects of Tax Reform on Labor Supply, Savings, and Investment," *Journal of Economic Perspectives* (Winter 1992): 3–25.

[7] Ironically, PATCO had been one of just three national unions to endorse Reagan during the election. The other two were the Teamsters and the Airline Pilots Association.

the public sector over the prior two decades (at the federal level, the most important strike was a 1970 walkout by the letter carriers), with the disputes generally being resolved by negotiations.

PATCO's leadership assumed that this conflict would follow the same pattern. They were wrong. After a forty-eight-hour grace period, Reagan fired the striking workers. He also had PATCO's leadership arrested and subjected to criminal prosecution. The striking controllers were replaced by supervisors and air controllers from the military. For a brief period, airlines were forced to fly a reduced schedule, but the union had been broken.

Reagan's confrontation with PATCO ushered in a new era in labor-management relations. Through the postwar period, firms generally accepted that they had an obligation to reach an agreement with striking workers. Although they may have attempted to maintain limited operations through a strike by relying on managers and supervisory employees, it was extremely rare for a firm to simply hire replacements for striking workers. This would have been viewed as unacceptable conduct by large segments of the population and would have created a public relations nightmare for any firm that chose to pursue such a confrontational path.

It was also strikingly evident that the rest of the labor movement proved completely ineffectual in doing anything in support of the fired controllers. While much of the airline industry was unionized at the time, no union in the industry walked out in solidarity with PATCO. Secondary walkouts are banned under the National Labor Relations Act, but in the past unions had often been willing to sidestep the law when important issues were at stake. In the case of PATCO, the labor movement looked like a paper tiger, with its leaders making angry comments about Reagan's actions but doing little to back up their words.

Reagan's decision to fire the air traffic controllers changed the basic norms surrounding labor-management relations. Within a year, there were several major strikes in the private sector in which employers opted to hire replacement workers rather than reach an agreement with striking workers. As the hiring of replacement workers became a standard practice, unions came to realize that going on strike could end up costing workers their jobs. This made the labor strike a far less effective weapon for unions in a wide range of industries.

The practice of hiring replacement workers also set the United States apart from the rest of industrialized world. Across Western Europe, the hiring of replacement workers during a strike was banned by law or long-standing tradition, and this has largely remained the case throughout the last quarter century. Most Europeans would still consider it outrageous that a worker would lose her job because she went on strike, as did most people in the United States before the PATCO strike.[8]

The changing norms surrounding strikes was not the only change to weaken labor in the Reagan era. Since the thirties, unions had turned to the National Labor Relations Board (NLRB) to protect their right to organize and engage in collective bargaining. While both labor and management had complaints about many NLRB decisions over the years, the board did have a large degree of independence, and there was relatively little difference in enforcement practices between Democratic and Republican administrations.

This changed with the Reagan administration. The Reagan appointees to the NLRB were markedly more pro-business than the appointees of preceding administrations.[9] In addition to becoming far more likely to rule in management's favor than prior boards, the NLRB also developed a huge backlog of more than 1,600 cases by 1984 (entailing a two-year delay in hearing cases) as budget cuts made the board unable to keep up with complaints being filed.[10] The combination of a more hostile board and long delays in hearings meant that the NLRB provided far less protection of workers' rights in labor-management disputes. It became a standard practice for firms to simply fire any workers who they believed to be part of a union organizing drive. Although such firings clearly violated the law, the penalties were so trivial that many companies gladly risked being found guilty in order to keep their workers from unionizing.

With an effective green light from the NLRB, firms adopted a much more aggressive posture toward union organizing drives. The unions

---

[8] For a brief summary of the rules governing industrial relations across Europe, see Federation of European Employers, *Industrial Relations Across Europe, 2004* (London: Federation of European Employers, 2004), http://www.fedee.com/condits.html.

[9] An examination of NLRB decisions in union-organizing disputes found that the board ruled in favor of business in 35 percent of the cases during the Ford administration, 46 percent of the cases during the Carter administration, and 72 percent of the cases during the Reagan administration (D. Vogel, *Fluctuating Fortunes: The Political Power of Business in America* [New York: Basic Books, 1989], 270).

[10] House Committee on Education and Labor, Subcommittee on Labor-Management Relations, *Oversight Hearings on the Subject "Has Labor Law Failed,"* 98th Cong., 2d sess., June 1984.

were unable to alter their tactics to adjust to a more confrontational environment. As a result, many organizing drives floundered. The share of the private sector workforce in unions fell from close to 20 percent in 1980 to just 12.1 percent by 1990. The importance of unions in the economy and society was seriously diminished as a result of Reagan's policies.[11]

The Federal Reserve Board and Inflation

While Reagan's tax cuts were boosting demand with record budget deficits, the Federal Reserve Board was pushing hard in the opposite direction. In the fall of 1979, Jimmy Carter appointed Paul Volcker, president of the Federal Reserve Bank in New York, to be chairman of the board of governors of the Federal Reserve Board. Volcker saw his main job as combating inflation, which clearly was a serious problem at the time. He quickly began raising interest rates in order to try to slow the economy and thereby weaken the labor market, which he hoped in turn would slow the growth in wages and prices. As noted earlier, this led to a short but steep recession in 1980, which certainly did not improve President Carter's reelection prospects.

Although Volcker eased up following the 1980 recession, he was not done tackling inflation. He began raising interest rates again even before the election. By the summer of 1981, the federal funds rate, the short-term interest rate that is most directly under the control of the Federal Reserve Board, was more than 19 percent. This run-up in interest rates had the intended effect. It led to a plunge in home construction and car sales, which in turn pushed the economy into a recession by the fourth quarter of the year. The unemployment rate rose rapidly, hitting 8.5 percent by the end of 1981. Unemployment continued to rise throughout 1982, finally peaking at 10.8 percent in December, the highest level of the postwar era.

Volcker's policies imposed a high cost on workers, but they did have the desired effect of slowing inflation. The inflation rate fell sharply, from 12.5 percent in 1980 to just 3.8 percent by 1982. As inflation eased, Volcker allowed interest rates to drop as well, and the economy

---

[11] See M. Goldfield, *The Decline of Organized Labor in the United States* (Chicago: University of Chicago Press, 1989), on the decline of unions during the Reagan years.

bounced back swiftly from the 1980–2 recessions. By the second half
of 1984, the unemployment rate was less than 7.5 percent. This was
still extremely high by postwar standards, but it was more than 3 full
percentage points below the peak unemployment rate of the 1981–2
recessions. In the minds of many economists and policy analysts, the
costs of Volcker's policies – higher levels of unemployment – were well
worth the benefits associated with lower inflation.[12]

As was noted in Chapter 1, the risk of unemployment is not borne
evenly by all segments of the population. The most disadvantaged
workers are the ones who face the greatest risk of unemployment. As
a rule of thumb, the unemployment rate for African Americans is twice
the overall unemployment rate. The unemployment rate for African
American teens is six times the overall rate. These rules of thumb held
reasonably well through the 1980–2 recessions. The unemployment
rate for African Americans peaked at more than 21 percent at the
beginning of 1983. The unemployment rate for African American
teens peaked at more than 52 percent.

There is another important aspect to the Federal Reserve Board's
high interest rate policy during this period. High interest rates in the
United States led to an inflow of foreign capital, as foreign investors
could now get better returns on U.S. bonds and interest-bearing
accounts than they could in their own countries. This inflow of foreign capital in turn raised the value of the dollar relative to the currencies of the trading partners of the United States. The dollar rose
almost continuously from the summer of 1980 until its peak in early
1985, increasing in value by close to 50 percent against most major
currencies.

The run-up in the dollar had the expected effect on trade. A higher
dollar means that a U.S. dollar will buy more units of a foreign currency.
For example, when the dollar rose in this period, it went from being
worth 1.8 German marks in 1980 to more than 2.9 German marks in
1985. If a dollar can buy more German marks, this means that goods
produced in Germany are cheaper for people in the United States.
If goods produced in Germany and other foreign countries become
cheaper, people in the United States will buy more of them. This is
exactly what happened in the eighties. The share of non-oil imports

---

[12] For an account of the internal politics at the Fed surrounding Volcker's anti-inflation
policy, see W. Greider, *Secrets of the Temple: How the Federal Reserve Runs the Country*
(New York: Simon and Schuster, 1987).

rose from 5.9 percent of GDP in 1979 to 7.5 percent in 1986. A higher dollar makes U.S. exports more expensive to people living in other countries, since they will have to spend more of their money to get dollars. Exports declined sharply during this period, falling from 9 percent of GDP in 1979 to 7.2 percent in 1986.

This pattern of trade helped contribute to the upward redistribution of income during this period, in addition to further weakening organized labor. By increasing imports and reducing exports, an overvalued dollar has the effect of putting downward pressure on the wages of workers in the traded goods sector. This disproportionately affects non-college-educated workers in the manufacturing sector, as better-educated workers are more likely to find themselves in an occupation protected from foreign competition. In addition, the manufacturing sector was heavily unionized at the start of this period, with more than 30 percent of workers belonging to unions. This meant that the loss of manufacturing jobs translated very directly into the loss of union jobs. Many of the country's most powerful unions lost a large share of their membership in these years as union jobs were lost to import competition.

Social Welfare Protections

In addition to pursuing a number of policies that had the effect of tilting the market in ways that redistributed income upward, the Reagan administration also substantially weakened government protections that were explicitly designed to improve the situation of those at the bottom. At the top of this list is the reduction in the value of the minimum wage. There had been regular increases in the federal minimum wage since it was first implemented in 1937, which had the effect of ensuring that even the lowest paid workers shared in the economy's productivity gains, or at least had their wages more or less keep pace with inflation.

This policy changed in the Reagan years. President Reagan first made the minimum wage an issue during the 1980 election, claiming that it was a major reason for the high unemployment rate among black teens. The last minimum wage law passed under Carter had provisions to raise the minimum wage to keep pace with inflation through 1982 but provided for no further increases in subsequent years. Reagan staunchly opposed any increase and was willing to allow the value of the minimum wage to be eroded by inflation. By the time the next minimum wage increase finally took effect in 1990, the real value of the minimum wage had fallen by 25.2 percent.

The sharp drop in the real value of the real wage that began under President Reagan was a clear break with the policies directed toward the bottom end of the labor force in the other wealthy countries. For the most part, these countries maintained the real value of their minimum wages, and in fact in most cases they actually increased the value of the minimum wage in step with overall wage growth. As a result, by 2005, the minimum wage was substantially lower in the United States than in most European countries, even though wages were on average somewhat higher in the United States.[13]

Reagan also pushed for cutbacks in a wide variety of government antipoverty programs that had been put in place over the prior two decades. Housing subsidies for low-income families stood out as being an especially vulnerable target. In 1979, Congress had appropriated $84.7 billion for rental housing assistance, but the appropriation fell to $26 billion in 1984 (both numbers in 2005 dollars).[14]

Usually programs were not directly cut. Instead, Reagan proposed combining several different federal programs and replacing them with block grants to state governments. With a block grant, the federal government gives a specific sum of money to state governments for a general purpose, such as training workers or community development, with the states deciding how to actually spend the money. This grant of money to the states replaces federally run programs that were designed to train workers or promote community development. The block grants would typically be set at levels that were considerably lower than the combined spending on the federal programs they replaced. More important, the block grants would not rise at the same rate as might have been the case if the programs had remained on the books, in general not even keeping pace with inflation. Through time, this

---

[13] For recent data on the value of the minimum wage in relation to the average wage, see Organisation for Economic Co-operation and Development, "Annex A: Structural Policy Indicators," in *Economic Policy Reforms: Going for Growth* (Paris: OECD, 2006), http://www.oecd.org/dataoecd/40/56/36014946.pdf. For a discussion of minimum wage policy in Europe, see J. Eekhoff, *Competition Policy in Europe* (Berlin: Springer-Verlag, 2004), 74–5.

[14] Congressional Budget Office, *The Challenges Facing Federal Rental Assistance Programs* (Washington, DC: Congressional Budget Office, 1994), table A-2, http://www.cbo.gov/ftpdocs/48xx/doc4850/doc54.pdf.

implied substantial cuts, but this method meant that no one's finger-prints had to be on program cuts.

In addition, distributing funds through block grants was consistent with another goal promoted by President Reagan – giving more control back to the states. Reagan argued that states were better situated than the federal government to determine their most important priorities. He also argued that detailed guidelines on spending from the federal government often led to unnecessary waste. In effect, block grants shifted responsibility to the states.

Reagan also made cutbacks in funding for enforcement that had the effect of reducing the value of laws intended to protect various segments of the population. For example, funding for the Occupational Safety and Health Administration (OSHA) was close to 10 percent less on average during the Reagan years than in the last Carter budget.[15] Similarly, the budget for the Equal Employment Opportunity Commission (EEOC) was cut by more than 10 percent in the first years of the Reagan administration.[16] These cutbacks in funding ensured that the agencies could not enforce workplace safety and discrimination regulations and laws as effectively as they had in prior administrations.

The net effect of the Reagan administration policies was to bring about an upward redistribution of both before-tax income and after-tax income. The lowering of tax rates on higher-income families probably received more attention in the media, but for most workers the policies that redistributed before-tax income upward and weakened their job security and bargaining position with management were probably of much more consequence.

Reagan and Social Policy

Reagan had won the presidency with the strong support of conservative Christians, who generally cared deeply about issues such as abortion and the public policy toward homosexual or bisexual behavior. Many of his supporters believed in a traditional family in which

---

[15] OSHA funding levels can be found in D. Weil, "OSHA: Beyond the Politics," *Frontline*, 2003, http://www.pbs.org/wgbh/pages/frontline/shows/workplace/osha/weil.html.

[16] The cutbacks in the EEOC budget and enforcement power are discussed in M. Meerepol, *Surrender: How the Clinton Administration Completed the Reagan Revolution* (Ann Arbor, MI: University of Michigan Press, 2000).

women stayed at home with their children and men went out and earned a living. Reagan's presidency provided these social conservatives with the reassurance that they had an ally in the White House, even if there was no way that he could turn back the major trends of the postwar era.

Perhaps the biggest item on the nation's social agenda at the time that Reagan took office was the equal rights amendment (ERA). This amendment to the constitution, which was approved by Congress and sent to the states for ratification in 1972, would have explicitly guaranteed women equal rights in the constitution. The amendment was quickly approved by a majority of state legislatures, but the momentum stopped short of the thirty-eight states needed for ratification. By 1980, thirty-five states had voted to ratify the amendment (eight had voted to rescind their ratification, a step of uncertain legal status). The ERA was originally supposed to have seven years in which to be ratified by the states, but Congress had passed an extension in 1979 (also of uncertain legal status), which pushed the deadline back to 1982.

The additional three years proved to be of little use to supporters of the ERA. They were not able to get a single additional state to ratify the amendment during this time period. By this point, the opposition to the ERA was well organized. The most prominent of the opposition groups was the Eagle Forum, led by Phyllis Schlafly. Schlafly first gained national prominence in 1964 when she wrote *A Choice, Not an Echo*, a book endorsing the presidential campaign of Barry Goldwater. She started the Eagle Forum in 1972 to promote the traditional family and to counter the perceived threat of the ERA. Schlafly argued that women, rather than focusing on their own careers, should be encouraged to stay at home with their children in order to ensure that they were given the necessary attention for a proper upbringing. The Eagle Forum continued to be an important voice for conservative Christians throughout this quarter century.[17]

One of the issues that aroused especially strong opposition to the ERA was the prospect that the amendment would subject women to any future military draft. The military draft had ended as the Vietnam

---

[17] For accounts of the growing political importance of conservative Christians, see J. Green, M. Rozell, and W. Wilcox, *The Christian Right in American Politics: Marching to the Millennium* (Washington, DC: Georgetown University Press, 2003), and C. Wilcox, *Onward Christian Soldiers* (Boulder, CO: Westview Press, 1995).

War was winding down in 1973, but President Carter had reinstated registration for the draft in 1980 after the Soviet Union invaded Afghanistan. With the cold war heating up, the possibility that the draft would return was taken quite seriously. If the ERA passed, its opponents insisted that it would require women to be drafted, a thought that many found hugely offensive at the time.

If social conservatives could declare victory on the ERA, their battle over abortion rights had a more ambiguous outcome in the Reagan era. Reagan had raised abortion as an issue in the election, coming out strongly against it. (In a debate with Carter, he scored points with many by pointing out that everyone who supported women's right to abortion had already been born.) Social conservatives counted on Reagan to appoint judges to the Supreme Court who would vote to overturn *Roe v. Wade*, the 1973 decision that prevented states from banning abortion. Reagan's appointments turned out to be a mixed group on this issue from the standpoint of social conservatives. The battle over the Supreme Court in the Reagan-Bush era is discussed more fully in the next chapter; at this point, it is only necessary to note that two of Reagan's four Supreme Court appointees voted to sustain *Roe v. Wade* when given the opportunity.

However, the survival of *Roe v. Wade* did not guarantee that women would have access to abortion. The federal government ended Medicaid funding for most abortions in 1977. (Medicaid is the federal program that provides health care to low-income families. It is administered by the states, which pay close to half of the cost.) While several states continued to provide Medicaid funding for abortions on their own, most states did not. Many states passed restrictions limiting access to abortion through parental consent requirements, mandatory counseling requirements, and early limits on the duration of a pregnancy that could be terminated. Most of these restrictions have been ruled unconstitutional, but the ones that survived have made it more difficult for some women to obtain an abortion.

The anti-abortion movement also adopted direct action tactics, picketing and harassing clinics that perform abortions. In some cases, these efforts turned violent. In particular, there were instances of women being attacked while seeking an abortion, several bombings of clinics, and even assassinations of doctors who performed abortions. Partially as a result of these actions, it became increasingly difficult for women living in many parts of the country (primarily the South and rural Midwest) to obtain an abortion. Few, if any, doctors perform abortions in these areas, so women are unable to get an abortion unless they have the resources to travel to another county or state.

If the outcome of the battle over abortion rights was ambiguous in this period, the direction of movement in regard to gay-lesbian rights was far clearer. In 1980, few political figures of any prominence were prepared to openly support measures that explicitly protected individuals from discrimination based on their sexual orientation. There were only a handful of openly gay elected officials, all in liberal bastions such as San Francisco.

This changed rapidly over the course of the decade. Same-sex relationships gained much more public acceptability. By the end of the Reagan era, two gay members of Congress had openly acknowledged their sexual orientation and managed to get reelected. Many other gay and lesbian politicians at the state and local level also acknowledged their sexual orientation, as did prominent figures in other occupations. While prejudices and discrimination based on sexual orientation were still deeply embedded in society at the end of the decade, support for gay-lesbian rights was much stronger than it had been at the start of the decade.

One of the factors that perversely helped to advance gay-lesbian rights was the spread of acquired immune deficiency syndrome, or AIDS.[18] The first confirmed incidents of AIDS occurred in the late seventies. It was found in gay men as well as intravenous drug users in the United States and heterosexual men in Haiti and Tanzania. It began to spread rapidly in the eighties. In 1981, there were 234 deaths attributed to AIDS. The yearly death toll had risen to 5,386 by 1985. Gay men bore the brunt of this disease, dying in hugely disproportionate numbers. This death toll was particularly striking because the vast majority of the victims were people who were relatively young and otherwise healthy. With no known cure for AIDS, being diagnosed with this new and mysterious disease was effectively a death sentence.

---

[18] For an account of the early politics around the AIDS epidemic, see S. Epstein, *Impure Science: AIDS, Activism, and the Politics of Knowledge* (Berkeley, CA: University of California Press, 1992); J. Andriote, *Victory Deferred: How AIDS Changed Gay Life in America* (Chicago: University of Chicago Press, 1999); and J. D'Emillo, *Making Trouble: Essays on Gay History, Politics, and the University* (London: Routledge, 1992).

Faced with this threat to their life and health, members of the gay community began to organize and assert themselves politically in ways that they had not previously done. They demanded that the threat of AIDS be taken seriously by public health officials and that resources be devoted both to caring for people already afflicted with AIDS and to seeking treatments and ultimately a cure. They also organized within the gay community to try to discourage sexual practices associated with the spread of AIDS.

This effort had considerable success. In 1982, President Reagan's press secretary joked about AIDS at a press conference. Four years later, President Reagan noted the AIDS epidemic in his State of the Union address and committed his administration to working for a cure to the disease and taking steps to slow its spread. In this short time span, political activity around AIDS, led by the gay community, had made it an issue that even a conservative political figure like Ronald Reagan had to take seriously.

In 1987, the U.S. Food and Drug Administration approved zidovudine (AZT) as a treatment for AIDS. AZT proved effective in substantially lengthening the lives of AIDS victims and improving their quality of life, but it was not a cure. Further breakthroughs in the nineties made AIDS a chronic illness that people could survive with for long periods of time, often in reasonably good health. The second-generation AIDS drugs are quite expensive, and affordability remains a major issue for people in the developing world, but they have proven largely effective in bringing the AIDS epidemic in the United States under control. While AIDS will likely remain a serious health threat for some time into the future, in the United States and other wealthy countries, it is not the same killer disease as when it was first identified at the beginning of the eighties.

The need to organize to counter the threat from AIDS enhanced the political power of the gay community in other areas as well. At the most basic level, many prominent figures in all walks of life publicly acknowledged their sexual orientation for the first time. Instead of viewing homosexuality as an unusual practice involving only a fringe element of society, the public began to recognize that homosexuality was commonplace. Emotional political battles continue to the present over the acceptance of homosexual activity, but the response to the AIDS epidemic qualitatively changed public perceptions of same-sex relationships.

Environmental Policies in the Reagan Years

Environmentalism had a rebirth out of the politics of the sixties. As young people became politically active and questioned many features of American life, one focus of their attention was the impact that economic growth was having on the environment. As a result, many took up environmental causes, leading to a huge expansion of many existing environmental groups and an explosion of new organizations committed to preserving the environment.

This movement quickly had an impact on mainstream politics. In 1970, the first "Earth Day" was held, guided by a Democratic senator from Wisconsin, Gaylord Nelson. It included school lectures, movies, protests, and other activities involving tens of millions of people across the country. While environmentalists tended to be on the left side of the political spectrum, President Nixon was determined not to let the environment become a Democratic issue. He supported the creation of the Environmental Protection Agency (EPA) in 1970, and three years later he signed the Endangered Species Act, a landmark piece of environmental legislation.

At the time of Reagan's election in 1980, there continued to be an active environmental movement, although it was more institution-alized than it had been in the sixties. While environmentalists were disproportionately Democrats, a substantial number of environmental activists were Republicans, and many prominent Republicans were anxious to be viewed as friendly to the environment.

In the area of environmental policy, the Reagan administration broke course with the broad bipartisan consensus that had been estab-lished over the prior decade. In his campaign and in public statements after the election, Reagan complained about regulatory abuses that were imposing an undue burden on business. While Democrats in Congress would have blocked any efforts to roll back environmental legislation, Reagan did have considerable power as president to reduce the impact of this legislation. Soon after taking office, Reagan issued an executive order requiring that federal agencies conduct a cost-benefit analysis before instituting any new regulations, including environmen-tal regulations.[19] He instructed agencies to implement the least costly

---

[19] This section is based on the discussion in R. Andrews, *Managing the Environment, Managing Ourselves: A History of Environmental Policy in America* (New Haven: Yale University Press, 1999), 255–83.

option unless explicitly mandated otherwise by law. This order had the effect of both delaying the implementation of new regulations, since cost-benefit analyses take time, and weakening any regulations that were eventually put in place.

Reagan also weakened the enforcement of regulations by cutting back funding for the EPA. He reduced its staff by 11 percent in his first year in office. Reagan put Anne Gorsuch (later Burford), a political supporter with no background in environmental policy, in charge of the agency. Other top appointments also went to people with no expertise in environmental policy. This demoralized the professional staff, causing many to leave the agency and further weakening its enforcement capacity.

Reagan's other key appointment to a post with major environmental responsibilities was James Watt as secretary of the interior. Watt had established a reputation as someone actively hostile to environmentalists, having created the Mountain States Legal Defense Fund in 1976 to combat environmental regulations. As secretary of the interior, Watt placed a priority on opening up government land for commercial uses, such as logging, mining, and tourism, rather than preserving areas in their natural state. Watt became something of a lightening rod because of his belligerent stance toward environmentalists as well as his off-the-cuff comments. (In one case, he divided the country into "liberals and Americans.") He was eventually forced to resign in the fall of 1983 after making a joke in public about a "cripple."

Although Gorsuch's reign at the EPA and Watt's reign at the Interior were both relatively brief, they did have a lasting impact on environmental policy. Throughout the seventies, the country had been moving in the direction of stricter environmental regulation and greater protection for the country's remaining natural areas. This progress was stopped and even partially reversed in the Gorsuch-Watt years. As environmental movements gained force in Europe and the rest of the industrialized world, the environmental movement in the United States ran into a serious roadblock. The country went from being a world leader in developing environment policy to being a major laggard.

Reagan and the World

Soon after he took office, Reagan set about asserting U.S. power in the world. Most immediately, this meant taking a more confrontational approach toward the Soviet Union. In keeping with his campaign promise, shortly after his inauguration, Reagan announced that he would not submit the SALT II agreement negotiated by President Carter for approval by Senate. Carter had signed the agreement in June 1979, but opponents managed to delay its approval in the Senate, raising concerns over verification and other issues. In spite of this opposition, there continued to be strong bipartisan support for the agreement, and when Reagan announced that he was withdrawing the treaty, this was a rebuke not only to Carter but also to the Nixon-Ford foreign policy teams that had laid the basis for the eventual agreement. (Reagan announced that the United States would temporarily abide by the terms of SALT II as long as he was satisfied that the Soviets were adhering to the treaty.)[20]

Reagan also accelerated a military buildup that had already begun in the last years of the Carter administration. Defense spending as a share of GDP fell substantially in the immediate aftermath of the Vietnam War, dropping from 9.5 percent of GDP at the peak of the war in 1968 to 4.7 percent in 1978. It had increased to 5.2 percent in 1981, as a result of the last budget prepared by the Carter administration. Reagan continued the upward trajectory for defense spending, which eventually peaked at 6.2 percent of GDP in 1986. (In 2005, 1 percent of GDP corresponded to approximately $125 billion in annual spending. This means that the increase in defense spending of 1.5 percentage points from 1978 to 1986 would be equivalent to an increase in the annual defense budget of approximately $187.5 billion in 2005.)

It is worth noting that Reagan was not able to convince U.S. allies of the need to increase defense spending to meet the Soviet threat. Defense spending fell relative to GDP in almost every country in Europe in the eighties. Even the United Kingdom, under the rule of the conservative Thatcher government, had a modest reduction in the share of the economy devoted to the military in the eighties. The

---

[20] For a conventional overview of arms control negotiations during this period, see R. Garthoff, *Detente and Confrontation: American-Soviet Relations from Nixon to Reagan*, rev. ed. (Washington, DC: Brookings Institution, 1994). For a discussion of the popular movement for arms control and its political impact, see D. Waller, *Congress and the Nuclear Freeze: An Inside Look at the Politics of a Mass Movement* (Amherst, MA: University of Massachusetts Press, 1986), and T. Rochon and D. Meyer, eds., *Coalitions and Political Movements: The Lessons of the Nuclear Freeze* (Boulder, CO: Lynne Rienner Publishers, 1997).

military buildup to meet the Soviet challenge was restricted to the United States.[21]

Much of Reagan's military buildup was focused on new weapon systems. The Carter administration had supported the development of three major weapon systems, the B-1 bomber, the Trident submarine, and the MX missile, but it had not made the decision to actually deploy any of these systems. (Carter had actually decided against deploying the B-1 bomber.) Each of these weapon systems was very expensive. In addition, in the case of the B-1 bomber, there were serious questions about its effectiveness, with some experts arguing that it would be unable to penetrate Soviet air defenses. (At the time, the Defense Department was already in the process of developing its next-generation B-2 bomber, which was designed with radar-evading "stealth" technology.)

Perhaps more important, the Trident submarine and the MX missile were potentially destabilizing weapon systems, since they could undermine the doctrine of "mutually assured destruction," or MAD, that had been the accepted basis of deterrence for the prior two decades. The MAD doctrine was simply that neither the United States nor the Soviet Union would ever launch a nuclear first strike because the remaining nuclear capacity of the victim of the attack would be large enough to destroy the initiator of the attack. This meant that initiating a nuclear war would be a sure path to self-destruction, so no rational government would ever do it.

The Trident submarine and the MX missile could undermine MAD because the two systems would put in place large numbers of missiles, each with highly accurate multiple warheads, that would be targeted on the Soviet Union's fleet of intercontinental missiles and bombers. The successful deployment of both systems would raise the possibility of a successful U.S. first strike that would leave the Soviet Union with very limited capacity to respond.

Many defense experts viewed such a scenario as dangerous because it radically altered the nature of deterrence and could lead to a more explosive situation. For example, if the Soviet leadership was no longer confident that it would retain sufficient second-strike capacity to make

---

[21] For data on defense spending in the United States and other wealthy countries, see H. Oxley and J. Martin, *Controlling Government Spending and Deficits: Trends in the 1980s and Prospects for the 1990s*, OECD Economic Studies no. 17 (Paris: OECD, 1991), http://www.oecd.org/dataoecd/33/12/34259242.pdf.

first use by the United States inconceivable, then it might adopt a "launch on warning" policy. This would mean that the Soviet Union would be prepared to launch an attack against the United States as soon as it had evidence (possibly inaccurate) that it was under attack.[22]

Before the end of his first year in office, President Reagan took a weeklong retreat with his top military advisors to review his options concerning these three big weapon systems. At the conclusion of the retreat, he announced that he would proceed with the development of all three. Whatever the military importance of these systems, this decision showed Reagan's willingness to commit himself to an expensive military buildup and to risk ending the détente with the Soviet Union that had developed over the prior two decades.

The United States and Central America

Reagan's foreign policy team turned their attention to Central America almost immediately after taking office. Their first goal was to ensure the survival of the governments in Guatemala and El Salvador, both of which were facing armed insurgencies. The government in El Salvador was especially threatened, as the regime's base mostly consisted of a small group of wealthy families, while the insurgency enjoyed wide support among unions, peasant organizations, and other segments of the population. Over the longer term, the Reagan administration also sought to overthrow the government in Nicaragua.

To sustain the government in El Salvador, the Reagan administration essentially gave it a green light to initiate a massive wave of repression, undermining most visible forms of opposition. This was done primarily through death squads that targeted union and peasant leaders, journalists, student activists, and even members of the clergy. In March 1980, Oscar Romero, the archbishop of San Salvador, was killed during a sermon. Romero had originally been allied with conservatives in the Catholic Church who were closely tied to the ruling elites, but he had come to sympathize with the poor and in the last years of his life was increasingly critical of the government. In his last sermon, Archbishop Romero effectively endorsed the insurgency.

The fact that even the archbishop could be killed with impunity made it clear to the Salvadoran people that no one was immune from

---

[22] This issue is discussed in detail in R. Ehrlich, *Waging Nuclear Peace: The Technology and Politics of Nuclear Weapons* (Albany, NY: SUNY Press, 1985).

the death squads. According to the human rights group Americas Watch, more than 30,000 people were killed by the death squads during the eighties.[23] This was equal to approximately 0.6 percent of the country's population, the equivalent of 1.8 million people in the United States. Officially, the government denied having any knowledge of the cause of these deaths, and it claimed that it was trying to crack down on the death squads. The Reagan administration repeated a similar line when its aid to the Salvadoran government came under attack. As a United Nations truth commission made clear after a peace agreement was negotiated in 1991, the military and the death squads were one and the same. The U.S. government, which was supplying arms, training, and intelligence to the Salvadoran military, surely was aware of this fact.

From its first days, the Reagan administration made clear that it would not accept the legitimacy of the government in Nicaragua. It organized and armed the remnants of Somoza's National Guard as a guerilla army positioned along the Nicaraguan-Honduran border. Although this operation began while President Carter was still in office, Reagan championed this group, which he called "freedom fighters." Most of the rest of the world referred to them as the "Contras," short for "counterrevolutionaries." With U.S. training, weapons, and logistical support, the Contras began to stage cross-border raids, attacking remote border regions that the Nicaraguan army could not easily defend.

In addition to its military efforts, the Reagan administration also sought to isolate the Nicaraguan government politically and economically. At the time the Sandinistas took power in Nicaragua, they commanded considerable sympathy and support through much of the Western world. Many groups throughout Western Europe were anxious to assist a revolution that they saw as offering real hope for improving the lives of Nicaragua's poor. Many of the Western European governments, most notably the socialist government elected in France in 1981, were also willing to lend support to Nicaragua's new government.

The Reagan administration used political pressure to limit the support for Nicaragua from Western European governments. Its biggest success in this area was stopping the flow of arms from France to

---

[23] Human Rights Watch: Americas: El Salvador, *El Salvador's Decade of Terror, 1981–1991: Human Rights Since the Assassination of Archbishop Romero* (New York: Human Rights Watch, 1991).

Nicaragua. By limiting any assistance from Western Europe, the Reagan administration made Nicaragua more dependent on the Soviet Union. While many in the leadership of the Sandinistas would have looked in this direction in any case, the Reagan administration's drive to isolate the Sandinistas internationally ensured that the country would have no alternative.

Ostensibly, the reason for the Reagan administration's hostility to Nicaragua was its lack of democracy and its ties to the Soviet Union and Cuba. The administration also charged that the Nicaraguan government was sending arms to the insurgents in El Salvador.[24] It is questionable whether these were really the issues of concern. The United States had supported and even imposed dictatorships throughout Latin America for most of the prior century, with the Somoza regime in Nicaragua being a prominent example. Even as it railed against the lack of democracy in Nicaragua, it was supporting a regime in El Salvador that was executing tens of thousands of its political opponents. When the Nicaraguan government did organize elections in 1984, the Reagan administration, instead of trying to set up conditions that would ensure fair and competitive elections, worked to ensure that the major opposition leaders would not take part.[25]

Overthrowing the Nicaraguan government became a virtual obsession of the Reagan administration. Its actions became a source of international embarrassment, as few countries were willing to publicly support Reagan in his effort to remove a sitting government that clearly enjoyed substantial popular support at the time. In 1984, information leaked out that Reagan had sanctioned the mining of Nicaragua's harbors, a blatant act of aggression.[26] The Nicaraguan government

---

[24] Since Nicaragua did not even share a border with El Salvador, it is implausible that there was any large-scale flow of arms from the government to the insurgents in El Salvador. It would have been necessary for arms to pass through Honduras, which had a large contingent of U.S. soldiers stationed near the border with Nicaragua, or through the Bay of Fonseca, which was patrolled by U.S. ships and planes.

[25] The 1984 elections held in Nicaragua were subject to foreign observation by the Latin American Studies Association as well as parliamentary groups from England and Ireland. The Reagan administration undoubtedly could have arranged more extensive foreign observation if holding fair elections had been its priority at the time. See T. Walker, *Nicaragua: Living in the Shadow of the Eagle* (Boulder, CO: Westview Press, 2003).

[26] The U.S. military also held training exercises with Honduran forces along the border with Nicaragua. It gave these exercises names like "Big Pine." This particular

subsequently brought a case against the United States in the World Court on this and other charges. The Court ruled in Nicaragua's favor on most charges, with the majority of even the Western European judges supporting Nicaragua on several of the charges.

There was also substantial domestic opposition to the Reagan administration's policies in Central America. Demonstrations against Reagan's policies toward Central America were held in cities across the country, attracting hundreds of thousands of people over his term of office. This movement placed pressure on Congress and eventually pushed it to put a halt to the flow of arms to the Contras.[27] In 1983, in a continuing resolution that provided funding for large segments of the budget, Congress included a clause that prohibited giving any assistance except humanitarian aid to the Contras. While this may have affected the president's ability to pursue the war against Nicaragua legally, it was not the end of Reagan's quest to overthrow the government.

The Middle East

The Reagan administration took office at a time of considerable turmoil in the Middle East, which continued throughout his administration. The revolutionary government in Iran was engaged in a bloody war with Iraq, which had invaded in 1980. Israel and Lebanon were engaged in a series of cross-border attacks that were escalating in intensity. And the Soviet Union was bogged down in Afghanistan trying to subdue an Islamic resistance movement.

While the specifics surrounding Iraq's invasion of Iran in 1980 are subject to dispute, there is little doubt that Iraq, under Saddam Hussein, thought it was taking advantage of a period of disarray in Iran to gain territory that was both rich in oil and strategically valuable. It is also clear that Iraq's attack had at least the tacit approval of the United States. The Reagan administration sold weapons to Iraq at various

example alluded to Theodore Roosevelt's "Big Stick" policy at the beginning of the twentieth century – a policy under which the United States repeatedly intervened to change Latin American governments that did not meet his approval.

[27] The political movement against U.S. intervention in Central America also prompted the Federal Bureau of Investigation to monitor its activities. See R. Gelbspan, *Break-Ins, Death Threats and the FBI: The Covert War Against the Central America Movement* (Boston: South End Press, 1991).

points during its long war. More important, the Arab kingdoms in the Persian Gulf, which were close U.S. allies, gave large amounts of money to support Iraq's war effort. The United States may not have been anxious to see Iraq secure a more powerful position in the region, but it was clearly content with a situation that had both Iraq and Iran tied up in a lengthy struggle that sapped their economies and led to hundreds of thousands of deaths on both sides.

Israel and Lebanon had been engaged in tit-for-tat attacks for years: forces in southern Lebanon, including guerillas of the Palestine Liberation Organization (PLO), would lob artillery shells into Israel, and the Israeli military, using artillery, planes, and occasional ground invasions, would inflict punishment on southern Lebanon. During this period, the central Lebanese government had little control over the southern part of the country. Power in the region had devolved to various militias that were organized primarily along sectarian lines. Some of the Moslem militias became increasingly aggressive, having been inspired by the revolution in Iran and in some cases also receiving training, arms, and money from the new Iranian government.

In June 1982, Israel used the occasion of the attempted assassination of its ambassador to Britain (by a group not affiliated with the PLO) to launch a ground invasion that did not stop in southern Lebanon but continued all the way to Beirut, the Lebanese capital. In occupying Beirut, Israel sought to accomplish two goals: first, to strike a blow against the PLO, which was then headquartered in Beirut, and second, to install a friendly government in Lebanon. The United States assisted in the first goal when it helped to broker an agreement providing for the evacuation of the PLO leadership and its armed fighters to Tunisia by the end of August.

Israel's hopes for a friendly government unraveled when Lebanon's newly installed president, Bachir Gemayel, was assassinated by a bomb in his party's headquarters on September 15. In immediate response to this assassination, Israel allowed allied Christian militias to enter the Sabra and Shatila Palestinian refugee camps on the west side of Beirut and to massacre at least 700 people and possibly as many as 2,700.[28]

---

[28] The estimate of 700 deaths is from an Israeli commission that subsequently investigated the massacre. The International Committee of the Red Cross estimated that more than 1,500 people were killed. See Y. Sayigh, *Armed Struggle and the Search for State: The Palestinian National Movement, 1949–1993* (Oxford: Oxford University Press, 2000), 539.

Prompted by international outrage over these massacres, the United States (which had assumed responsibility for protecting the Palestinian population following the departure of the PLO fighters) agreed to send more troops into Beirut on an ill-defined peacekeeping mission under the auspices of the United Nations. Over the next year, the U.S. troops came to be seen as playing an increasingly partisan role, acting in support of the Christian-dominated government on several occasions. As a result, the U.S. forces became the targets of attacks by Moslem militias. The worst of these attacks took place in October 1983, when a suicide bomber drove a truck laden with explosives into a marine barracks, killing 241 marines. Reagan insisted that such attacks would not drive the United States out of Lebanon. However, less than four months later, he announced the redeployment of U.S troops to ships stationed off the coast, bringing this ill-fated venture to a close.

The largest covert operation of the postwar era took place in Afghanistan in the eighties. The Reagan administration, continuing a policy inherited from Jimmy Carter, pursued the goal of making Afghanistan the Soviet Union's Vietnam. This meant arming and training the guerilla forces resisting the government installed by the Soviet Union. The annual cost of this operation ranged as high as $500 million by some estimates.[29]

While this cost was extraordinarily high for a covert operation, the mission was successful in making the Soviet Union pay a high price for its occupation. The Soviet Union and its Afghan allies often used brutal repression to try to subdue the resistance and in doing so managed to create more enemies. The result was a war that was enormously costly to the Soviet government in economic, political, and human terms. The war in Afghanistan also had a demoralizing effect on the Soviet military, which had managed to avoid any extended conflicts in the post–World War II era. Further, it was a major source of discontent among civilians, since families were unhappy to see their children drafted and soon risking death in Afghanistan.

If the U.S. policy was successful in making the Soviet Union pay a price for its invasion and occupation, it was less successful in helping to transform Afghanistan into a viable country. The Reagan administration had little interest in the country except as a convenient

---

[29] See S. Coll, *Ghost Wars: The Secret History of the CIA, Afghanistan, and Bin Laden, from the Soviet Invasion to September 10, 2001* (New York: Penguin Books, 2004), 102.

battleground. There was little coherence in the vision being pursued by the resistance fighters. While many no doubt objected to the brutal features of a foreign occupation, some of the most effective fighters were Islamic fundamentalists reacting to the government's efforts to liberalize the treatment of women – for example, allowing them to expose their face in public places or to work or go to school. Afghanistan became a magnet for Islamic extremists from all over the world who were anxious to have an opportunity to defend the faith. One of the people who came to Afghanistan from Saudi Arabia for this purpose was Osama bin Laden.

Terrorism and Grenada

One of the unifying themes that the Reagan administration used in promoting its foreign policy was opposition to terrorism. It routinely denounced its political opponents in other countries as terrorists or supporters of terrorism. This was the case in Central America, the Middle East, and even South Africa. (The Reagan administration was extremely hostile to the African National Congress and regarded Nelson Mandela as a terrorist.) While in many cases, guerilla groups seeking to topple regimes allied with the United States did use terrorist tactics, deliberately targeting civilians, this hardly distinguished them from groups allied with the United States. For example, the guerillas fighting to oust the Soviets in Afghanistan routinely bombed restaurants, movie theaters, and other civilian targets.[30] They even blew up a bus carrying the Afghan national field hockey team. The U.S.-backed governments in El Salvador and Guatemala killed tens of thousands of political opponents, making little distinction between armed insurgents and the civilian opposition.

Although the characterization of the United States as the leader in a worldwide drive against terrorism may have carried little weight in the rest of the world, the national media in the United States largely accepted this framing of the foreign policy debate. Even in 2005, the 1983 bombing of the U.S. marine barracks in Lebanon (obviously a military target) was routinely referred to as a "terrorist" attack. (A "terrorist" attack usually means the deliberate targeting of civilians.)

[30] For a discussion of some of the tactics pursued by the Afghan resistance to the Soviet occupation, see J. Cooley, *Unholy Wars: Afghanistan, America, and International Terrorism* (London: Pluto Press, 2002).

The 1983 invasion of Grenada, which occurred just two days after the bombing of the marine barracks in Lebanon, provides another example of a disconnect between how events were portrayed in the United States and how they were perceived in the rest of the world.[31] Grenada is a small former British colony in the Caribbean that had a population of 90,000, the size of a small city in the United States. It had been ruled since 1979 by Maurice Bishop, a charismatic left populist who came to power in a military coup against a government that was widely viewed as corrupt and dictatorial.[32]

Bishop had angered the Reagan administration by developing close relationships with the governments of Cuba and Nicaragua. He had also made expanding Grenada's airport so that it could land planes flying directly from Europe a top priority. This was a reasonable development goal given that the island's major industry was tourism. But the Reagan administration raised the alarm, pointing out that the expanded runway could also be used to land Soviet military planes and that Cuban construction workers were assisting with the project.

The situation in Grenada suddenly became explosive when Bishop was killed in a coup staged by his former political allies, who also claimed to be Marxists. The Reagan administration quickly raised concerns about several hundred U.S. students who were attending a medical school established on the island to serve U.S. citizens. Ostensibly to prevent the students from being taken hostage, as had happened with the staff at the embassy in Iran, the Reagan administration sent in a military force to take over the island and overthrow the recently installed regime. The rescue of the students and the successful use of force was widely celebrated in the United States, fitting well with Reagan's theme that "America is back." In fact, President Reagan declared October 24, 1984, "Freedom Day" in commemoration of the liberation of Grenada one year earlier.

The reality was very different. The students were not being held hostage. In fact, they faced no obvious threat whatsoever until the U.S forces began their assault on the island. Rather than holding the

---

[31] For an account of the invasion of Grenada, see M. Kryzanek, "The Grenada Invasion: Approaches to Understanding," in *United States Policy in Latin America: A Decade of Crisis and Challenge*, ed. J. Martz, 58–79 (Omaha, NE: University of Nebraska Press, 1995).

[32] On the regime preceding Bishop's rise to power, see R. Pastor, *Exiting the Whirlpool: U.S. Foreign Policy Toward Latin America and the Caribbean* (Boulder, CO: Westview Press, 2001).

students hostage, the new regime was actually anxious to get rid of the U.S. students to eliminate this potential source of conflict with the Reagan administration. They had been trying to negotiate the evacuation of the students just prior to the invasion.

The invasion itself was chaotic by any measure. Eighteen U.S. soldiers were killed and more than a hundred were injured, even though the U.S. forces encountered only scattered resistance from a small military force that was already collapsing due to internal dissent at the time of the invasion. In the course of the invasion, the military accidentally bombed a psychiatric hospital, killing seventeen patients and one staff person. In spite of the mishaps, the Pentagon still awarded almost 9,000 medals in connection with the invasion, more than the number of troops who had landed on the island.

The invasion was widely condemned throughout the world, with the United Nations General Assembly voting in favor of a resolution of condemnation of the U.S. invasion by a wide margin. In the Security Council, the U.S. veto was the lone dissenting vote. Even British Prime Minister Margaret Thatcher, President Reagan's conservative political soul mate, strongly opposed the invasion. The rest of the world largely saw the invasion as an unnecessary exercise of force, one in which the United States took advantage of its enormous military power to eliminate a government that did not meet its approval.

Politics in the Reagan Era

Reagan's election in 1980 left the Democratic Party in a state of shock. Losing the presidency was a large blow in itself, but virtually no one had expected the Democrats to lose control of the Senate. The Democrats had controlled the Senate for twenty-six years, usually by a comfortable margin. The sudden shift to minority status, which was accomplished through the defeat of several long-serving senators, badly shook the party. The Democrats also lost thirty-four seats in the House, cutting their majority by more than half, in addition to losing numerous offices at the state and local level.

After getting elected, Reagan enjoyed the honeymoon that newly elected presidents always get from the media. This period of largely uncritical coverage was extended by an assassination attempt that seriously wounded the president in March 1981.[33] However, the president's main policy proposals were not proving very popular, and with the economy falling back into recession by the middle of year, Reagan's popularity was slipping badly. The 1982 elections were held when the unemployment rate was at a postwar peak of more than 10 percent.

In addition to high unemployment, there was also an immediate problem facing the Social Security program: the trust fund was running empty. (It actually did run out of money for a period of time, and it was necessary for the retirement fund to borrow from the disability fund in order to meet its expenses.) This was partly due to a long-term trend – an increase in the ratio of retirees to workers associated with the aging of the population – but the shortfall was also driven by a falloff in Social Security tax revenue resulting from the economic downturn. Reagan did not help Republican congressional prospects in the 1982 election went he suggested cutting benefits in order to deal with the shortfall.

As a result of anger over the economy and concerns about Social Security, as well as some concern about Reagan's aggressive foreign policy, the Democrats had a solid victory in the November elections. They picked up 27 seats in the House, giving the party a 103 vote majority in that chamber. The Senate was a somewhat different story. The Democrats managed to pick up just a single seat in the election, leaving the Republicans with a 54 to 46 majority.

The political controversy over Social Security did lead to a resolution of its funding problems. President Reagan and the Democratic leadership in Congress agreed to appoint a bipartisan commission to strengthen the program's finances. The commission, which was chaired by future Federal Reserve Board Chairman Alan Greenspan, agreed to a phased increase in the retirement age to sixty-seven over the next forty years, as well as an increase in the payroll tax. This plan, which Congress approved nearly unanimously in 1983, was supposed to leave the program completely solvent for the program's full seventy-five-year planning period (according to the 2005 projections by the Congressional Budget Office, the program appears to be almost on target to meet this goal).

---

[33] John Hinckley Jr., the would-be assassin, was not politically motivated. He was a mentally disturbed man who apparently tried to kill the president out of a desire to impress an actress whom he did not know. He was subsequently found not guilty by reason of insanity. He remained institutionalized in a psychiatric hospital in 2005.

When it was time for Reagan to run for reelection himself in 1984, the economy was in much better shape than it had been in 1982. At 7.2 percent, the unemployment rate was still relatively high by election day, but it was far below its double-digit peaks at the bottom of the recession. More important, the economy was clearly moving in the right direction, having bounced back sharply from the worst slump of the postwar era. Much of the public was willing to give Reagan credit for the recovery while holding Carter responsible for the downturn.

In addition to good news on the unemployment rate, inflation, the nemesis of the seventies, seemed to be largely under control. After soaring into double-digit territory in the late seventies, inflation was less than 4 percent in each year from 1982 to 1984. Mortgage interest rates followed the inflation rate down, dropping 2 to 3 percentage points from their recent highs by election day. Of course, this drop in the inflation rate had been brought about at a substantial cost – the high unemployment during the 1980–2 recessions. When unemployment hit postwar peaks, workers had little bargaining power and ended up taking large cuts in real pay.

Another part of the picture was falling energy prices. The inevitable market response to the surge in energy prices at the end of the seventies included a cutback in demand as firms and consumers adjusted to higher prices and an increase in supply as new sources of energy came online. President Reagan had the good fortune to be sitting in the White House as this adjustment was making voters happy with lower gas prices rather than during the period when the cutoff of oil from Iran was sending oil prices through the roof.

The improved economic performance, combined with President Reagan's skills as a politician, made him a solid favorite for reelection. Nonetheless, there was a heated contest among the Democrats for the right to challenge Reagan. The frontrunner in this race was Walter Mondale, who had served as Jimmy Carter's vice president after two terms in the Senate. Mondale managed to hold off a challenge from Colorado Senator Gary Hart by relying on the support of the party's establishment. However, the most notable feature of the Democratic contest was the role of Reverend Jesse Jackson, a civil rights leader who had worked alongside Martin Luther King Jr. in the sixties. Jackson managed to gain solid support from the African American community, racking up 3.5 million votes in the primaries, far more than any previous African American candidate.

During the general election, Mondale opted to position himself as a fiscal conservative, making the Reagan era deficits his major issue. He kicked off his acceptance speech at the Democratic convention by announcing that taxes would have to be raised regardless of who got elected president. Mondale distinguished himself from President Reagan by saying that even though taxes would be raised regardless of who won, "He won't tell you. I just did." Although Mondale promised a less confrontational foreign policy and there were important differences between the two candidates on social policy, his campaign did not highlight these issues.

Mondale's 1984 campaign was noteworthy in that he selected Geraldine Ferraro, a three-term representative in Congress from New York, as his running mate. Ferraro was the first woman to run on the national ticket of a major political party. While the inclusion of a woman on the ticket was a historic event, the vice-presidential selection process detracted somewhat from its significance. Mondale was publicly seen interviewing a number of potential candidates, most of whom were women, African Americans, and/or people of Hispanic ancestry. The media highlighted this aspect of the selection process, portraying the selection of Ferraro as an exercise in tokenism.

Placing tax increases at the center of his platform did not prove to be a successful political strategy for Mondale. Reagan insisted that he had no intention of raising taxes. He dubbed Mondale "Coach Tax Hike" and held him up as a relic of failed liberalism. With Mondale seemingly offering little more than the promise of higher taxes, he never seriously challenged Reagan in the polls. Reagan won reelection in a landslide, getting just under 59 percent of the popular vote. He won every state except Mondale's home state of Minnesota and the District of Columbia.

Reagan's landslide victory did little for Republicans lower down the ticket. The Republicans managed to gain seventeen seats in the House, but this did not come close to offsetting the Democrats' gains in 1982. The Democrats still held a majority in the House of more than seventy seats after the election. In the Senate, the Democrats actually managed to pick up two seats, narrowing the margin of Republican control to fifty-three versus forty-seven. In effect, the election did little to change the balance of power in Washington: the Republicans controlled the White House and the Senate, and the Democrats remained firmly in control of the House of Representatives.

In spite of his overwhelming reelection, Reagan continued to be a polarizing figure in many respects. In particular, his military buildup and aggressive foreign policy prompted considerable criticism and protest. Most of organized labor remained staunchly opposed to Reagan because of the breaking of PATCO, the appointment of people who were pro-business to the National Labor Relations Board, and other antiunion measures. African Americans and Hispanics were similarly angered over the Reagan administration's policies toward civil rights enforcement, the cutbacks in many domestic spending programs, and Reagan's conservative judicial appointments.

Incumbent presidents usually get reelected, especially if they have the good luck to be running at a time when the economy is growing at a healthy pace. Reagan's reelection prospects were also helped by the fact that he was an extremely effective politician, especially when placed alongside a longtime Washington insider such as Walter Mondale. However, during most of his presidency, Reagan did not enjoy especially high approval ratings. People usually tell public opinion pollsters that they approve of the president in office, and this was the case with Reagan, but his approval ratings were generally in the fifties. He did not often get approval ratings in the sixties or seventies achieved by presidents who are enjoying surges in popularity.[34] Although most voters may have liked Ronald Reagan, many obviously were concerned about the direction he was taking the country.

This was perhaps best demonstrated in the 1986 election, when the Democrats padded their majority in the House by gaining another five seats and managed to regain control of the Senate with a net pickup of eight seats, giving them a fifty-five to forty-five majority. Five Republican senators who had been swept into office on Reagan's coattails in 1980 were defeated in their 1986 reelection bids. This election left the Democrats as firmly in control of Congress as they had been prior to the 1980 election.

However, the Democratic Party had been changed by the Reagan era. It had become markedly more conservative. Most candidates for

[34] The *Washington Post*'s polls gave Reagan an average approval rating of 57 percent over the course of his presidency, tying him with Bill Clinton. This is far below the 70 percent average for John Kennedy or the 65 percent average for Dwight Eisenhower. In fact, it is only 1 percentage point above the 56 percent average approval rating for Lyndon Johnson, who enjoyed a far lower disapproval rating than President Reagan. http://uspolitics.about.com/gi/dynamic/offsite.htm?site=http://abcnews.go.com/sections/politics/DailyNews/poll%5Fclintonlegacy010117.html.

national and even statewide offices felt the need to position themselves as moderates, especially on fiscal issues. This meant, for example, a reluctance to push major new social programs, such as national health care insurance. Also, Reagan's positions on foreign policy, many of which had been viewed as extreme even by many Republicans in 1980, were treated as respectable by most prominent Democrats, even if they did not actually embrace them.

The growing conservatism of the Democratic Party likely reflected in part the changed finances of political campaigns. Money has always been important in politics, but it became increasingly important in the eighties. The average Democratic candidate for the U.S. House of Representatives spent $150,000 on his campaign in 1980. By 1986, average spending had risen to $220,000, and it hit $240,000 by the 1990 cycle (all figures in 2005 dollars).[35] These numbers actually hugely understate the cost of a congressional campaign, since the vast majority of races are not seriously contested and therefore do not lead to large campaign expenditures. In order to raise the sort of money needed for a contested campaign, it is necessary to appeal to wealthy contributors. Insofar as wealthier citizens, or corporate contributors, have more conservative views on policy, their attitudes are likely to be reflected in the range of candidates elected to public office. Furthermore, the opportunities to offset a disadvantage in financing with grassroots organizing dwindled in the eighties, as the old city-based Democratic machines had largely collapsed and labor unions were shrinking rapidly in size and influence. This meant that Democrats increasingly had to rely on large contributors if they hoped to get elected.

Tax and Spending Policy in the Later Reagan Years

After Reagan's reelection in 1984, politicians from both parties were prepared to acknowledge the seriousness of the deficit problem and to take steps to bring it under control.[36] One of the key tools to

---

[35] Data on campaign spending can be found in the U.S. Census Bureau's Statistical Abstracts of the United States from 1982 (table 810), 1989 (table 493), and 1993 (table 446). For a discussion of the importance of the growing cost of campaigns, see R. Hague, "The United States," in *Power and Policy in Liberal Democracies*, ed. M. Harrop, 95–122 (Cambridge: Cambridge University Press, 1992).

[36] Interestingly, budget deficits increased substantially in most wealthy countries during the Reagan years, although spending growth was more important in driving

accomplish this goal was the Gramm-Rudman-Hollings Balanced Budget Act, initially passed in 1985. This act set out a series of gradually declining deficit targets intended to lead to a balanced budget in 1990. Under the act, if Congress failed to reach the targets, the president was supposed to order spending in large areas of the budget to be sequestered (not spent). Effectively, the act imposed across-the-board reductions in most areas of nondefense spending (Social Security and Medicare were also put off limits for cuts) as a backup means of achieving deficit reduction if Congress did not make progress toward a balanced budget.

While the sequestration part of the bill was declared unconstitutional in 1986 – the Supreme Court ruled that it violated the separation of powers between Congress and the president – the initial act and its subsequent version (approved in 1987) probably did help reduce the deficit. The budget deficit was equal to 4.8 percent of GDP in 1984, a clearly unsustainable level. It had fallen to 2.8 percent of GDP by 1989, a level that is within the bounds of sustainability. In other words, the country could have maintained a deficit of the size that it was running in 1989 for a long period of time into the future.

The reduction in the deficit over this period was attributable in roughly equal parts to lower spending and higher taxes. The reduction in spending involved some savings from the beginning of the end of the cold war and from substantial cuts in some areas of social spending. The higher tax revenue was attributable in part to a tax reform bill that swept through Congress in 1986. (Half of the rise in tax revenue between 1984 and 1989 was attributable to the increase in Social Security taxes put in place by the Greenspan Commission.)

The 1986 tax reform grew out of a desire to make the tax code simpler by eliminating many of the loopholes that had been added over the decades. Since wealthy taxpayers benefit the most from loopholes, the trade-off was that they would get lower income tax rates in exchange for fewer loopholes. While the drive to lower tax rates was usually associated with Republicans, the bill that finally passed was pushed largely by two Democrats, Richard Gephardt in the House of Representatives and Bill Bradley in the Senate. The key features of this

deficits elsewhere than in the United States. See H. Oxley and J. Martin, *Controlling Government Spending and Deficits: Trends in the 1980s and Prospects for the 1990s*, OECD Economic Studies no. 17 (Paris: OECD, 1991), http://www.oecd.org/dataoecd/33/12/34259242.pdf.

bill were a top marginal tax rate of 29 percent and the elimination of the special treatment of capital gains income.[37] Although only half of capital gains income on stocks or businesses had previously been subject to the income tax, the 1986 tax reform taxed capital gains income at the same rate as wage income.

The idea of a simpler, fairer tax code that also gave a modest tax break to most middle-income families had considerable appeal. President Reagan enthusiastically signed the bill less than two months before the 1986 midterm election, proclaiming that the new tax law would require people to make money by working or investing rather than by gaming the tax code. It is not clear whether President Reagan recognized it at the time, but the 1986 tax code did at least partially reverse the tax cut for higher-income individuals that was the centerpiece of his 1980 campaign. Nonetheless, upper-income taxpayers still faced substantially lower effective tax rates than they had before he took office.

---

[37] In reality, the top tax rate varied due to the phasing out of some exemptions. Also, the bill maintained favored tax treatment for capital gains on homes.

4

The Reagan Revolution Becomes Institutionalized

Every administration has its share of scandals. There are always people who will abuse power. But the number of scandals that shake an administration to its core – that involve the president and actually bring its survival into question – is relatively small. The Iran-Contra scandal, which was exposed in the last two years of the Reagan administration, fits the bill. It directly involved two top cabinet officers (the secretary of state and the secretary of defense), the director of the Central Intelligence Agency, and two of President Reagan's national security advisors.

While President Reagan's personal knowledge of illegal conduct may never be known, it is clear that he was aware of the broad outlines of a plan that sought to subvert the law as passed by Congress and signed by the president. In assessing the case for impeaching President Reagan, Lawrence Walsh, the special prosecutor appointed in the case, noted that "President Reagan created the conditions which made possible the crimes committed by others by his secret deviations from announced national policy as to Iran and hostages and by his open determination to keep the contras together 'body and soul' despite a statutory ban on Contra aid." However, he concluded that a case could not be made for impeachment because, "fundamentally, it could not be proved beyond a reasonable doubt that President Reagan knew of the underlying facts of Iran-Contra that were criminal or that he made criminal misrepresentations regarding them."[1]

---

[1] L. Walsh, *Final Report of the Independent Counsel for the Iran/Contra Matters*, vol. 1, *Investigations and Prosecutions* (Washington, DC: United States Court of Appeals for the District of Columbia Circuit, 1993), 445, http://www.fas.org/irp/offdocs/walsh/.

The Iran-Contra scandal was in fact two scandals in one. The Iran part involved selling arms to Iran as a way to secure the freedom of American citizens being held hostage by Iran's allies in Lebanon. Under the direction of Lieutenant Colonel Oliver North, an assistant to the national security advisor, Israel acted as an intermediary in selling two loads of U.S.-made antitank and antiaircraft missiles and other weapons to Iran.

This activity was carried out in strict secrecy because exchanging arms for hostages is generally viewed as a bad practice (it can encourage hostage taking) and it certainly contradicted the image of toughness that the Reagan administration sought to project to the world. Providing weapons to Iran also contradicted the official position of the Reagan administration toward Iran. Iran was viewed as a supporter of terrorism and was the subject of a strict U.S. economic embargo.

The Contra part involved using the profits from the arms sales to support the Contras fighting to overthrow the government in Nicaragua. This backdoor method of financing was made necessary by the fact that Congress had explicitly prohibited funding for the Contras in an appropriations bill signed by President Reagan in 1983. This law, the Boland Amendment, explicitly prohibited using government funds to support the Contras. It was approved by Congress after some of the Contras' tactics (which included attacks directed against the civilian population) and the Reagan administration's support for them came to light.

Both the sale of arms to Iran and the use of the profits to finance the Contras raised serious legal issues. However, the financing of the Contras was more obviously a violation of the law since it used government funds for a purpose explicitly prohibited by Congress. In addition, the scandal involved the large-scale destruction of evidence as well as repeated lying to congressional committees in order to conceal the administration's actions from Congress and the Federal Bureau of Investigation. The sale of arms for hostages also raised serious questions of judgment and certainly contradicted the public posture of the Reagan administration, with its hard-line stand against Iran and hostage takers.

There had been accounts in the alternative media of arms shipments to the Contras throughout the period in which the Boland Amendment was in effect, but the Iran-Contra scandal first began to receive substantial attention in the mainstream media in November 1986, just after the midterm election. The story first broke in a Lebanese newspaper that reported the United States had sold weapons to Iran in exchange for the release of hostages.[2] The Reagan administration originally denied both sides of the Iran-Contra scandal. In late November, as more evidence came to light, it was forced to acknowledge the central facts about its arms-for-hostage deals. Eventually, the Reagan administration was forced to acknowledge the backdoor funding of the Contras as well.

Evidence of questionable conduct continued to grow, and Reagan's attorney general, Edwin Meese, agreed to appoint an independent counsel in late December of 1986. He picked Lawrence Walsh, a former federal judge and a moderate Republican. Over the next seven years, as Walsh carried through an investigation that led to several sets of indictments and trials, he became a hated figure among stalwart conservatives, who accused him of pursuing a vendetta against the Reagan administration. For the most part, Walsh's pursuit of prosecutions through the criminal justice system did prove to be an exercise in futility, although not necessarily because he was prosecuting innocent people.

In response to the public concern over a scandal that involved officials at the highest level of the Reagan administration, both the House and Senate created special committees to investigate the scandal. The Democratic leadership in both houses filled the committees with moderate Democrats, excluding more liberal members of the party, ostensibly in the interest of maintaining bipartisanship in the conduct of the investigation. Following the example of the Senate Watergate hearings held in the summer of 1973 (which attracted enormous national attention), the special committees decided to hold televised public hearings. These hearings would both provide the public with direct insight into the nature of the scandal and also allow the members to spend time in the public spotlight. To solve the problem of competing House and Senate hearings, the committees agreed to hold joint hearings.

The Watergate hearings elicited facts furthering an investigation that led to numerous indictments and successful prosecutions and eventually the resignation of a president. The Iran-Contra hearings had the

---

[2] After the scandal finally broke, there was some questioning within the media as to whether they had done their job, having been scooped on this important story by small alternative media outlets and foreign newspapers (e.g., see "The Reagan White House; Missing the Iran Arms Story: Did the Press Fail?" *New York Times*, March 4, 1987, A15).

opposite effect. The leadoff witness was Lieutenant Colonel Oliver North, the person at the center of the scandal. He was unapologetic in his testimony before the committee, arguing that he had served the president in protecting the country's national security. Most of the Democratic members of the committee were defensive before this decorated Vietnam War veteran, in some cases almost apologetic for the restrictions that led the Reagan administration to pursue illicit means to finance the Contras' military operations. The media coverage of the testimony transformed North into a hero for large segments of the public.

After North, the testimony of other witnesses received less attention. Although some interesting and important details of the scandal did come to light, for the most part the Democrats on the committee felt the need to be cautious in their questioning of the witnesses, while many of the Republican members effectively played the role of defense attorneys. The evidence presented to the committee did show that President Reagan was informed about the general course of the events comprising the scandal, but they did not establish that he had direct knowledge of specific illegal acts.

Perhaps more important, the hearings effectively thwarted Lawrence Walsh's efforts to bring the participants in the scandal to justice. The committee had granted Oliver North and several other top figures in the scandal immunity from prosecution in exchange for their agreement to testify before the committee instead of using their Fifth Amendment right not to incriminate themselves. Walsh had asked the committee not to grant immunity, but because it did, he presented sealed files to the court prior to each witness's testimony in order to preserve his ability to prosecute witnesses. These files included all the relevant evidence he had at the time, which would provide the basis for his case at trial. By presenting sealed files to the court, Walsh could show that his evidence was not derived from the testimony given by the immunized witnesses to Congress.

With this evidence, Walsh was able to secure convictions of North and several other top officials. However, the convictions were overturned on appeal. The courts ruled that some of the witnesses in the trial may have had their testimony affected by the immunized testimony of the defendants. Therefore, the prosecution violated their grants of immunity.

The final chapter in Walsh's long effort to legally pursue those involved in the scandal was the 1992 indictment of Caspar Weinberger,

President Reagan's secretary of defense. Weinberger was indicted after Walsh discovered that he had kept a detailed diary that covered the events surrounding the scandal. Walsh had already subpoenaed all documents that Weinberger possessed related to the scandal, but Weinberger had not turned over the diary until Walsh found out about it from another source. Based on evidence in the diary, Walsh indicted Weinberger for lying to Congress. Just before Weinberger was due to come to trial, President Bush, who had already lost his reelection bid, pardoned Weinberger and the other top officials tied to the scandal. This act ensured that virtually no one would be held criminally accountable for any crimes committed as part of the Iran-Contra affair.[3]

U.S.-Soviet Relations in the Late Reagan Years

The leadership of the Soviet Union had undergone major changes between 1980 and 1985. Leonid Brezhnev, who had been general secretary of the Communist Party since 1964 (the top position in the Soviet hierarchy), died in November 1982. His two immediate successors both died very shortly after assuming power. In March 1985, Mikhail Gorbachev became general secretary of the Communist Party. Gorbachev was considerably younger than his predecessors and had a reputation as a reformer.

In his first year in office, Gorbachev announced his plans for "glasnost," a political opening that was supposed to allow more room for expression of dissent, and "perestroika," an economic restructuring that was intended to create a space for privately owned businesses inside of the Soviet system. Both were clear breaks from the path pursued by previous leaders.

Gorbachev also anxiously sought to ease cold war tensions. Soon after taking power in 1985, he met with British Prime Minister Margaret Thatcher, Reagan's conservative ally in England. He won her enthusiastic endorsement as "someone we can do business with."

---

[3] For accounts of the Iran-Contra scandal, see L. Walsh, *Firewall: The Iran-Contra Conspiracy and Cover-up* (New York: W. W. Norton and Co., 1998); P. Kornbluh and M. Byrne, eds., *The Iran-Contra Scandal: The Declassified History* (New York: New Press, 1993), and D. Inouye and L. Hamilton, eds., *Iran-Contra Affair: Report of the Congressional Committees* (New York: Three Rivers Press, 1998).

In the fall of 1986, Gorbachev followed up this meeting with a summit with Reagan in Reykjavik, Iceland, in which they discussed a wide range of arms control issues.

While they did not end up reaching an agreement at this meeting, they came close on several key topics, including restrictions that would prevent the deployment of intermediate-range U.S. missiles in Europe. They also began discussions of actual reductions in the number of nuclear missiles on both sides rather than just limitations on the construction of new weapons, meeting a Reagan administration demand for arms reduction talks. Previously, the demand for arms reduction talks was widely viewed as a pretext for evading serious negotiations on arms limitations. Whatever Reagan's motives, Gorbachev treated his proposal as a serious negotiating position.

The talks ultimately deadlocked because Reagan refused to abandon plans for his Strategic Defense Initiative (SDI), an antimissile system that was intended to protect the United States from nuclear attack. There were serious questions about the technical feasibility of such a system (it was derided as "Star Wars" by its opponents), but if it could have been developed, it would certainly have undermined the mutual assured destruction deterrence doctrine. A functional SDI would have meant that the Soviet Union would no longer have the ability to inflict massive damage on the United States, meaning that it no longer could be sure of discouraging a U.S. first strike.

In spite of the initial deadlock, the following fall Reagan and Gorbachev reached an agreement on arms reduction. This agreement called for a substantial reduction in long-range missiles over the next decade and the elimination of short- and intermediate-range missiles that had already been deployed. Reagan did not back down on his commitment to SDI, but he did offer to share the system with the Soviets. It is not clear whether Gorbachev took this offer seriously or simply assumed (like most experts) that the prospect of a workable SDI was sufficiently far off in the future that there was no reason for it to be a major factor in arms control talks.

The Gorbachev negotiations marked an end to a period of growing cold war tensions that had begun with the Soviet invasion of Afghanistan and accelerated with the election of Reagan. This was best measured by the growth and later decline in the size of the defense budget. Relative to the size of the economy, military spending had risen by nearly a third, from 4.7 percent of GDP in 1979 to 6.2 percent of GDP in 1986. It had already fallen back to 5.7 percent of GDP

in 1989, the last year for which the Reagan administration developed
a budget.[4]

The 1988 Presidential Campaign

There are generally few important initiatives put forward in the last
two years of a two-term president's tenure. This was especially true
in Reagan's case. This was partly due to his diminished stature as a
result of the Iran-Contra scandal, which showed top officials in his
administration trading arms for hostages and engaging in actions of
questionable legality. The fact that the Democrats had retaken control of the Senate meant that Reagan faced an increasingly hostile
Congress. His advancing age (he was seventy-two at the start of his
second term) may have also limited his ability to drive the political
agenda. He was often described as "disengaged," and one reporter
expressed fears that he was senile after a private interview.[5]

By 1986, many of the harder-line conservatives had left the Reagan
administration, replaced by more traditional Republicans. However,
if the rightward momentum of the administration appeared to have
waned, this was in large part because the administration had accomplished much of what it had intended. The country had shifted sharply
to the right in both international and domestic affairs, and there was
little threat that this shift would be reversed, regardless of the outcome
of the 1988 election.

With Reagan not eligible for reelection, both the Republican and
Democratic nominations were up for grabs in 1988. George H. W.
Bush, who had been vice president throughout the Reagan years, was
considered the overwhelming favorite for the nomination, although

---

[4] For an interesting account, written just prior to the collapse of the Soviet Union,
of Reagan's seeming shift on arms control toward a more conciliatory policy, see
C. Bell, *The Reagan Paradox: American Foreign Policy in the 1980s* (New Brunswick,
NJ: Rutgers University Press, 1989). See also the account of negotiations between
Gorbachev and Reagan in J. Smith, *The Cold War 1945–1991*, 2nd ed. (Oxford:
Blackwell Publishers, 1997).

[5] Leslie Stahl, a reporter for CBS News, recounted in her memoirs a 1986 meeting
with President Reagan in which he seemed disoriented and appeared to fade out at
several points (*Reporting Live* [New York: Touchstone Press, 1999]). Reagan suffered
from Alzheimer's disease after leaving the White House. If he was experiencing
any symptoms while still in office, it has not been publicly acknowledged by his
doctors or any members of his administration.

he did face some surprisingly stiff opposition in the first primaries. Bush had never been very popular among those in the more conservative faction of the Republican Party, and they were reluctant to back his candidacy. This led to a stinging defeat for Bush in the Iowa caucuses, the first contest in the race for the nomination. Robert Dole, the minority leader in the Senate at the time, won the caucus, while Pat Robertson, a conservative minister who had built his reputation hosting a national television show, edged out Bush for second place. However, Bush quickly bounced back from this loss, using the advantages of the vice presidency to gain the support of most of the Republican party apparatus. He managed to wrap up the nomination relatively early in the primary season.

The Democratic nomination was much more hotly contested. The big surprise was the performance of Reverend Jesse Jackson. Jackson first gained national prominence as a young minister working alongside Martin Luther King Jr. in the Southern Christian Leadership Conference. Jackson was with Dr. King in Memphis on the night he was assassinated. Jackson went on to form his own civil rights organization, People United to Save Humanity (PUSH), which was based in Chicago. The 3.5 million votes he won in the 1984 race for the Democratic presidential nomination established Jackson as a serious force in the Democratic Party.

His 1984 race also gave him a solid base for contesting the 1988 primaries. In the 1988 race, he reached far beyond the African American community, winning support by making a populist economic appeal. Although most of the Democratic Party establishment lined up behind other candidates, Jackson was able to appeal over their heads to the party's base. In a race against a group of white career politicians with little charisma, Jackson clearly stood out. He was a highly articulate outsider with a long history at the forefront of the civil rights movement.

In the early contests, Jackson was able to do well even in states with very small African American populations, such as Iowa and New Hampshire. Then he stunned the political establishment by getting the largest number of votes on "Super Tuesday," a clustering of state primaries and caucuses, mostly in the South, held in early March. The Democratic leadership had hoped that by having the more conservative states voting together early in the primary process, they could derail more liberal candidates. Instead, by building on the large African American vote in these states, Jackson was able to use Super Tuesday to catapult to the top of the pack. Jackson gave the party's leadership

another jolt when he won a landslide victory in the Michigan caucuses, a state where he was not even expected to be among the top
two contenders.

At that point, it actually appeared possible that Jackson could win
the Democratic presidential nomination. Determined to prevent this
prospect, the party establishment rallied behind Massachusetts Governor Michael Dukakis. Dukakis was able to carry most of the rest
of the primaries after Michigan and win the nomination, although
some of the remaining races were strongly contested. The three-way
race in the New York primary stood out in this regard, as Senator Al
Gore, who was also pursuing the nomination, made a special point of
attacking Jackson's qualifications for the presidency.

Like Mondale before him, Dukakis was determined to run a centrist
campaign. In his acceptance speech at the convention, he proclaimed,
"This election is about competence, not ideology." (One joke after
the election was that, unfortunately for Dukakis, he turned out to
be right.) Dukakis ran an uninspired campaign. To the chagrin of his
advisors, he took a long vacation immediately after the Democratic
convention, allowing the political bounce from the convention to
dissipate. When he did take to the campaign trail, he sought to make
an issue out of the persistently large budget deficits that had resulted
from Reagan's tax cuts and military buildup.

In contrast, the Bush campaign portrayed Dukakis as an extremist
liberal who could not be trusted to defend the country. Bush also
warned that Dukakis would raise taxes if he was elected. To emphasize
this second point, Bush took a no-tax-increase vow in his acceptance
speech at the Republican Convention, saying, "Read my lips, no new
taxes."

Throughout the campaign Bush repeatedly referred to Dukakis's
membership in the America Civil Liberties Union, his opposition to
the death penalty, and his veto of a bill passed by the Massachusetts
legislature that would have required public schools to begin each day
with the pledge of allegiance. In the same vein, the Bush campaign
sponsored a television advertisement that warned about "Willie Horton," a black man who was serving a life sentence in Massachusetts
after being convicted for murder.[6] Under Dukakis, Massachusetts had
a weekend furlough program that was used to reward prisoners for

---

[6] Al Gore had actually first raised the issue of the Willie Horton furlough during a
     debate in the Democratic primaries.

good behavior. When he was released as part of this furlough program, Horton staged a home invasion in which he beat and stabbed
a man and then raped his fiancée. To take advantage of white fears
of black crime, the Bush campaign sought to make Willie Horton a
household name and link him indelibly to Dukakis.[7]

Bush ended up winning the race by a comfortable margin, although
the Democrats managed small gains in both the House and Senate. This
left the status quo in place: a Republican president and a Democratic-
controlled Congress.

To a remarkable extent, foreign policy events that were not in
the least anticipated dominated the attention of the administration
of George H. W. Bush. These events included the establishment of
democratic regimes in Eastern Europe, the first war against Iraq, and
the collapse of the Soviet Union.

The Collapse of Communism in Eastern Europe

The collapse of the regimes in Eastern Europe was an immediate outgrowth of the process of glasnost that Gorbachev had adopted in the
Soviet Union. In prior decades, the Soviet Union had supported its
client states in Eastern Europe in cracking down on dissent and was
even prepared to intervene directly itself (for example, in Hungary in
1956 and Czechoslovakia in 1968) when governments proved unwill-
ing or unable to rein in opposition.

Just as he allowed for a greater range for dissent within the Soviet
Union, Gorbachev also sanctioned increased tolerance for dissent in
the Eastern bloc countries. This had its first noticeable impact in
Hungary, where elections with non-Communist candidates were held
in June 1985, resulting in the election of forty-three independents to
Hungary's parliament. The opposition continued to grow in strength
over the next four years, as the Communist Party gradually eased

---

[7] Lee Atwater, one of George H. W. Bush's top political consultants, made the
decision to highlight the Willie Horton incident. In order to insulate the Bush
campaign from charges of racism, he arranged for an independent committee to
actually run ads on Willie Horton. Apparently, Mr. Atwater was also the person
who gave him the name "Willie." Mr. Horton's legal name is "William," and
apparently that is how he referred to himself. The media followed Mr. Atwater's
lead in using the name "Willie." See J. Feagin, H. Vera, and P. Batur, *White Racism*
(London: Routledge, 2001), 152–85.

restrictions on dissent and introduced economic reforms. The party eventually agreed to full multiparty elections, which took place in 1990.

A parallel process was occurring in Poland. In 1988, after a series of strikes, the government entered into a dialogue with Solidarity, the independent trade union. Solidarity first gained notoriety in the late seventies as militant workers under the leadership of Lech Walesa went on strike at the huge Lenin Shipyards in the city of Gdansk. At that time, the government agreed to negotiate with the workers, giving in to many of their demands. The union grew quickly, pulling together a broad range of opponents of the government, including a peasant union that took the name "Rural Solidarity."

As the number of strikes increased and the demands grew, the government finally cracked down, declaring martial law in December 1981 and arresting much of Solidarity's leadership. However, the Polish government never succeeded in destroying Solidarity's base of support. In the late eighties, when the government eased up on dissent in the wake of Gorbachev's glasnost policy, Solidarity reemerged as an important political force.

The negotiations led to an agreement to hold multiparty elections in the summer of 1989, which allowed the opposition to gain representation in Parliament while still assuring a majority for the Communist Party. When the opposition won all but one of the seats up for election, the limited base of support for Communist regime became clear. By the end of the year, Walesa had managed to persuade the small parties allied with the Communists to join an alliance with Solidarity, creating a non-Communist government in Poland.

The collapse of the Communist government in East Germany followed directly from the decision by Hungary to open its borders in 1989 to allow free travel to Austria. After Hungary officially opened its border with East Germany in September 1989, East Germans could freely leave their country and migrate to the West for the first time since the building of the Berlin Wall in 1961. Thousands of people soon took advantage of this opportunity.

Remarkably, the East German government did nothing to try to crack down on this flow of emigrants. This emboldened people to protest against restrictions on movement more generally and other restrictions on civil liberties. The regime did little to suppress these protests, which grew progressively larger and eventually forced the resignation of Erich Honecker, the long-serving head of the Communist

Party. On November 9, the Berlin Wall collapsed. Guards no longer prevented East Germans from passing through the barriers, and people on both side of the border used sledge hammers to physically demolish portions of the wall.

After the fall of the wall, there were some efforts to preserve a separate East German state, but these soon collapsed. By the spring of 1990, the new East German government was engaged in reunification talks with West Germany. These talks required the participation of the Soviet Union, which still had legal authority over Germany as one of the occupying powers following World War II. Gorbachev did not attempt to impose any major barriers to German reunification, which required, among other conditions, the withdrawing of Soviet troops who had been stationed in East Germany since the end of World War II. The reunification legally took place on October 3, 1990, less than a year after the fall of the Berlin Wall.

The collapse of the Communist government in Czechoslovakia was even quicker than in the other three countries. A series of protests demanding democracy began in November 1989, led by a group of dissident intellectuals who had been periodically jailed over the prior two decades. By the middle of December, the government had collapsed, leaving the path open to democratic elections. Before the end of the year, Vaclav Havel, a writer and the country's most prominent dissident, had been elected president by the Federal Assembly.

The remaining two Eastern bloc countries, Romania and Bulgaria, had also installed democratically elected governments by the middle of 1990, completing a set of events that caught the entire political establishment by surprise. The map of postwar Europe, with NATO confronting the Warsaw Pact countries, had been completely transformed in less than a year, with barely a shot being fired. (There had been some fighting in Romania, as hard-line supporters of Nicolae Ceausescu, the long-serving head of the Communist Party, tried to hang on to power.) The Soviet bloc was now essentially just the Soviet Union.

The Winding Down of Conflicts in Central America

The first years of the Bush administration also saw the resolution of the wars in Central America. In the case of Nicaragua, the government agreed to move up to February 1990 the elections that had been scheduled to be held later in the year. Although the U.S.-backed opposition had boycotted the 1984 elections, they energetically contested the 1990 race. The Bush administration pledged to end the U.S. embargo of Nicaragua, but only if the opposition won. Similarly, it was not clear that the Contra war would come to an end unless the U.S.-backed coalition won the election. Faced with the prospect of continuing war and further economic decline if the Sandinista government remained in power, the country voted for the opposition.

In the next two years, peace agreements were signed in El Salvador and Guatemala between the governments of these countries and the armed opposition. In both cases, the opposition agreed to lay down its arms in exchange for the opportunity to take part in democratic elections, with the United Nations supervising the reintegration of the guerilla forces back into society. The agreements also established "truth commissions" that were assigned the responsibility of investigating the tens of thousands of killings that had occurred in both countries during the previous decade.

While these agreements did not bring an end to conflicts in the region, and they certainly did not usher in a period of prosperity (the countries in the region remain extremely poor, even in comparison to the rest of Latin America), they probably succeeded about as well as could have been expected given the violence of the struggles. Interestingly, the truth commissions in both countries largely corroborated the views of the critics of the Reagan administration's policy – specifically, that the Salvadoran and Guatemalan governments had been responsible for the tens of thousands of death squad killings.[8] In both countries, the commissions documented ties between the death squads and officials at the highest levels of the government, but this fact received almost no attention from the U.S. media.

There was one other important episode involving Central America and the United States in this period. The United States indicted the head of state of Panama, Manuel Noriega, on drug-smuggling charges

---

[8] See United Nations Commission on the Truth for El Salvador, *The Report of the United Nations Commission on the Truth for El Salvador* (New York: United Nations, 1993), http://www.hrw.org/reports/pdfs/e/elsalvdr/elsalv938.pdf, and Guatemala's Historical Clarification Commission, *Guatemala: Memory of Silence* (New York: United Nations, 1999), http://shr.aaas.org/guatemala/ceh/report/english/.

in February 1988. It is not clear whether Noriega's involvement in drug smuggling was the real motive, since many other figures in the region had been involved in drug smuggling with at least the tacit consent of the United States.[9] In addition, Noriega had long-standing ties with the CIA, which presumably had been aware of his activities all along. Noriega had also acted as an important ally of the United States on several occasions; for example, he provided a refuge for the shah of Iran after he was forced to flee in the midst of the Iranian revolution.

Whatever the cause of the falling out between the United States and Noriega, relations became progressively more hostile over the next year and a half. During this time, Noriega was linked by a former associate to the murder of a prominent critic and more importantly to the plane crash that killed Omar Torrijos, a widely respected nationalist leader who had negotiated the turnover of the Panama Canal by the United States. Noriega cancelled internationally supervised elections scheduled to be held in May 1989 after it became clear that the opposition was going to win. A gang of thugs loyal to Noriega attacked and nearly killed one of the opposition candidates.

There were also a series of minor confrontations with U.S. military personnel stationed in the Canal Zone. After an incident in which a U.S. soldier was shot and killed, President Bush launched an invasion of Panama on December 20, 1989. The stated purpose was to arrest Noriega, but his arrest also necessitated the overthrow of the Panamanian government and the installation of a new regime. The task was accomplished with relatively few casualties on the U.S. side. The civilian death toll in Panama numbered at least 200 (the estimate of the U.S. military) and possibly more than 300 (according to an analysis by Physicians for Human Rights).[10] Another 15,000 people were displaced, with most of the civilian casualties being the result of the shelling of a neighborhood adjacent to Noriega's headquarters.

---

[9] The Contras had used drug sales to help finance their war against the Nicaraguan government. See, for example, "Contra Arms Crews Said to Smuggle Drugs," *New York Times*, January 20, 1987, A1, and P. Scott and J. Marshall, *Cocaine Politics: Drugs, Armies and the CIA in Central America* (Berkeley, CA: University of California Press, 1991). For an account of Noriega's relationship with the United States in the years leading up to the invasion, see K. Buckley, *Panama* (New York: Touchstone, 1992).

[10] Physicians for Human Rights, *"Operation Just Cause": The Human Cost of Military Action in Panama* (Boston: Physicians for Human Rights, 1991).

The First Iraq War

While the cold war was coming rapidly to an end in 1990, the Bush administration did not have to look far for new enemies. In July, Saddam Hussein invaded Kuwait, annexing it as a province of Iraq. The invasion was a direct outgrowth of the Iraq-Iran war, which had finally come to an end two years earlier, after more than 1 million people had been killed.

Iraq had been on the offensive in the first stages of the war, catching the revolutionary government in Iran in a state of disarray. Iraq had managed to occupy a significant slice of Iranian territory, giving it control over the Shatt al-Arab waterway, which separates the two countries, and some of the oil-rich regions in the western part of Iran. However, an Iranian counteroffensive had pushed the Iraqi forces back behind their border in 1982, leaving the countries to fight out a brutal World War I–type war of attrition over the next six years.

With a larger population, and many recruits willing to die for their country, Iran had an advantage in such a conflict. However, the Iraqi government enjoyed considerable international support. The United States provided some weapons to Iraq (in addition to the weapons that it was secretly selling to Iran) and intelligence information to assist in battlefield coordination. The United States also allowed Iraqi oil to be shipped on U.S.-flagged tankers protected from attack by Iran. The other important source of international support for Iraq consisted of the oil-rich monarchies of the Persian Gulf region. These countries were anxious to see the Iranian revolution contained in Iran. Toward this end, they lent Iraq tens of billions of dollars to help finance its war.

When the war came to an end in 1988, Iraq suddenly faced the burden of repaying its war debt. Saddam Hussein argued that Saudi Arabia, Kuwait, and the other Arab states of the region should forgive all or part of the debt, since Iraq had been serving a common Arab interest in fighting the revolutionary government in Iran. In addition, Iraq had specific grievances against Kuwait. Kuwait was producing oil at a rate that far exceeded the quota assigned by the Organization of Petroleum Exporting Countries (OPEC), thereby depressing world prices. Iraq also complained that Kuwait was engaging in slant drilling near the border that allowed it to tap oil fields on the Iraqi side, effectively stealing oil from Iraq.

When Iraq was unable to get Kuwait to give ground on these issues, it simply overran the country, easily defeating its tiny army. In announcing that it was annexing Kuwait, Iraq was both appealing to Arab nationalism and challenging the makeup of the postcolonial world. The division of the Gulf region into various states was primarily the work of the colonial powers (mainly Britain), with little basis in earlier history. Hussein's annexation of Kuwait amounted to a challenge to the colonial divisions.

It is not clear what sort of response Hussein anticipated from the United States, but the Bush administration quickly declared its intention to remove Hussein from Kuwait.[11] Toward this end, Bush almost immediately began a buildup of U.S. forces in Saudi Arabia near the Kuwaiti border (ostensibly sent there to defend Saudi Arabia). He also went to the United Nations, where he got the Security Council to pass a resolution demanding the withdrawal of Iraqi forces from Kuwait. The council also imposed economic sanctions on Iraq that were to be maintained until its troops left Kuwait. The use of the Security Council in this case was one of the dividends for the United States from the end of the cold war. While in prior years the Soviet Union might have vetoed measures directed against Iraq, a cold war ally, at this point Gorbachev was largely supportive of the Bush administration's efforts.

To garner domestic support for its war drive against Iraq, the Bush administration felt the need to embellish the facts somewhat. For example, it purported to have evidence that Iraq had plans to continue

---

[11] There were questions raised in the media at the time as to whether the Bush administration had made clear to Hussein that it would not tolerate an invasion of Kuwait. April Glaspie, the U.S. ambassador to Iraq, had met with Hussein immediately before the invasion. She had indicated the Bush administration's desire to have closer relations with Iraq while at the same time urging that Iraq's disputes with Kuwait be settled peacefully. There are differing accounts as to how clear her warnings against an invasion were to Hussein. See M. Khadduri and E. Ghareeb, *War in the Gulf, 1990–91: The Iraq-Kuwait Conflict and Its Implications* (Oxford: Oxford University Press, 1997), for an account of the Glaspie–Saddam Hussein exchange as well as an excellent background discussion of the factors leading up to the war. Glaspie contended in congressional testimony that she made it very clear in her conversation that the Bush administration would not tolerate military action against Kuwait. The cables sent to the State Department by Glaspie at the time seem to indicate that she had not been entirely clear about the Bush administration's opposition to the use of force; see "Envoy's Testimony on Iraq Is Assailed," *New York Times*, July 13, 1991, A1.

its offensive south to Saudi Arabia, threatening the world's largest exporter of oil. In reality, its satellite photos showed the Iraqi troops stationed primarily in the northern and central portion of Kuwait, not poised near the border waiting for the signal to invade Saudi Arabia.[12]

The Bush administration's allies also sought to embellish the brutality of the invasion. In conjunction with a major U.S. lobbying firm, the Kuwaiti government invented a story about the Iraqi soldiers removing babies from incubators in Kuwaiti hospitals and leaving them to die. This story was picked up by Amnesty International, the highly respected human rights organization, and circulated widely through the media.[13] The small element of truth in the story was that electricity in some of the hospitals had gone off during the battle for Kuwait City. Although this power failure undoubtedly jeopardized the lives of babies in incubators, causing a power failure during a battle is very different from deliberately removing babies from incubators.

Throughout the fall, the United States built up its forces in Kuwait and assembled a large alliance of countries, including several Arab countries, that gave symbolic or substantive support to the effort to remove Iraq's forces from Kuwait. The Iraqi government lacked any major allies, although the Soviet Union was willing to act as a mediator to try to negotiate acceptable terms for a withdrawal.

As the deadlines imposed by the United States grew closer, the Bush administration was determined that Hussein not be given any cover for his withdrawal, explicitly refusing any proposals that allowed Iraq to retain any portion of Kuwait or offering any other concession in exchange for its withdrawal.[14] Having helped to build up Iraq as a major regional power during its war with Iran, many in the Bush administration viewed a war with Iraq as an opportunity to cut Saddam Hussein's military down to size.

The United States began its attack in mid-January 1991, after Hussein had failed to withdraw his troops from Kuwait by the deadline Bush had given him. Once the war began, there was little doubt as to

[12] This incident is discussed in D. Kellner, *Media Culture: Cultural Studies, Identity and Politics Between the Modern and the Postmodern* (London: Routledge, 1995), 199–226.

[13] An account of this episode can be found in J. MacArthur, *Second Front: Censorship and Propaganda in the 1991 Gulf War* (Berkeley, CA: University of California Press, 2004).

[14] See "Standoff in the Gulf; A Partial Pullout by Iraq Is Feared as Deadline Ploy," *New York Times*, December 18, 1990, A1.

its outcome. The United States enjoyed unchallenged air superiority –
Hussein sent much of his air force to Iran in a desperate effort to preserve some air power for the aftermath of the war. (Iran confiscated
the planes.) The U.S.-led forces had a month-long campaign of bombing and missile strikes against troops in the field and military targets in
Iraqi cities. The campaign also targeted the basic civilian infrastructure,
knocking out the power and sanitation systems in Baghdad.[15] After
more than a month of this air attack, the coalition's ground forces
quickly defeated the Iraqi forces, most of whom were draftees who
surrendered at the first opportunity. Hussein was prepared to sign a
ceasefire on Bush's terms almost immediately after the ground war
began. An agreement was reached on March 3, bringing an end to the
fighting.[16]

Although the U.S. forces penetrated deep into the predominantly
Shiite region of southern Iraq, they did not go near Baghdad. The decision not to directly remove Hussein was the result of a prior agreement
with the U.S. allies on the issue and the desire not to be bogged down
in a prolonged occupation in Iraq.[17] Furthermore, from the standpoint
of the Bush administration, it was not clear that leaving a weakened
Saddam Hussein in power in Iraq was a bad outcome.

The Bush administration did provide encouragement to an uprising
by Shiites in the south against Hussein, in addition to a rebellion
by Kurds in the north. The latter quickly succeeded, largely because
the Kurds had years of experience fighting for their independence as
guerillas. In addition, the United States warned Hussein against taking
any major military actions in the region. The Shiites were not so lucky.
Although the United States imposed a "no-fly" zone that prohibited
Hussein from using his remaining air power in the southern part of the

---

[15] See "War in the Gulf: Iraq; Raids Said to Cut Power in Baghdad," *New York Times*,
January 19, 1990, A10.

[16] For an analysis of the military strategy pursued in the war, see N. Friedman, *Desert
Victory: The War for Kuwait* (Annapolis, MD: Naval Institute Press, 1991).

[17] At the time, there seemed to be general agreement in political circles and among
military leaders that overthrowing Hussein would likely involve the United States
in a long and potentially bloody occupation. See R. Atkinson, *Crusade: The Untold
Story of the Persian Gulf War* (New York: Houghton Mifflin, 1994). In a news
conference shortly after the conclusion of the war, President Bush himself used the
phrase "Vietnam-style quagmire" in rejecting the notion that the United States
should overthrow Saddam Hussein and occupy Iraq. See "After the War: Excerpts
from Bush's News Conference: Relief Camps for Kurds in Iraq," *New York Times*,
April 17, 1991, A12.

country, it did not prevent him from ruthlessly suppressing the Shiite revolt with tanks and other heavy weaponry.

The conclusion of the war left Hussein in control of Iraq, but the country was far weaker both militarily and economically than it had been prior to the war. In addition to the damage its military suffered during the war, Iraq was also obligated to destroy much of its weaponry as a condition of the peace treaty. It was also required to destroy weapons of mass destruction, whether biological, chemical, or nuclear, and the precursors and equipment used to make such weapons.

The United States also imposed economic sanctions that prohibited Iraq from importing a wide variety of goods. The ostensible purpose of these sanctions was to prevent Hussein from rebuilding his military and producing weapons of mass destruction. However, the sanctions also prevented Iraq from importing items that were essential to maintaining and rebuilding the country's infrastructure, including the electrical system and the water and sanitation systems. Largely as a result of these sanctions, Iraq's economy deteriorated further following the war. The relatively generous (for a developing country) welfare state that Hussein had put in place with Iraq's oil money collapsed, and most Iraqis experienced a serious decline in their standard of living. In fact, many had to go without basic necessities and medical care.

One aspect of the first Persian Gulf war that distinguished it from prior wars fought by the United States was that the media was almost entirely dependent on the military for its news accounts. Just before the war began, the White House warned journalists that it could not ensure their safety once the air attack began, and it urged all of the reporters stationed in Iraq to leave the country. With very few exceptions, the press complied with this request. This meant that the only news that reporters could get about the progress of the war came from the daily press briefings held by top military personnel. At these briefings, the military would show videotapes of successful missile strikes, maps of targets that had been hit, and other news that it wished to share with the public. There was little discussion of bombs that had missed their targets, civilian casualties, or other features of the war that might not have been received well by the American public.

The one major news crew that did make a point of remaining in Iraq and reporting from Baghdad was a contingent from CNN led by Peter Arnett, a veteran war correspondent. His reports documented both the accuracy of many of the guided bombs used by the U.S.

military and also several incidents of either mistargeted or misfired bombs that destroyed civilian sites with no obvious military value. For these accounts, Arnett and CNN were vilified by supporters of the war, many of whom wanted to prohibit this sort of independent reporting for the duration of the war.[18]

From the standpoint of the Bush administration, the war in Iraq had been an enormous success. The United States had used military force to accomplish its goal – removing Saddam Hussein from Kuwait. There was massive celebration of this victory. Many pundits were anxious to pronounce the end of the "Vietnam syndrome" – the American public's resistance to the use of U.S. troops in foreign wars. Bush's approval rating soared, hitting 91 percent immediately following the war, the highest presidential approval rating ever recorded.

The Collapse of the Soviet Union

There was one other extraordinary foreign event during President Bush's first term – the collapse of the Soviet Union. At the end of 1991, the Soviet Union ceased to exist, broken up into its fifteen member republics. Mikhail Gorbachev, the Soviet leader who had begun the reform process in the Soviet Union, was suddenly out of a job. Boris Yeltsin, a former political ally, was now the president of the Russian Federation, the main successor state to the Soviet Union.

There were two separate forces that led to the dissolution of the Soviet Union. The first was the reform process that Gorbachev had unleashed, a drive for democratic rights and a greater role for private businesses. The second force was nationalism. The Soviet Union was a conglomeration of hundreds of different national groups that had come under the control of the Russian Empire over a period of four centuries. After the Russian Revolution, these groups became part of the Soviet Union.

---

[18] Arnett was subject to Iraqi censorship in his reporting (he has subsequently claimed that they rarely interfered), which was clearly indicated in all his reports by a line across the bottom of the screen. For more on the media coverage of the war, see W. Bennet and D. Paletz, eds., *Taken by Storm: The Media, Public Opinion, and U.S. Foreign Policy in the Gulf War* (Chicago: University of Chicago Press, 1994); R. Weiner, *Live from Baghdad: Making Journalism History Behind the Lines* (New York: St. Martins Press, 2002); and P. Arnett, *Live from the Battlefield: From Vietnam to Baghdad, 35 Years in the World's War Zones* (New York: Touchstone, 1995).

In some cases, the non-Russian national groups had been integrated reasonably well into the Soviet system. In other cases, Russian domination was generally accepted, even though there may still have been some resentment. However, in several of the Russian republics, anti-Russian nationalism remained a powerful force that was unleashed as soon as Gorbachev began to open up the political system. At the top of the list were the Baltic republics, Lithuania, Latvia, and Estonia, which began to push for independence not long after Gorbachev came to power. There were comparable, if less well organized, movements for independence or autonomy in many of the other republics. In 1989, in a move to decentralize authority, Gorbachev allowed democratic elections in each of the Soviet Union's fifteen republics. In Russia, Boris Yeltsin won control of the government, leading a slate of candidates openly critical of Gorbachev for not pushing reform faster.

The reform and nationalist dynamics came together in 1991 to bring about the dissolution of the Soviet Union. The final episode began with a clumsy coup attempt in August, when several high-ranking generals briefly detained Gorbachev while he was on his summer vacation. They sent tanks into the streets in Moscow, ostensibly to intimidate the population and discourage protests. The coup quickly fell apart when it became clear that most of the military was not prepared to take part and that the troops could not be counted on to fire on protestors. The tanks in Moscow became a platform for Yeltsin – literally, as he addressed a crowd of protestors standing on top of one of them – and other speakers to denounce the coup.

Yeltsin's position was hugely strengthened by his role in opposing the coup, while Gorbachev appeared increasingly irrelevant. Throughout the fall, Yeltsin seized more instruments of power within Russia. In December, he arranged with the presidents of the Ukraine and Belarus to jointly leave the Soviet Union, effectively bringing about its dissolution.

Given the centrality of the cold war in both foreign and domestic politics in the United States, this was a remarkable and almost completely unexpected turn of events. The United States had suddenly lost its major enemy in the world. While the underlying causes of the collapse can be debated, there is one striking irony worth noting. An argument often made by the hard-liners in the Reagan administration was that totalitarian regimes such as the Soviet Union must be met with force because they could never be reformed peacefully. In contrast, they claimed that the authoritarian regimes that were U.S. allies could gradually be transformed into democracies through persuasion. As it turned out, the Soviet Union and Eastern Europe were transformed into democracies with barely a shot being fired.[19]

Trouble at Home

While the course of international events could not have gone much better for the Bush administration, its domestic record was not nearly as encouraging. Unlike Reagan, Bush assumed office without any pressing domestic agenda. He campaigned on the slogan of promoting a "kinder, gentler nation," but there was little obvious substance to this promise. President Bush's domestic agenda, or lack of one, posed a political problem for him throughout his term of office.

Just two months after President Bush took office, an oil tanker, the *Exxon Valdez*, ran aground off the southern coast of Alaska, leading to the largest oil spill in the history of the world. The spill threatened the wildlife in one of the most pristine areas of the country. Subsequent investigations showed that there had been few precautions taken to prevent spills and little preparation for cleanup in the event of a spill. It turned out that the tanker captain had been drinking when the spill occurred and that the ship was being piloted by a person who was not even licensed to pilot a tanker. This disaster led to considerable public anger, both against Exxon and the oil industry more generally. The fact that President Bush had been in the oil business himself and had maintained close ties to it did not encourage public confidence in the president's commitment to the environment.[20]

The other big domestic policy item that President Bush had to deal with shortly after taking office was the budget deficit, which continued to raise serious concerns in policy circles and, at least occasionally, among the larger public. The budget deficit had been reduced from its levels during the high-deficit years of the Reagan administration through spending cuts on the domestic side and some tax increases,

[19] On the collapse of the Soviet Union, see G. Suny, *The Revenge of the Past: Nationalism, Revolution, and the Collapse of the Soviet Union* (Stanford, CA: Stanford University Press, 1993), and D. Remnick, *Lenin's Tomb: The Last Days of the Soviet Empire* (New York: Vintage, 1994).

[20] On the *Exxon Valdez* spill, see J. Keeble, *Out of the Channel: The Exxon Valdez Oil Spill in Prince William Sound* (Spokane, WA: Eastern Washington University Press, 1999).

most notably an increase in Social Security taxes that was phased in beginning in 1983. Also, the 1986 tax reform package managed to raise revenue by closing a number of loopholes. Still, the unified budget deficit never fell below 2.8 percent of GDP, a level hit in 1989 at the peak of the business cycle.[21] Prior to the Reagan era, the deficit only became this high during recessions. Furthermore, with the economy soon slumping into a recession in the summer of 1990, the budget deficit was again on the rise.

As a matter of economic policy, a recession is the worst time to raise taxes or to cut government spending. During a recession, the economy badly needs demand from any source. If a tax cut spurs consumption or the government employs people through additional spending, this is a clear gain for an economy with too few jobs. Raising taxes or cutting spending is likely to make a recession worse. Nonetheless, in the summer of 1990, with projections showing the deficit back on the rise, there was strong pressure to take measures to reduce the deficit. (It also was not apparent at the time that the economy had slumped into a recession.)

President Bush insisted on bringing down the deficit through spending cuts, while congressional Democrats argued that tax increases had to be included as part of the mix in any deficit reduction package. With the Democrats controlling Congress and refusing to pass a budget bill that did not include some tax increases, and President Bush threatening to veto any bill that did not have spending cuts, it seemed inevitable that there would be a compromise that would include a mix of the two. Eventually, President Bush agreed to sign a bill that included a modest increase in the tax rates paid by those in the top tax brackets, fewer than 10 percent of all taxpayers.

This deal gave the Democrats a political victory since they could claim that Bush had been forced to back down from the "no new taxes" pledge that he had used so effectively in the 1988 campaign. The tax increase also infuriated conservative Republicans, who felt that Bush had double-crossed them. The back and forth worked to the advantage of the Democrats in the 1990 election, where they had

---

[21] The budget deficit gets smaller at the peak of a business cycle because when the employment is high, the government collects more money in tax revenue. Also, its spending falls when the economy is strong because it has to pay out less money for unemployment compensation, welfare, and other forms of spending that increase when more people are unemployed.

a small gain of seats in both the House and Senate, giving them their largest majorities in both chambers since before Reagan took office.

The Battle over the Supreme Court

During the 1980 presidential campaign, Reagan had often talked about the courts, railing against liberal activist judges who he claimed were overriding the public's will. This was intended as a criticism of the role that the judiciary had played over the prior three decades in promoting civil rights, protecting civil liberties for criminal defendants, and legalizing abortion. In these areas, the courts had often overturned laws passed by legislatures, arguing that constitutional rights took precedence. Reagan promised to appoint judges who were "strict constructionists," which was taken to mean that they would generally defer to the judgment of elected officials.

During his two terms in office, Reagan had the opportunity to appoint hundreds of judges at all levels of the federal judiciary who reflected his general philosophy, but Supreme Court appointees are obviously the most visible and have the greatest impact. To the great frustration of many conservatives, even after eight years of the Reagan administration, the Supreme Court was still thwarting their efforts on many issues they considered important, most notably abortion, where it refused to overturn the *Roe v. Wade* decision that prevented states from outlawing abortion.

Although Reagan had the opportunity to appoint three of the nine justices during his administration (he also elevated a sitting justice, William Rehnquist, to the position of chief justice), his appointments had not completely shifted the composition of the court. Reagan's first appointment was Sandra Day O'Connor, the first woman to serve on the Supreme Court. Justice O'Connor established a reputation as a moderate conservative, not very different from the justice she replaced. President Reagan's second appointment was Antonio Scalia, who filled the associate justice position vacated by Rehnquist when he became chief justice. Scalia has consistently taken conservative positions, but so had the departing Chief Justice Warren Berger.

Reagan's third opportunity for a Supreme Court appointment came in 1987 when another one of the Court's moderate conservatives resigned. Reagan initially nominated Robert Bork, an appellate court judge who had developed a national reputation as a conservative legal scholar. Under pressure from women's groups, civil rights groups, and civil liberties organizations, the Democratic-controlled Senate refused to go along with Bork's nomination. When it became clear that he did not have the votes to be approved, Bork asked that his nomination be withdrawn. This was an important turn of events. In the past, the Senate had generally voted up or down on judicial nominees based on their competence for the position. No one had questioned Bork's qualifications as a legal scholar. He had been voted down based on his conservative ideology. The justice who was eventually approved in Bork's place, Anthony Kennedy, was another moderate conservative, not very different from the justice he replaced.

President Bush got his first opportunity to make an appointment to the Court when William Brennan, one of the most liberal justices, stepped down in 1990. He chose to nominate David Souter, a relatively unknown figure who he had just recently appointed as an appellate court judge. Once on the Court, Souter proved to be a moderate liberal, which meant that his appointment also did not hugely change the balance of the Court.

The next vacancy opened up in 1991, when Thurgood Marshall, the first and only African American justice, stepped down. Marshall was the most liberal justice on the Court at the time, so this vacancy provided a real opportunity to shift the Court's balance. Toward this end, President Bush nominated Clarence Thomas, a strongly conservative African American who had been appointed to the appellate court the previous year.

The appointment of Thomas immediately prompted the same sort of mobilization among liberal groups that had defeated the Bork nomination. However, many senators who had opposed Bork were reluctant to veto another presidential appointee, especially an African American such as Thomas, who had a very compelling personal story of rising out of poverty.

After an initial round of hearings, it seemed that Thomas had the votes needed to get his nomination out of the Judiciary Committee, which virtually guaranteed his approval by the full Senate. At that point, one of the committee's staffers leaked testimony to the media from one of Thomas's former assistants, Anita Hill, in which Hill claimed that Thomas had repeatedly subjected her to sexual harassment during the time she had worked with him. When these reports became public, there was an enormous public outcry over what appeared to be an effort by an all-male Senate committee to sweep serious allegations of sexual harassment under the rug. In response to this pressure, the committee reopened the hearings to examine the allegations.

The committee had several more days of televised hearings in which they heard from Hill, Thomas, and several other witnesses who had been familiar with one or both of them during the period in question.[22] Hill stood by her allegations, while Thomas angrily denied them. With the supporting witnesses giving occasionally comical but ultimately inconclusive testimony, the committee eventually voted to send the nomination to the floor of the Senate, where Thomas was narrowly approved.

Although the conservatives succeeded in getting Thomas approved, they still felt wronged by the battle. With so much importance now attached to judges, the battle over judicial appointments at all levels was far more intense than it had ever been in the past.[23]

The Rodney King Incident

There was one other important episode during the Bush administration that is worth noting: the beating of Rodney King by the Los Angeles police in March 1991 and the three days of civil unrest that followed the acquittals of the police officers responsible in March 1992. The Los Angeles Police Department (LAPD), like many major city police departments, had a reputation in the African American community for brutality. Daryl Gates, the department's long-serving chief of police, was always a staunch defender of his officers when charges of brutality were raised. In fact, he once suggested that the explanation for the large number of African Americans who died from chokeholds at the hands of the LAPD was that the anatomy of blacks differed from that of whites.[24]

The beating of Rodney King was an extraordinary event because it was captured on videotape by someone who witnessed the scene.

---

[22] The committee did not take public testimony from other former aides who had also alleged that Thomas had sexually harassed them.

[23] For an interesting collection of essays examining the social significance of the Thomas confirmation hearings, see A. Hill and E. Jordon, eds., *Race, Gender, and Power in America: The Legacy of the Hill-Thomas Hearings* (New York: Oxford University Press, 2005).

[24] See "Tape of Beating by Police Revives Charges of Racism," *New York Times,* March 7, 1991, A18.

Usually, when there is an incident involving police brutality, there are
no other witnesses except other police officers. If a person accused of
a crime makes an allegation against a police officer without corrobo-
rating evidence, he will generally not be successful in pressing his case.

King, who had been drinking at the time, had led the police on
a high-speed chase across the city. According to the police accounts,
after King was apprehended, he was acting erratically and refused to
follow their orders. The initial portion of the arrest was not captured
on videotape. What was captured was a black man lying face down on
the ground surrounded by police. He was repeatedly hit with batons
by one officer after another. Not one of the twenty-four police officers
at the scene saw anything sufficiently unusual in the arrest to report to
their superiors. In fact, the arrest was a topic of humor on the police
radio band that night.

However, when the videotape was shown on local and national
television, it prompted outrage, both in Los Angeles and across the
country. In response to public pressure, the Los Angeles district attorney dropped the charges he had filed against King and indicted the
four police officers who had been filmed doing most of the beating.
The trial took place the following year in Simi Valley, a largely white
suburban area. The defendants had argued successfully that the case
should be moved outside of Los Angeles in the interest of getting an
unbiased jury.

On April 29, 1992, a jury with no African Americans voted to
acquit the four officers.[25] This led to angry protests in the African
American community in South Central Los Angeles, which quickly
turned violent. Over the next four days, hundreds of stores and buildings were vandalized and set afire. Dozens of motorists were pulled
out of cars and beaten. With the police unable to regain control, the
National Guard was called in. When things finally settled down, 44
people had been killed, more than 1,700 had been injured, and more
than 6,000 had been arrested.

The set of events around the King beating and the later trial of the
police officers demonstrated yet again the extent to which much of the
African American population remained alienated from the rest of society. While African Americans had made progress by many measures,
the unrest in Los Angeles in 1992 was not qualitatively different from

---

[25] In the case of one officer, the jury was unable to reach a verdict on one of the
charges.

the urban riots of the sixties, many of which were also sparked by incidents of police brutality. The King arrest and the subsequent acquittals of the police officers seemed to show that police brutality against African Americans was still acceptable.

The 1992 Election

The international events of 1991 played a huge role in the 1992 election even though the state of the economy dominated the fall campaign. The main impact of international events was to scare most of the Democratic Party's big-name candidates out of the race. The prospect of running against an incumbent president with a 91 percent approval rating did not look very promising. As a result, well-known figures such as the House majority leader Richard Gephardt and Tennessee Senator Al Gore, both of whom had run in the 1988 primaries, opted not to run. Jesse Jackson also decided against another run. This left the field open to less-known candidates.

It is likely that the "top tier" candidates came to regret their decision. The triumphal celebrations following the Iraq war did not last long. The economy had fallen into a recession by the summer of 1990, which officially continued until March 1991. However, the official end of the recession did not put an end to workers' insecurity about their economic situation. The economy ended 1991 with fewer jobs than had existed at the beginning of the year. While it finally started creating jobs in the spring of 1992, at the time of the November election the economy still had not regained all the jobs lost in the recession.

And it was not only the lack of jobs that worried workers. Wages were not keeping pace with inflation, which meant that workers' paychecks were not going as far as they had previously. After adjusting for inflation, the average hourly wage was 4 percent lower on election day than it had been before the onset of the recession two and a half years earlier. In addition, rapidly rising health care costs were imposing a growing burden on workers and companies. An increasing number of companies were dropping health insurance coverage for workers and/or their dependents, leaving nearly 40 million Americans uninsured. Health insurance rocketed to the top of the national agenda after a special senatorial election in Pennsylvania was fought largely over the issue.

This was the context in which Bill Clinton managed to win the Democratic nomination and then capture the White House, becoming the first Democrat to be elected president in sixteen years. Clinton entered the Democratic presidential race as a relative unknown. He had been elected five times and served for twelve years as governor of Arkansas, one of the smallest and poorest states in the country. While there was little about his record as governor to distinguish him, Clinton was an extraordinarily talented politician with far more charisma than any other figure of his time.[26]

He also had been planning his run for the presidency from his college days, constantly building up his list of political connections. In positioning himself for the race, he billed himself as a "new kind of Democrat." By this he meant that he was pro-business, he favored an aggressive foreign policy (unlike most of the Democrats in Congress, he had supported Reagan's military buildup), and he favored tough anticrime measures like the death penalty. These positions made him acceptable to many centrists who may have objected to the positions of more traditional Democrats. It also made Clinton an acceptable candidate to many members of the business community, which gave him a large advantage in fundraising.

Clinton also had a genuinely first-rate campaign organization. They responded vigorously to any attacks. Early in the campaign, before the first primary in New Hampshire, stories came to light concerning Clinton's extramarital affairs. A letter was also leaked in which Clinton explained that he had enlisted in the National Guard to escape the draft (a common practice in the Vietnam era). Clinton managed to turn both of these issues to his advantage. At a time when most of the public knew virtually nothing about any of the candidates, the news was filled with stories about Clinton's affairs and draft record. When the first primary was finally held, the media portrayed it as a referendum on how the public felt about Clinton's marital infidelity and avoidance of service in the Vietnam War. The other candidates were barely even mentioned.

In spite of his soaring popularity at the conclusion of the Iraq war, President Bush faced a challenge for the Republican nomination from

---

[26] On Clinton's rise to the presidency see D. Maraniss, *First in His Class: A Biography of Bill Clinton* (New York: Touchstone, 1996); G. Stephanopoulos, *All Too Human* (Boston: Back Bay Books, 2000); and W. Clinton, *My Life* (New York: Knopf, 2004).

conservative television commentator Patrick Buchanan, who attacked him for being insufficiently conservative. First and foremost, Buchanan mocked Bush for having broken his "no new taxes" pledge. With many people still feeling considerable hardship from the recession, Buchanan's message had some resonance. Although he never stood a real chance of winning, Buchanan made a surprisingly strong showing in some of the early primaries, forcing Bush to fight to hold on to the party's nomination.

Although Clinton and Bush managed to lock up their parties' nominations early in the primary season, there was one additional factor in the 1992 race. Ross Perot, an eccentric billionaire, decided to run for president as an independent. Perot portrayed himself as a straight shooter who was above politics. He wanted to focus on the country's real problems, with the federal budget deficit being top on his list. Perot spent substantial amounts of his own money on the campaign and was able to get his message about the importance of deficit reduction to a wide audience. As a result of his strong showing in the polls, he was included in the fall presidential debates.

Clinton succeeded in keeping the weak economy front and center throughout the campaign. Bush's foreign policy successes ended up carrying little weight. Clinton won by a comfortable margin. As a sign of voters' extraordinary disaffection, Ross Perot managed to get more than 18 percent of the vote as an independent, in spite of very erratic behavior over the course of the campaign.[27] This was the largest share of the vote garnered by a candidate not running on a major party ticket since 1912, when a former president, Theodore Roosevelt, ran on a third-party ticket. President Bush was unable to even cross the 40 percent threshold in his reelection bid.

The Early Clinton Years

When he took office in 1993, Clinton had a solid Democratic majority in both houses of Congress. This should have given him ample

---

[27] Perot withdrew from the campaign unexpectedly in the middle of the summer. He then reentered the race in the fall. He later claimed that the reason he had withdrawn in the summer was that he had been told by his contacts that the Republican Party had plans to disrupt his daughter's wedding, which was scheduled for the late summer. He never presented any evidence to support this strange allegation.

opportunity to push through his main policy proposals, but this turned out not to be the case. Clinton pursued three major policy initiatives in his first two years: the passage of a budget plan for deficit reduction, the passage of the North American Free Trade Agreement (NAFTA), and the implementation of national health care insurance. He succeeded on the first two, although both required extensive efforts from the White House.

Clinton took on the battle over the budget soon after taking office. During the campaign, he had made largely contradictory campaign pledges. He had promised a major public investment initiative that would include spending more money on education and training, infrastructure, and research and development. He also had promised to bring the deficit down to a manageable level, setting the target of cutting it in half by the end of his first term in office. Although he did propose raising taxes on the wealthy, the additional tax money would not be enough to support a substantial boost in public investment while also bringing down the deficit.

After some internal debate among his top advisors, Clinton came down clearly on the side of deficit reduction.[28] This meant that the public investment agenda was largely abandoned. There was a serious element of bait and switch in this decision. Clinton had highlighted his support of public investment during the nomination process and in the general election. Other candidates in the primaries and the general election had championed the cause of a balanced budget. Voters had consciously rejected this strong focus on deficit reduction when they cast their vote for Clinton, yet this is exactly what they ended up with.

As a rhetorical matter, Clinton always maintained his support for public investment. In his speeches, he would often highlight modest budget increases in various programs for education or training. But the actual budget numbers told a different story. Spending in the areas that the Office of Management and Budget regards as investment, measured relative to the size of the economy, fell slightly from 1.8 percent of GDP in 1993 to 1.7 percent of GDP in 1997, the year of the last budget of Clinton's first term.[29]

---

[28] See R. Woodward, *The Agenda: Inside the Clinton White House* (New York: Simon and Schuster, 1994), for an account of the internal debates over economic policy in the first year of the Clinton administration.

[29] Office of Management and Budget, *The Budget for the Fiscal Year 2006: Historical Tables* (Washington, DC: U.S. Government Printing Office, 2005), table 9–1.

Clinton had to tinker with his budget package repeatedly to get it through Congress. He originally included a small stimulus package that included some of the investment items he had promised during the campaign. This failed to pass. He also floated the idea of an energy tax, which would have had environmental benefits and helped to reduce dependence on foreign oil in addition to raising money. This was scuttled and replaced with a modest increase in the national gas tax. The main tax increases were increases in the taxes paid by the highest-income taxpayers, and these affected less than 10 percent of the population.

The bill ended up passing by a single vote in both houses of Congress. Not a single Republican in either chamber supported the budget. Most of the Democrats who defected were conservatives, disproportionately from the South. The liberal and centrist wings of the party remained solidly behind Clinton, even though the budget package offered them little. They were committed to ensuring the success of the first Democratic president since Jimmy Carter.

The Battle over NAFTA

Clinton's push to get NAFTA through Congress was at least as contentious as his budget battles, even though the lineup of opposing forces was very different. The purpose of NAFTA was to more completely integrate Mexico into the U.S. economic sphere. While the agreement was labeled a "free trade" agreement, the pact actually had relatively little to do with free trade. The Clinton administration was interested in Mexico as a source of low-cost labor. The point of NAFTA was to put in place a set of rules that would make U.S. investments in Mexico more secure. Toward this end, the treaty included numerous clauses to ensure that future Mexican governments could not expropriate the property of U.S. corporations or put in place restrictions on repatriating profits. The treaty also sought to extend U.S. patent and copyright protections into the Mexican market. This was done both to increase the profits of the U.S. pharmaceutical and entertainment industries and to set up a model that could be imposed on other developing countries through comparable agreements.

It is worth briefly contrasting NAFTA with the simultaneous efforts in Europe to consolidate the European Union. While NAFTA was intended strictly as a commercial treaty, the members of the European

Union sought to craft a unified social and political structure. In 1989, the European Union approved a "social charter" that guaranteed a wide set of rights, including freedom of movement, to all citizens of the European Union.[30] In addition, the European Union set up a fund that was used to funnel money for economic development from the wealthier regions in Europe to the poorer regions. The explicit intention was to hasten growth in poorer regions to rapidly bring their living standards to levels comparable to those in the richer areas. Some countries, most notably Ireland, have used this support very effectively in the last two decades. Ireland is now among the wealthiest countries in the European Union.

NAFTA included no provisions explicitly intended to raise living standards in Mexico to U.S. levels. Nor did it provide for free movement among the member countries. And it certainly did not obligate any of the signatories to guarantee any basic rights to their citizens.

Since one of the main purposes of NAFTA was to place U.S. manufacturing workers in direct competition with low-wage workers in Mexico, unsurprisingly the agreement was not very popular. NAFTA had been largely negotiated in back rooms by the Bush administration. Like prior trade agreements, it originally attracted little public attention. This changed as a result of the 1992 presidential campaign, where Ross Perot had railed against it, warning of the "giant sucking sound" of jobs being pulled south of the border by the attraction of low wages in Mexico. Perot warned that the country could lose 6 million jobs to Mexico because of NAFTA.

While Perot's warnings were certainly gross exaggerations of NAFTA's potential negative effects, the Clinton administration had no qualms about making outlandish claims about the potential benefits of NAFTA. They publicized a study by well-respected economists showing that the treaty would lead to a large trade surplus with Mexico, thereby creating 200,000 jobs in the United States.[31]

---

[30] For a brief discussion of the European Social Charter, see European Union, *Activities of the European Union: Summaries of Legislation: Social Charter* (Brussels: European Union, 2005), http://europa.eu.int/scadplus/leg/en/cha/c10107.htm.

[31] The 1994 *Economic Report of the President* cites a study by economists Gary Hufbauer and Jeffrey Schott that claimed that NAFTA would create 200,000 additional jobs (Council of Economic Advisors, *Economic Report of the President* [Washington, DC: U.S. Government Printing Office, 1994]). In standard trade theory, the impact of trade on jobs is indirect and almost invariably small. The potential efficiency gains from a treaty such as NAFTA would be expected to have a trivial impact

Party allegiances in Congress reversed with NAFTA. Most of the support for NAFTA came from Republicans, whereas most Democrats opposed the agreement. The congressional Democrats were largely responding to pressure from labor and environmentalists, the latter group being concerned about the potential impact of the agreement on the environmental regulations in the United States. However, the opposition to NAFTA was also very deeply based. Even with a massive public relations campaign from President Clinton and the Republican leadership, the business community, and the elite media (major news outlets such as the *Washington Post* and the *New York Times* printed columns that were almost exclusively pro-NAFTA), NAFTA remained unpopular with the public.

To get a majority in Congress, Clinton was forced to engage in old-fashioned horse trading; for example, he talked to members one at a time and committed to various pork-barrel projects for their districts. In the end, he was able to secure a comfortable margin of victory. NAFTA passed in the House by a margin of 234 to 200. House Republicans voted for the treaty by a margin of 132 to 42, and Democrats in the House were opposed to NAFTA by a margin of 156 to 102.[32]

Striking Out on Health Care

Although Clinton was able to stumble to victories with his budget plan and NAFTA, his health care reform plan was almost a textbook case in how not to advance legislation. He got off to a bad start with the decision to put his wife, Hillary Rodham Clinton, in charge of the effort. Hillary Clinton was a very intelligent and articulate woman (like President Clinton, she was a graduate of Yale Law School) who had tied her own ambitions to her husband's political career. Over the course of the presidential campaign, she had become a lightening rod for the Far Right. Her prominence in designing the policy guaranteed a strong base of opposition from the onset.

on employment. Hufbauer and Schott later disavowed this conclusion from their study, which had been used widely in the NAFTA debate.

[32] For a critical account of the political efforts to pass NAFTA, see J. MacArthur, *The Selling of "Free Trade": NAFTA, Washington, and the Subversion of American Democracy* (Berkeley, CA: University of California Press, 2001). For a more sympathetic account of both the politics and economics surrounding NAFTA, see G. Hufbauer and J. Schott, eds., *NAFTA Revisited: Achievements and Challenges* (Washington, DC: Institute for International Economics, 2005).

Instead of setting out general principles and letting Congress deal with the details, as Reagan had done with his tax cut plan, Clinton took it upon herself to produce a highly detailed proposal for health care reform. She assembled a commission of health care policy experts, who then met in secret for several months crafting a proposal. They also set as their target a compromise plan that they hoped would appease most of the powerful interests in the debate. This was an alternative to a universal Medicare-type system, which would have offered enormous efficiencies but essentially put the health insurance industry out of business. While the commission was meeting, those who were excluded from the process – most importantly, the health insurance industry – began taking shots at the Clinton health care team and whatever substantive items became public.

When the nearly completed plan finally was made public (through a leak), it was almost impossible for anyone to understand it. Although there was broad public support for extending coverage to the 40 million people who were uninsured, most people did have insurance already. It was easy to play on the fears of the insured majority that the Clinton plan would worsen the quality of their care.[33] At the time, most health insurance was still traditional "fee-for-service," which meant that patients would go to the provider of their choice and send the insurance company the bill. The restrictions on choices of doctors and treatment that are now standard under most insurance plans were first put in place for most people later in the decade.

When it became clear that the never-completed plan produced by Hillary Clinton's commission was going nowhere, President Clinton threw the issue back to Congress. He used his 1994 State of the Union address to demand that Congress produce a health care bill that insured every American. As this seemed less likely over the course of the year, President Clinton gradually scaled back his target, at one point suggesting that nearly universal coverage might be acceptable. Without strong presidential leadership or a clear message, the health insurance effort floundered. No bill was ever brought to the floor in either chamber.

---

[33] The health insurance industry funded an extraordinarily successful ad campaign around a fictional couple, Harry and Louise. Harry and Louise were shown reading about aspects of the Clinton health care plan (which did not yet exist in final form) and expressing concern about their loss of choice regarding doctors and about the type of health care they would receive.

Going into the fall elections in 1994, President Clinton had won on two of his three major policy initiatives, but his .667 batting average did not look very good in political terms. He won his budget battle, but only by abandoning the public investment agenda that proved popular in his presidential campaign. Most of the public saw it as a tax increase, even though only a small segment of the public actually faced an income tax increase.[34] He had won on NAFTA, but this meant primarily overcoming the strong opposition from core Democratic constituencies. And he had lost on the one commitment that would have had a visible impact on most people's lives – by giving them the security that they would always have health care coverage.

The economy, though much improved from 1992, still left many workers feeling insecure. Unemployment had fallen just below 6 percent (the level considered to be full employment at the time), but real wages remained stagnant, as price increases eroded the value of workers' wage gains. Most workers did not feel that Clinton had yet delivered on his promises of prosperity.

---

[34] The budget agreement did impose a three-cent-per-gallon increase in the federal gas tax. While this had a minimal impact on people's living standards, it provided a basis for Republican claims that Clinton had raised taxes on the middle class.

5

The Republican Tidal Wave and the Clinton Boom

By the 1990s, Democratic control of the House of Representatives had gone on so long that most people in political circles took it as almost a basic fact of life. Congressional incumbents always enjoy a large advantage in fundraising, name recognition, and access to the media. In addition, the congressional districts had been drawn to ensure that most incumbents would not face a real race. For these reasons, when House Republican whip Newt Gingrich (the second-ranking House Republican) spoke of his plans to gain a majority, it was usually assumed that he was just trying to boost morale among the faithful. Few people thought that he was actually serious.

Gingrich was an aggressive and innovative politician who quickly moved up in the Republican leadership structure by challenging the party's complacency in the House of Representatives. Prior to Gingrich, the Republican leadership had largely accepted its status as a permanent minority party, usually seeking out compromises as a way to gain influence in an institution where the majority has almost absolute control.

Gingrich went in the opposite direction, seizing every opportunity to make a political point. He was the first to discover the value of C-SPAN cable telecasts of sessions of Congress, often making impassioned speeches to an empty chamber; these speeches reached a substantial audience of hardcore political junkies through the new cable television network. In 1989, Gingrich managed to force the resignation of Democratic House Speaker Jim Wright by exposing the fact that he was using the sales of a book he authored as a way to evade the House's limit on speaker's fees.

Gingrich continued his confrontational tactics in 1994, when he forced the resignation of House Republican leader Robert Michael by announcing his plans to challenge him for the party's leadership in the next session of Congress. This placed Gingrich in effective control of the party caucus even though he was still just the minority whip. In this capacity, he came up with a plan for "nationalizing" the 1994 congressional elections by drafting a "Contract with America," which listed ten specific measures that he made a commitment to passing in the first 100 days after assuming control of Congress. Getting Republican candidates across the country to run on a single platform was a sharp departure from the traditional pattern, in which races were contested on issues that were often narrowly focused on the concerns of the particular congressional districts. In this way, the Contract with America was an extraordinarily bold and risky strategy.

Most of the Contract with America consisted of long-standing Republican positions, such as tax cuts, tougher rules for welfare, balancing the budget, and restrictions on federal mandates to the states, but one of the measures directly attacked the way Congress had been managed for the last several decades. Congress is generally exempted from the laws it passes, including antidiscrimination measures and labor standards such as the minimum wage and forty-hour workweek. The rationale for this exemption is based on the separation of powers between the executive and legislative branches of government. This could be endangered if the president has the authority to freely order investigations of members of Congress to examine their compliance with federal statutes.

The congressional exemptions to federal statutes came to play a large role in the 1994 elections after the public became aware that the House had established a bank that was exclusively for its members and that allowed them to run overdrafts on their checking accounts at no cost. It turned out that most members had taken advantage of the opportunity to bounce checks at zero cost at least a few times. Many members had bounced dozens of checks, and some had bounced literally hundreds of checks, taking full advantage of the system to get zero-interest loans for themselves. In a context in which many families were struggling to make ends meet, the idea that members of Congress did not even have to balance their checkbooks infuriated millions of people. Gingrich was anxious to seize on this sentiment in drafting the Contract with America.

The election results from 1994 stunned most political observers. The Republicans had a net pickup of 54 seats in the House, going from being at the minority end of a 258–176 split to having a majority in a House divided 230–204. The Republicans managed to defeat many long-serving Democrats, including House Speaker Thomas Foley, without having a single Republican incumbent unseated. The Republicans also won back control of the Senate, with a net gain of 8 seats, giving them a 52–48 majority, later increased to 54–46 after two Democratic senators switched party affiliations. The "tsunami," as Gingrich dubbed it, was felt at the state and local levels as well. Republicans won control of numerous state houses, with several prominent Democrats, such as New York Governor Mario Cuomo and Texas Governor Ann Richards, going down to defeat. (Richards lost to George W. Bush.)

The 1994 election totally reshaped U.S. politics. The Republicans were now in control of both houses of Congress for the first time since the early fifties. They also had the sense of being ascendant, with a clearly defined conservative agenda. Given that the Republicans were now in control of Congress and that Clinton had openly split with historic Democratic positions on many issues, it was no longer clear what the Democratic Party stood for.

Clinton and the Republican Congress: Triangulation

Clinton's initial response to the Republican takeover of Congress was largely one of accommodation. He indicated his willingness to cooperate with Gingrich on issues such as welfare reform, tougher penalties for criminals, and balancing the budget. In his 1996 State of the Union address, he even called for having children wear school uniforms, apparently in the hope of preempting the Republicans on a push for more order in the schools. In these areas and others he consciously distanced himself from the congressional Democrats, a positioning his advisors characterized as "triangulation."

Gingrich initially managed to get through many of the items on his agenda. Congress quickly passed the Taking Back Our Streets Act, which Clinton signed; this act toughened sentences for many federal crimes and sharply restricted grounds for appeals. The direct effect of this law was limited, since the vast majority of criminal offenses are prosecuted at the state level. However, the decision of a Democratic president to support this sort of tough anticrime law undermined the ability of Democratic legislators in the states to resist more punitive legislation for minor crimes. Such measures played an important role in the rapid growth in the prison and jail population during this period.

Congress also passed measures that put new restrictions on lawsuits, limiting the ability of individuals and their lawyers to collect damages from corporations, ostensibly to curb abuses by trial lawyers.[1] In one case, the Gingrich Congress succeeded in overriding a veto by President Clinton on a bill, the Private Securities Litigation Reform Act, restricting litigation in cases alleging manipulation of stock prices.

On taxes, Clinton agreed to go along with a measure creating a $500 per child tax credit in addition to a cut in the capital gains tax. The latter was especially important to wealthy taxpayers since a large share of their income is typically in the form of capital gains, especially if the tax code gives them an incentive to have their income appear as capital gains. As a result of the cut in the capital gains tax, the wealthiest taxpayers saw a marginal tax rate of 20 percent on their capital gains income, compared with the 28 percent rate that many middle-class workers paid on their wage income.

Clinton also agreed to a bill that put strict time limits on the period that a family could receive welfare benefits, restricting most families to two consecutive years of benefits and a maximum of five years of benefits over a lifetime. The argument behind this change was that the country had built up a welfare culture in which families stayed on welfare indefinitely, seeing it as a regular means of support. In reality, the vast majority of welfare spells were relatively short and usually the result of job loss, family breakups, or illness.[2] But the image of the lazy welfare mother had become almost a cultural icon, at least since Reagan's days, so the proposal for strict time limits had considerable public support.

---

[1] Bringing a lawsuit against a major corporation is extremely expensive, since it can delay any suit for years by bringing motions of questionable relevancy. Therefore, only very wealthy individuals or other corporations will typically be able to pay for their lawyers in advance when suing a corporation. This is why plaintiff lawyers typically bring suits on a contingency basis, collecting fees only if they win. Since this means that the lawyers are themselves facing considerable risk (often incurring large expenses with no return if they lose the case), they will often demand high contingency fees. Republicans have sought to limit fees as a way of preventing suits from being brought against corporations.

[2] Two useful accounts of the impact of the 1996 welfare reform act are I. Sawhill, R. Haskins, and R. Weaver, eds., *Welfare Reform and Beyond: The Future of the Safety Net* (Washington, DC: Brookings Institution, 2003), and National Research Council, *Evaluating Welfare Reform in an Era of Transition* (Washington, DC: National Academies Press, 2001).

To reflect the intention behind this new limit, the name of the program was changed from Aid to Families with Dependent Children to Temporary Assistance to Needy Families (TANF). In principle, the time limits were also supposed to be accompanied by increased work support in the form of child care and health insurance for low-wage workers. While some federal money was appropriated for these purposes, it was ultimately the responsibility of state governments to carry through with this commitment. TANF and other funding to support low-income families was structured in the form of "block grants," which meant that states had a large degree of discretion in determining how the money was used. Previously, federal welfare funding was associated with rigid guidelines that laid out how the states should administer the program.

Gingrich had less success in other areas. One of the items in the Contract with America was an amendment to the constitution requiring a balanced budget. He was easily able to get the two-thirds vote needed in the House but fell one vote short in the Senate. (Actually, several senators who voted for the politically popular amendment probably would have voted against it if their votes had been necessary to defeat the measure.) The Contract with America also called for term limits for members of Congress, a measure that the signers rejected once in office.

However, his biggest setback came in his drive to balance the budget by 2002. Gingrich had seized on the idea of achieving a balanced budget in seven years and insisted that Clinton go along. At the time of the election, the budget projections still showed large and increasing budget deficits over this seven-year time horizon, driven primarily by projections of higher health care costs. Gingrich was adamantly opposed to raising taxes, and he was also opposed to further cuts in the military budget, so this meant that the budget had to be balanced primarily by attacking domestic spending.

Gingrich's main mechanism for cutting domestic spending was to prevent spending in most areas (such as education, the national parks, and transportation) from rising in step with inflation and economic growth. This translated into cuts in government services over time, since it is generally not possible to provide the same level of services with dollars that are worth less due to inflation (for example, the salaries of government workers typically rise in step with inflation) and where the economy is growing and demanding more services. But the cuts in these areas were still not large enough for a balanced budget to be achieved by 2002. Thus, it was necessary to go after one of the big areas of federal spending.

Gingrich chose to go after Medicare and Medicaid. Medicare, the program that provides universal health care coverage to people older than age sixty-five, offers key benefits to the middle class and was hugely popular. Medicaid provides health insurance coverage to the poor but also to many of the middle-income elderly. It also was popular, both for the services it provided and because many voters did not clearly distinguish Medicaid from Medicare.

Gingrich came up with a proposal that would have led to several hundred billion dollars in savings in Medicare and Medicaid over the budget planning period through a process of partial privatization. It turned out that he had seriously overreached. The opposition to this measure was led by the Democrats in the House of Representatives, especially minority leader Dick Gephardt. They refused to go along with Gingrich's privatization proposal, and working with labor and senior citizens groups, they were able to build a national movement in opposition. Seeing the strength of this movement, President Clinton eventually joined in and vowed to protect Medicare and Medicaid from the Gingrich Congress.

The episode eventually came to a head in October, at the end of the 1995 fiscal year. Gingrich insisted on the inclusion of his Medicare and Medicaid cuts in a bill that would maintain funding for the government into the new fiscal year. Clinton refused to sign the bill, which led to a shutdown of most areas of government service, as the government lacked funding. This period effectively amounted to a high-stakes game of chicken, with Clinton and Gingrich fighting for the high ground and seeking to blame the other for any inconveniences caused by the government shutdown.

Clinton proved to be far more effective in this game, standing on the principle of protecting Medicare and Medicaid as essential public programs. At one point, Gingrich made himself the subject of national ridicule when he complained about a personal slight by President Clinton (Gingrich claimed that Clinton had not greeted him when he was returning from a foreign trip aboard Air Force One, the president's plane) and implied that this slight would prolong the government shutdown. In the end, Gingrich backed down, producing funding bills that did not contain the Medicare and Medicaid cuts to which Clinton had objected. This episode had blunted the main thrust of Gingrich's conservative push.

The extent to which the political momentum had shifted following the confrontation over the government shutdown is probably best demonstrated by the passage of a bill raising the minimum
wage in 1996. The minimum wage is anathema to most Republican
conservatives; President Reagan obstructed any legislated increases in
the minimum wage during his entire term of office. In 1989, Congress
did push through an increase in the minimum wage that partially
restored the purchasing power that had been lost due to inflation in
the Reagan years, but by 1995 inflation had again eroded the purchasing power of the minimum wage almost back to its 1989 level.

Raising the minimum wage had not been a priority for Clinton
during his first two years, when a Democratic congressional majority
would have quickly approved a bill submitted by their new president.
The momentum for a minimum wage hike in 1996 began with a push
on the issue by the AFL-CIO. The labor federation had elected a new
leader, John Sweeney, who looked to revitalize a labor movement that
had seen its strength and membership rapidly erode over the prior
fifteen years. Sweeney decided to push for a higher minimum wage as
one of the first items on his national political agenda. He soon enlisted
the support of Clinton's labor secretary, Robert Reich.

As the issue got more attention, it was clear that there was overwhelming public support for helping out workers at the bottom. This
had particular resonance in the context of the welfare debate – if welfare recipients were to be forced into the labor market, it was argued
that they should earn a decent wage from working. After the battle over
the government shutdown, many Republicans were anxious to have
something positive to show before the 1996 election. As a result, one
of the last major pieces of legislation passed by the Gingrich Congress
was a 90-cent-an-hour increase in the minimum wage, which was to
be raised from $4.25 to $5.15 over two years. This was not an outcome
many would have predicted immediately following the 1994 election
tsunami.

The 1996 Election

After the seismic shift that resulted from the 1994 election, the 1996
election turned out to be relatively uneventful. President Clinton had
regained his standing with the public following his showdown with
Gingrich, but he had no compelling new agenda to put forward in
his second term. The congressional Democrats were no longer on the

defensive, but they also had no positive agenda with which to rally the public. As a result, the election did little to change basic political alignments.

Robert Dole, the majority leader in the Senate, was the Republican nominee for president.[3] Dole was a long-standing Washington insider who had first gained national prominence in 1976 as Gerald Ford's vice-presidential candidate. Dole was not a charismatic figure, but he was able to secure the nomination by virtue of the many political connections that he had made over the years. While he was generally conservative, he did not inspire the right wing of the Republican Party in the same way as Ronald Reagan had done or as George W. Bush would four years later. It also did not help that he was already seventy-three years old at the time of the election, the oldest major party candidate ever to run for a first term as president.

Dole's platform consisted of proposals for tax cuts, along with complaints that Clinton had allowed the military to deteriorate (Dole was a World War II hero). Clinton ran largely against the Gingrich Congress, promising that he could be counted on to protect Medicare, Medicaid, education, and the environment. He also denounced Dole's tax cut plan as a "risky scheme."

Ross Perot again entered the presidential race, this time at the head of his newly created Reform Party. In his second try, he got just 8 percent of the vote, down a full 10 percentage points from his 1992 total. While a large part off this falloff was probably attributable to the fact that he was excluded from the presidential debates in 1996 (and also spent much less of his own money), the level of public disaffection with politics was also not as great as it had been in 1992. With the economy moving along at a healthy pace, the public felt comfortable keeping the status quo.

Perot did manage to pull in enough votes to deprive Clinton of an absolute majority in the election. Although Clinton had a comfortable margin of victory over Dole, he was the first two-term president since Woodrow Wilson to never capture a majority of the popular vote.

The Clinton Boom Takes Off

At the time of the 1996 election, the economy was quite strong relative to its performance during the prior two decades. The unemployment

---

[3] Dole resigned his Senate seat in May, after he had secured the nomination, in an effort to appear as less of a Washington insider.

rate was 5.2 percent, just slightly above its twenty-year low. Also, real wages had begun rising for most workers, as a tighter labor market allowed workers to achieve wage gains. But this was just the beginning. Over the next four years, the United States had it most impressive burst of prosperity since the sixties.

There were three key parts to this boom. The first important factor was the role of the Federal Reserve Board. The Federal Reserve Board, through its control of interest rates, has enormous ability to affect the rate of economic growth. This is especially true on the downside. While it is not always possible to boost the economy quickly by lowering interest rates, higher interest rates can almost always be counted on to slow the economy – or to push it into a recession if interest rates are raised too much. Higher interest rates make home mortgages more expensive, thereby discouraging homebuilding. They also make it more expensive to buy a new car, since people usually borrow money to buy cars as well. Higher interest rates also slow investment. These sectors make up a large enough share of the economy that the Fed can usually slow the economy effectively by raising interest rates.

The important role of the Fed in the late nineties boom stemmed from the fact that its chairman, Alan Greenspan, opted not to raise interest rates. At the time, the conventional view among economists was that if the unemployment rate fell much below 6 percent, the inflation rate would begin to increase; further, it would continue going up as long as the unemployment rate remained below this percentage. At some point, the inflation rate would reach dangerous levels and do great harm to the economy. This is known as the nonaccelerating inflation rate of unemployment (NAIRU) doctrine.[4]

The Fed had adhered to this doctrine closely over the prior decade. In the late eighties, Greenspan had raised interest rates sharply when the unemployment rate fell below 6 percent, causing the 1990–1 recession. He began to raise interest rates again in 1994 when the unemployment rate began to fall to the 6 percent level that was considered the economy's NAIRU. However, in the second half of 1995, he broke with the NAIRU doctrine. The economy was slowing but the unemployment rate was at 5.7 percent, slighter lower than the standard estimates of

---

[4] The basic theory of the NAIRU can be found in most standard macroeconomic textbooks. See, for example, A. Blinder and W. Baumol, *Macroeconomics: Principles and Policies* (Mason, OH: Thomson South-Western, 2005).

the NAIRU. Seeing little evidence of inflationary pressures, Greenspan opted to lower interest rates.

To the great concern of many economists, including some of his colleagues at the Federal Reserve Board, Greenspan allowed the unemployment rate to continue to fall further below the NAIRU without taking steps to slow the economy. It fell below 5 percent for the first time in May 1997. The unemployment rate dropped to 4.5 percent in April 1998, and it reached 4 percent in December 1999. The year-round average unemployment rate for 2000 was 4 percent, the lowest level since 1969. Throughout this episode, there was little change in the underlying rate of inflation. The consensus within the economics profession proved to be wrong.

Greenspan's actions at the Fed are not the whole story of the late nineties boom, but they were an extremely important part, because his actions could have prevented the boom from ever occurring. His decision not to raise interest rates was a policy decision that had enormous consequences for the country. It is worth noting that his interest rate policy was partly influenced by international events. He probably would have raised interest rates at various points during this period had foreign financial crises, such as the 1997 East Asian financial crisis, not intervened. It is especially striking that Greenspan, who was originally appointed by President Reagan, made the decision to allow the unemployment rate to fall to thirty-year lows in defiance of the conventional wisdom in the economics profession. Ironically, his main opponents on this policy at the Fed were Janet Yellen and Laurence Meyer, two economists appointed to the Fed's Board of Governors by President Clinton.

The second major factor in the boom was a completely unexpected surge in productivity growth. Over the long term, productivity, the economic value produced in an hour of work, is the main determinant of living standards. For reasons that are not fully understood, productivity growth slowed sharply in 1973. The average annual rate of productivity growth had been 2.8 percent from 1947 to 1973.[5] It fell to 1.4 percent in the years from 1973 to 1995. Most economists had come to accept that the economy had permanently moved to a slower rate of productivity growth.

---

[5] These numbers refer to the Bureau of Labor Statistics estimates of productivity in the nonfarm business sector. These data be found in the *Economic Report of the President*, 2006, table B-49.

However, in the second half of 1995, the rate of productivity growth accelerated and has remained high ever since. From the second half of 1995 through the second half of 2000, productivity growth averaged 2.7 percent annually. Although the mid-nineties upturn, like the earlier downturn, is not fully understood, clearly the huge advances in information technology (IT), like the development of the Internet, played a major role. This more rapid pace of productivity growth allowed for more rapid growth of wages without any increase in the rate of inflation.

The third factor sustaining the late nineties boom was the stock market bubble. The stock market had been in a long-term rally since 1982. There was a sharp one-day plunge in October 1987, but Greenspan, who had just recently been installed as Fed chairman, took extraordinary measures to stabilize the market. It quickly recovered most of its losses, and by 1989 it was already above its precrash peaks. This episode increased the willingness of investors to put money in the stock market, since many came to believe that any major downtowns could be rectified by the Fed.

The bull market had gone on for so long that by 1996 many middle-class workers had come to view a rising stock market as a basic economic fact. The percentage of the population with a direct stake in the stock market had soared during this period, with nearly half of all families holding shares of stock either directly or through a mutual fund by 1998. As a comparison, just 31.6 percent of families held stock directly or indirectly in 1989.[6] Most of these new investors had no experience with stock apart from this long bull market.

The main force pushing up rates of stock ownership was the rapid disappearance of traditional defined benefit pension plans, which paid workers a pension based on their wages during their working years. A change in the tax code in the late seventies facilitated the growth of defined contribution pensions, such as 401(k) accounts, in which workers and/or their employers put money in a tax-sheltered retirement account.[7] With these accounts, workers' pensions would depend

---

[6] Data on stock ownership are taken from A. Kennickell, M. Starr-McCluer, and B. Surette, "Recent Changes in U.S. Family Finances: Results from the 1998 Survey of Consumer Finances," *Federal Reserve Bulletin*, January 1998, 1–29.

[7] The rationale for creating this sort of tax-privileged account was that many workers at smaller firms did not have traditional defined benefit pensions. It was argued that 401(k)-type accounts would allow these workers to better support themselves in retirement. Few proponents of these accounts recognized that they would eventually displace defined benefit pensions.

on the performance of their investments. Firms were anxious to transfer the risk of bad stock returns to workers. As a result, almost no new firms offered defined benefit pensions, and many of the firms that had previously provided a defined benefit pension converted to defined contribution plans. This switch meant that most middle-class workers who had any retirement savings at all were at least partly dependent on the stock market.

The run-up in the stock market in the eighties was largely a correction from the extraordinarily low levels it had hit in the seventies. By the end of the eighties, the ratio of stock prices to corporate earnings (the price-to-earnings ratio) was close to its long-term average. However, stock prices continued to grow more rapidly than corporate earnings in the nineties so that by 1996 the ratio of stock prices to earnings was at an extraordinarily high level, reaching 20, much higher than the long-term average of 14.5. It should have been possible to recognize that such high price-to-earnings ratios could not be sustained unless stockholders were willing to accept much lower returns in the future than they had in the past. This was an implausible proposition, since many people were clearly betting on getting rich in the stock market.[8] At the time, investors seemed completely unconcerned about mundane matters like profits and price-to-earnings ratios. They talked of a "new economy" where the normal rules of economics and arithmetic no longer applied.

Instead of correcting to more traditional levels, stock prices continued to soar in the late nineties. This run-up was led by the high-technology sector, where investors had seen huge fortunes made in companies such as Microsoft and other leaders of the IT revolution. Stock investors were anxious to jump into companies that they hoped would be the next Microsoft, often paying large sums for the stock of companies that were not even making a profit and in some cases did not even know how they could make a profit. The most extreme overvaluations occurred in the high-technology sector, especially overvaluations of Internet-based retailers at the very end of the bubble in 1999 and 2000, but the market as a whole had become ridiculously

---

[8] There were economists who tried to warn of the dangers of the stock bubble, most notably Yale University Professor Robert Shiller; see his book *Irrational Exuberance* (Princeton, NJ: Princeton University Press, 2000). See also D. Baker, "Bull Market Keynesianism," *The American Prospect*, January-February 1999, 78–83; and D. Baker, *Double Bubble: The Implications of the Over-valuation of the Stock Market and the Dollar* (Washington, DC: Center for Economic and Policy Research, 2000).

overvalued. At its peak in March 2000, the price-to-earnings ratio had risen above 30. At this level, the market was overvalued by more than $10 trillion (approximately the output of the economy over a full year) in comparison with its historic price-to-earnings ratio.

The stock bubble propelled the economy in two ways. The most important mechanism was through its effect on people's consumption. As people saw the value of their stock portfolio soar, they felt comfortable spending more money and saving less for retirement and other needs. Private savings rates plunged in this period, as stockholders splurged on cars, vacations, and other luxuries. This consumption splurge helped sustain the extraordinary growth rates of the late nineties.

The second way in which the stock bubble boosted the economy was through its impact on investment. Typically, the stock market has relatively little impact on investment. Most firms finance their investment either through profits or through bank loans or bond issues. Only a small portion of new investment is financed directly by issuing stock. However, this changed in the late nineties. With high-tech startups able to raise hundreds of millions of dollars through new stock issues, much of the money from new stock issues was going directly into investment in the high-technology sector. As a result, there was a boom in investment in the last part of the nineties that amplified the impact of the consumption boom.

The stock bubble was not confined to the United States. There was a substantial run-up in stock prices throughout most of the industrial world during this period. Germany even established a short-lived "Neuer Markt" for high-tech companies that was intended as a counterpart to the NASDAQ in the United States. However, the stock bubble did not foster as much growth in Europe on the way up, nor did it create as much damage when it deflated in the years 2000–2.

Needless to say, growth based on a financial bubble cannot be sustained. The crash of the bubble and the resulting fallout are discussed in the next chapter. But as long as it lasted, the stock bubble was a major force sustaining high rates of growth and pushing unemployment down to thirty-year lows.

There is one other important aspect to the late nineties boom that should be noted. The dollar rose in value by more than 15 percent compared to the currencies of the U.S. trading partners. This had two important short-term effects, one positive and one negative. The positive effect is that it lowered the price of imported goods. In the simplest case, if a dollar buys 15 percent more yen (or euros), then the price of goods produced in Japan (or Europe) falls by 15 percent for people in the United States. In reality, prices do not change by quite as much as currency values do, but as a rule, the higher the value of the dollar, the lower the cost of imports. This increases the purchasing power of people in the United States and helps to reduce the rate of inflation.

The negative effect is simply the flip side of the positive effect. The workers who produce goods in industries that compete with imports lose jobs and see lower wages because lower-priced imports became available. This primarily affects workers in manufacturing, who produce goods that must directly compete against imports. As a result of the run-up in the dollar, the U.S. trade deficit soared, reaching a record 4.1 percent of GDP at the end of 2000. The number of production jobs in manufacturing peaked in February 1998. This sector subsequently lost 670,000 jobs over the next two years (5.2 percent of total employment in manufacturing), even as the rest of the economy was booming.

Whatever the benefits of cheap imports in the short run, it is impossible for a country to run large trade deficits indefinitely. The country must borrow to cover its trade deficit, and there is a limit to how much it can borrow. At some point, the dollar must fall to correct the trade imbalance, leading to higher import prices, which means more inflation and lower living standards. The high-dollar policy of the late nineties, which continued into the next decade, might have been desirable as short-term policy, but it comes with substantial long-run costs.

But the country did not see these costs in the nineties. It did see very real benefits from the strong growth and low unemployment of the period.[9] Unemployment is not evenly distributed; the least advantaged workers are the most likely to be unemployed, which means that when the unemployment rate falls, they are the ones who are most likely to benefit. Whereas the overall unemployment rate fell from 6.1 percent in 1994 to 4 percent in 2000, for African Americans, the drop was

[9] A fuller discussion of the benefits of the nineties boom can be found in J. Bernstein and D. Baker, *The Benefits of Full Employment* (Washington, DC: Economic Policy Institute, 2004), and A. Blinder and J. Yellen, *The Fabulous Decade: Macroeconomic Lessons from the 1990s* (New York: Century Foundation, 2001).

from 11.5 to 7.6 percent.[10] For Hispanics, the unemployment rate declined from 9.9 percent in 1994 to 5.7 percent in 2000. For African American teens, the unemployment rate fell 10 percentage points, from 34.6 percent to 24.5 percent. Even though black teens still faced high unemployment in 2000, their likelihood of getting a job had vastly improved from 1994.

The tighter labor market also meant that workers were in a position to push up their wages. The years from 1996 to 2000 were the first period of sustained growth in real wages for workers at all points along the wage distribution since the late sixties. After adjusting for inflation, wages rose at a rate of about 1.5 percent a year for workers in the middle of the wage distribution and even more rapidly for those near the bottom. With workers in short supply, employers regularly complained about being forced to reach out to new groups of workers. Hotels and restaurants in the suburbs were chartering buses to take workers who lived in inner-city neighborhoods to and from work each day. Employers were also being forced to accommodate the family care needs of workers, in some cases offering flexible work schedules to allow workers to deal with child care arrangements or to attend to sick family members. Although its foundation in the stock bubble and the overvalued dollar might have guaranteed that the late nineties boom could not continue indefinitely, it did provide real benefits for most of the country's workers while it lasted.

Politics in the Second Clinton Administration

With the status quo left intact by the 1996 elections, the central issue in the national political debate was again the deficit, as Clinton and Congress struggled with plans to reach the Gingrich target of a balanced budget by 2002. In the period immediately following the election, this still appeared to be a daunting target. One scheme that played a prominent role in this debate was a plan to change the indexation formula for Social Security benefits and tax rates. This plan would have moved the budget most of the way toward balance through a technical fix, allowing Congress to avoid taking the blame for cutting benefits and increasing taxes.

---

[10] Unemployment data are from the Bureau of Labor Statistics and can be found on its website (http://www.bls.gov).

Social Security benefits for retirees are indexed to the consumer price index (CPI). If the CPI shows that inflation was 3 percent last year, then benefits will rise by 3 percent this year. Similarly, the tax brackets will rise by 3 percent. This means that if $100,000 was the cutoff last year for the 35 percent tax bracket, then this cutoff will rise to $103,000 this year.

The technical fix considered by Congress involved changing the indexation formula for both Social Security and the tax brackets to a measure that was 1 percentage point less than the CPI. Under this proposal, if the CPI showed 3 percent inflation, then Social Security benefits for retirees would only rise by 2 percent. The same would be the case for tax brackets. This change would not make much difference after one year, but after five years retirees would see their benefits cut by close to 5 percent, and after ten years the reduction would be close to 10 percent. The same would be the case with the tax bracket cutoffs. In short, this was real money.

If everyone went along, it would probably have been possible to slip this technical change by the public without causing much of a political backlash, since its impact would only be felt gradually over time. President Clinton and the Republican congressional leadership had actually reached such an agreement in the spring of 1997. However, the change never took effect because not everyone did go along. Richard Gephardt, the leader of the Democrats in the House of Representatives and, more importantly, a potential contender for the 2000 Democratic presidential nomination, refused to sign on to the deal.

Gephardt's opposition was sufficient to quell this plan for large cuts in future Social Security benefits and a substantial increase in taxes. Clinton's vice president, Al Gore, was planning his own run for president in 2000. Gore had an enormous advantage going into this election as a two-term vice president. However, Gephardt would have relished the opportunity to challenge him in the Democratic primaries, running as the person who tried to defend Social Security against the man whose administration had cut benefits. Gephardt's opposition forced Clinton to back down, and the plan was dropped.

Soon after this indexing scheme collapsed, the whole debate over balancing the budget suddenly was overtaken by events. The economic boom, coupled with lower than expected growth in health care costs, radically altered budget projections. The budget picture for 1997 brightened to the point that the budget was nearly balanced without any major new taxes or spending cuts. Furthermore, the new budget projections issued in January 1998 showed that the budget was in surplus for the indefinite future. After holding a central place in national politics ever since the Reagan tax cuts, the budget deficit no longer existed.

With the sudden switch from deficits to surpluses, the focus of the debate went from how to balance the budget to what to do with the surplus. The Republicans had a simple answer: cut taxes. President Clinton took the opposite tack. He argued that the government should use the surplus to "save Social Security." His administration had been working on plans for partially privatizing the Social Security system. In the short run, these plans would require additional money to cover the lost revenue as Social Security taxes were diverted into private accounts. In an era of large deficits, it would have been difficult to make up for this shortfall. However, the projected government surpluses provided a unique opportunity to finance Social Security privatization. While President Clinton did not publicly commit to Social Security privatization, he used his 1998 State of the Union address to argue against tax cuts, insisting that Social Security should be the first priority.

The Impeachment Scandal

President Clinton's plans for Social Security were quickly derailed by an unexpected turn of events. News of a sexual affair between President Clinton and an insecure young intern had leaked to the media just as he was preparing his State of the Union address. The origin of the leak was a deposition given in a sexual harassment lawsuit that a former employer of the state of Arkansas had filed against Clinton. This suit had been financed by various right-wing groups who saw it as an opportunity to embarrass President Clinton. They used the suit as a fishing expedition, trying to find information about extramarital affairs or anything else that could prove damaging.

In the beginning of 1998, they finally struck pay dirt when they found a former intern, Monica Lewinsky, who had had a brief sexual relationship with President Clinton. Lewinsky testified about this relationship in depositions connected with the sexual harassment suit. The details of the testimony were leaked to the media and shared headline space with accounts of the president's State of the Union address.

Clinton responded to the allegations in what proved to be the worst possible way. Instead of telling the truth about the relationship, or simply refusing to speak about private matters, as politicians have done since the beginning of time, Clinton vehemently denied any relationship. His aides tried to portray the young woman as a psychopathic stalker who had bizarre fantasies about her relationship with President Clinton.

Although Clinton and his supporters clung to his denials, the Far Right pressed the case against Clinton, using sympathetic media outlets, such as the relatively new Fox News channel, various right-wing talk radio shows, and political blogs on the Internet, which had suddenly emerged as a new feature of political life. The anti-Clinton forces also had the help of Kenneth Starr, a former appellate court judge and solicitor general under President Bush. Starr had been given the job of independent counsel in 1994, with responsibility for investigating a questionable real estate deal that Clinton had been involved with when he was governor of Arkansas. Starr gradually expanded his responsibilities to other alleged scandals. When news of the Lewinsky affair came to his attention, he quickly got himself assigned to the case.

Clinton's denials might have been sufficient to get him through the onslaught. Most of the public did not care about the affair, and the Far Right could not prove its case. This changed in the summer of 1998, when though a strange turn of events Starr was able to produce DNA evidence establishing that an affair had indeed occurred. In August, Clinton was finally forced to acknowledge the affair in a speech to the nation.

The Republicans seized on the new evidence to begin impeachment hearings. The Republican-controlled House Judiciary Committee approved several articles of impeachment related to the Lewinsky affair just before the fall election. In what many took as a rebuke of their conduct, the Republicans lost five seats in the House in the 1998 election. With the Democrats in control of the White House, the normal pattern would have been for the Republicans to win seats in the midterm election. Nonetheless, the House held a lame-duck session in December to finish the job. They voted to impeach Clinton based on his efforts to conceal the Lewinsky affair. It was only the second time in the country's history that a president had been impeached by Congress.

When the new session of Congress convened in January, its first order of business was President Clinton's trial by the Senate, to determine if he should be removed from office. To remove a sitting president, the constitution requires that the Senate vote by a two-thirds majority in favor of removal. With the Democrats standing solidly behind Clinton, and several Republicans wavering, there was no real chance that he would actually be removed. On February 12, the episode finally came to a close when the Republicans proved unable to muster even a simple majority in support of either of the two articles of impeachment that the House had approved.

Although Clinton remained in power and still had to deal with a Republican-controlled Congress, much had changed as a result of this peculiar scandal. There was a strong public reaction against investigations into what were clearly the private lives of public figures. In a tit for tat, several affairs involving high-level Republicans were made public, including one involving Bob Livingston, who was the Republicans' original choice to be House Speaker after Gingrich stepped down in the wake of the party's poor election performance. Both sides seemed anxious to have a truce, at least with regard to discussing their sexual conduct.

The other big change was that President Clinton's second-term agenda had been derailed. The public never got to see his plans for restructuring Social Security. As the scope of the Lewinsky scandal expanded to the point where it actually jeopardized the survival of his presidency, Clinton was forced to turn to the traditional Democratic base, African Americans, labor, and women's groups, in order to ensure the support he needed to survive in office. Since these were exactly the groups that would have most strongly opposed any effort to privatize Social Security, President's Clinton's plans in this area were effectively killed.

President Clinton still had nearly two full years left in office, but he faced a hostile Republican Congress and had no clear agenda. Furthermore, many of his closest political allies felt betrayed, having publicly defended Clinton in his denials, only to later find out that he was not telling the truth. At this point in his presidency, Clinton was very much a lame duck.

Foreign Policy in the Clinton Years

With the end of the cold war, foreign policy in the Clinton years was much more explicitly focused on economic policy than in the past. The military budget shrank from 4.4 percent of GDP when Clinton took office in 1993 to just 3 percent of GDP in 2001, the year of his last budget, a drop equivalent to approximately $165 billion in annual spending at the 2005 level of GDP. With the collapse of the Soviet Union, even this level of spending vastly exceeded the combined spending of any conceivable collection of potential enemies.

Clinton's economic program for developing countries centered on promoting the economic polices that came to be known as the "Washington Consensus."[11] This agenda involved removing many types of trade barriers and subsidies and increasing reliance on foreign investment to promote development.[12] The Washington Consensus called for privatizing state-owned industries and in many cases public services such as Social Security. This set of policies also involved the freeing of capital flows so that foreign investors could freely move money into and out of developing countries. The Washington Consensus also discouraged countries from pursuing industrial policies to promote the growth of key industries. Most of the currently industrialized countries had used some form of industrial policy to promote growth in the early stages of their development.

The Clinton administration continued a policy developed in the first Bush administration: promoting the Washington Consensus model through bilateral trade agreements such as the North American Free Trade Agreement (NAFTA), regional trade agreements such as the administration's "Caribbean Basin Initiative," and international agreements such as the Uruguay Round agreement of the World Trade Organization.[13] In addition to directly promoting the Washington

---

[11] John Williamson, an economist at the Institute for International Economics, is generally given credit for coining the phrase "Washington Consensus" to refer to a specific set of policies. See J. Williamson, "What Washington Means by Policy Reform," in *Latin American Adjustment: How Much Has Happened?* ed. J. Williamson, 5–20 (Washington, DC: Institute for International Economics, 1990). For a critical assessment of the effect of these policies, see J. Stiglitz, *Globalization and Its Discontents* (New York: W. W. Norton and Co., 1990), and N. Birdsall, D. Rodrick, and A. Subramaman, "How to Help Poor Countries?" *Foreign Affairs* 84, no. 4 (2005): 136–52.

[12] It is important to note that the Washington Consensus did not call on countries to reduce barriers in all areas. The Clinton administration fought to increase patent and copyright protections in developing countries. While patent and copyright protections impose costs on developing countries, they increased profits for the U.S. pharmaceutical, entertainment, and software industries, all of which vigorously lobbied for stronger protections.

[13] The Uruguay Round agreement created the World Trade Organization as a permanent body to moderate trade disputes. It succeeded the General Agreement on Tariffs and Trade (GATT), which was established in 1947, shortly after the end of World War II.

Consensus model, the Clinton administration also used its influence at the International Monetary Fund (IMF) and the World Bank to promote it. These institutions typically made the adoption of Washington Consensus policies a condition of receiving loans and aid.

The record of the Washington Consensus model is at best mixed. Most developing countries have made little economic progress over the last fifteen years. In particular, the countries of Latin America, many of which had eagerly embraced the model, have had very poor growth rates during this period. Many critics have also raised concerns about the impact of these policies on inequality and the environment. Proponents of the Washington Consensus attribute the weak growth performance to the failure of many countries to go far enough in adopting the required reforms. They also point to China and India, whose populations make up close to half of the developing world, both of which have seen very strong growth since 1990. However, the extent to which these countries can be viewed as following the Washington Consensus model is questionable, given that both continue to have very extensive government involvement in wide areas of the economy.

As the Clinton administration pursued the promotion of Washington Consensus policies, it faced a series of brushfires in the form of financial crises around the developing world. The first of these crises was the "Tequila Crisis" in Mexico, which hit in January 1995, ironically just as NAFTA was going into effect. The basic problem was relatively simple – Mexico had maintained an overvalued currency that it could no longer sustain. It had no choice but to reduce the value of the currency, which at the time had been fixed against the dollar by the Mexican government. The devaluation of the currency caught investors by surprise. There had been a massive inflow of foreign capital into Mexico in prior years as investors sought high returns in what they considered to be a sound currency. In the 1995 Tequila Crisis, there was suddenly a massive outflow of money from Mexico as investors (both foreign and domestic) sought to flee the Mexican peso before it lost even more of its value.

The Clinton administration was able to arrange a package of loan guarantees that shored up Mexico's currency and stemmed the immediate financial crisis, although it could not prevent a sharp falloff in its economy and a surge in unemployment. Even more important, the crisis undermined investors' confidence in developing countries more generally, leading to a sharp rise in interest rates throughout the developing world.

The next serious crisis took place in East Asia in the late summer of 1997. East Asia had been the poster child of the developing world. Countries such as South Korea and Taiwan had gone from being among the poorest countries in the world just after World War II to enjoying living standards that were comparable to the poorer countries in Western Europe. Other countries in the region, such as Thailand, Indonesia, and Malaysia, seemed to be following the same path.

This success seemed to be on the edge of unraveling as first Thailand and then Malaysia, Indonesia, and South Korea saw runs on their currency, forcing sharp devaluations. Instead of being touted as role models, these countries were being denounced for their "crony capitalism" and the lack of transparency in both private sector and government accounting. These criticisms were more than a little hypocritical, given that institutions such as the IMF had just given all of them a clean bill of health in their most recent reviews. It also was peculiar to be criticizing a lack of transparency when foreign investors who controlled large pools of capital had voluntarily invested hundreds of billions of dollars in the region. If these countries had kept such shoddy books, why would huge banks opt to risk money there?

As financial panic spread through the region, the Clinton administration's first concern was to stabilize the financial situation. This was done most importantly by ensuring that China did not devalue its currency, which could have set off a second round of competitive devaluations. A second key goal was to stay in control by keeping the IMF in charge of the situation. Japan and Taiwan (both of which managed to escape the direct effects of the crisis) laid out plans for an East Asian bailout fund, to which they would be the major contributors. Clinton quickly nixed this idea before it could get any traction.

The third goal was to protect the interests of Western banks. The vast majority of Western bank loans to the region were made to private banks and corporations. In many cases, these companies were now bankrupt, which should have meant that the loans were essentially worthless. (The countries in the region did not have well-developed bankruptcy laws, so creditors had little obvious recourse.) As a condition of receiving aid, the IMF required the governments of the region to take responsibility for much of this private debt.

The fourth goal was to require these countries to further open their capital markets so that it would be easier for foreign investors to buy up domestic companies. These countries all had substantial restrictions (many of which were informal) that made it difficult for foreign

investors to take over domestic companies. This was part of the industrial policy that the countries of East Asia had used to foster growth
for four decades. The Clinton administration wanted to remove these
restrictions so that foreign investors could more readily buy up corporations in the region. With both the currencies and the stock markets
of the region in a free fall, this condition essentially required the countries to hold fire sales for their major corporations.

Although most of the region did recover relatively quickly (after a
sharp downturn), there were substantial repercussions from the crisis.
First, investors became more wary of developing countries in general,
leading to a reduced flow of funds to the developing world. Second,
there came to be more widespread suspicion at all levels of the goals and
competence of the IMF and World Bank. Third, countries throughout
the developing world, and especially in East Asia, began to accumulate
massive foreign exchange reserves (primarily dollars and euros) in order
to ensure that they would not face the sort of crisis of confidence that
hit the East Asian region in the fall of 1997.

The next big crisis took place in Russia. After the breakup of the
Soviet Union, Russia's economy went into a tailspin. Following the
advice of the World Bank and the IMF, Russia adopted a policy of
"shock therapy" as a means of rapidly converting from a centrally
planned economy to a market economy. This policy involved quickly
privatizing the country's vast assets by selling off factories and land.
As was the case elsewhere in the former Communist countries, the
process of privatization was massively corrupt, with many of the most
valuable assets falling into the hands of politically connected investors at
fraction of their real value.[14] Russia suffered much more in this process
than the rest of Eastern Europe. Its economy shrank by 40 percent,
an unprecedented economic decline for a country not suffering from
either war or natural disaster.

After experiencing modest growth in 1996 and 1997, Russia's economy faced severe strains in 1998, as it had difficulty sustaining the
value of its currency. Investors became worried that the country would

---

[14] According to data from the World Bank, Russia collected just $8.3 billion from
privatizing virtually its entire economy (World Bank, *Global Development Finance*
[Washington, DC: World Bank, 2001], 186). By comparison, the market value of
General Electric alone hovers near $400 billion, more than forty times as much as
Russia earned from selling off the bulk of its industrial and agricultural assets.

devalue its currency, forcing the Russian central bank to raise its interest rate ever higher in order to compensate investors for the risk. While the obvious solution was to devalue the currency, Clinton's economic team did everything they could to prevent devaluation. Finally, in August 1998, Yeltsin abandoned the effort to support the currency, causing it to fall sharply, and he temporarily suspended payments on the country's debt.

Russia was dubbed an international pariah, and its economy took a sharp plunge. However, by the beginning of 1999, Russia's economy was growing again, and it has maintained a robust rate of growth ever since. Robert Rubin, Clinton's treasury secretary at the time, classified his efforts in Russia as a failure because he could not get the government to accept conditions that would have allowed it to avoid devaluing its currency and temporarily defaulting on its debt.[15] However, from the standpoint of promoting Russian economic growth, the change in policies that summer was by far the most positive turn of events since the collapse of Communism in Eastern Europe.

The fallout from this series of crises had an important domestic consequence. The decision of foreign central banks to acquire large amounts of dollars helped to drive up the value of the dollar. This reinforced the high-dollar policy consciously pursued by the Clinton administration. As noted earlier, this high-dollar policy led to a massive U.S. trade deficit in this period. The efforts of developing countries to acquire large reserves of dollars effectively meant that poor countries were lending money to the richest country in the world – the exact opposite of what standard economic theory predicts should happen in the normal course of economic development.

The War over Kosovo

While President Clinton's foreign policy was focused on economics, he did bring the country into one major military conflict near the end of his second term. This involved a battle against Serbia over the future of Kosovo.

---

[15] This episode is discussed in Rubin's autobiography (coauthored with Jacob Weisberg), *In an Uncertain World: Tough Choices from Wall Street to Washington* (New York: Random House, 2003).

The war over Kosovo was a late chapter in the unraveling of Yugoslavia. Yugoslavia was a country that was created by the victorious powers after World War I. It pulled together several distinct ethnic and religious groups in the Balkans with a long history of conflict between them. Not long after the creation of Yugoslavia, World War II devastated the country, as a German-backed government led by Croats engaged in genocidal killings of Serbs, Jews, and Gypsies. A powerful guerilla resistance force developed during the war, led by Josip Broz Tito, and as the war was coming to an end, the guerilla resistance succeeded in pushing back the German forces assigned to Yugoslavia in support of the Croat regime.

With the resistance largely responsible for the liberation of the country, Tito took power, determined to protect Yugoslavia's independence. He steered a middle path between the Soviet Union and the West, allying with neither bloc. In economics, he also steered a middle path: Yugoslavia had a substantial state sector but also some private businesses and worker-owned enterprises. Further, although it was hardly a democracy, and there were political prisoners in the country, the population enjoyed far more freedom than in any of the Eastern bloc countries. Tito also worked hard to tame nationalistic sentiments and promote a Yugoslav identity.

After Tito died in 1980, it was not long before nationalism again became a major force in Yugoslavia. In Serbia, the most populous republic in the Yugoslav federation, Slobodan Milosevic became the leading figure in national politics by trumpeting the cause of Serbs within Kosovo, a province of Serbia where most of the population was ethnic Albanian. Milosevic's nationalism was fueled by the rise of nationalism elsewhere in Yugoslavia, most importantly Croatia, where Franjo Tudjman had come to power. Tudjman's party used the symbols of the party that was responsible for mass killings in Croatia during World War II. He also had authored a revisionist history of the period, denying that any mass killings had taken place. It could not have been very reassuring to Serbs when a newly reunited Germany rushed to give diplomatic recognition to Tudjman's regime after it unilaterally declared its independence from Yugoslavia in December 1991.

The breakup of Yugoslavia continued over the next several years as other republics declared their independence. This resulted in repeated conflicts over the boundaries of the new republics, the most bloody of which was in Bosnia, where Croats, Serbs, and Moslems all sought to consolidate control over portions of the country where they were the dominate ethnic group. There were atrocities committed by all three ethnic groups, but the Bosnian Serbs were guilty of the largest number by far (mostly notably the June 1995 massacre at Srebrenica), pursuing a policy of "ethnic cleansing," which led to the deaths of thousands of Bosnian Croats and Moslems. In November 1995, after more than two years of fighting and several headline-grabbing atrocities, the Clinton administration helped to broker a peace agreement that ended the conflict and installed a NATO-led peacekeeping force.

With the other republics having already separated from Yugoslavia and boundary disputes largely settled (the small Republic of Montenegro was still tied to Serbia in a weaker federation), Kosovo was the last major issue. There had been long-standing tensions between the Albanians, who made up about 90 percent of the province's population, and Serbs, who accounted for the remaining 10 percent. Milosevic had taken away the province's autonomy in 1989, which fed resentment by the Albanian population.

In the nineties, a guerrilla resistance force, the Kosovo Liberation Army, began to stage attacks and take control of a portion of the province. However, the Serbian army enjoyed a huge advantage in heavy weaponry and would often respond to attacks with massive force, killing many civilians in the process. As this war escalated and the number of deaths increased, the Clinton administration sought to negotiate a solution involving a pullback of Serbian troops and autonomy for Kosovo.

Faced with the explicit threat of U.S. military force, Milosevic was prepared to agree to Clinton's demands. However, Clinton then added an additional clause that would have essentially given the U.S. military a free hand to inspect any site within Serbia proper (not just Kosovo) for heavy weapons at any time. Milosevic refused to accept this condition, and in March 1999, the United States began a two-month-long bombing campaign against Serbia.[16]

Immediately after this bombing campaign began, the Serbian military began mass expulsions of the Albanian population from large sections of the province. Remarkably, in the reporting at the time, this sequence was usually reversed. Many news accounts implied that Clinton had initiated the bombing in retaliation for the expulsions.[17]

---

[16] For an account of the history leading up to the Kosovo war, see T. Judah, *Kosovo: War and Revenge* (New Haven, CT: Yale University Press, 2002).

[17] For example, a *New York Times* editorial asserted that "NATO bombed Serbia for seventy-eight days to combat lethal ethnic cleansing, to reverse the expulsion of more than a million ethnic Albanians from their homes and to prevent Slobodan

Most of the public probably was not aware of the reason that President Clinton had gone to war.

While it clearly was only a matter of time before the unanswered U.S. airpower would force Milosevic to surrender, his forces proved far more resilient than had been expected. Milosevic had apparently found relatively effective methods of concealing his tanks and other heavy weaponry, limiting the damage sustained from U.S. air strikes. Eventually, the military took to bombing key civilian targets, such as power plants and the state-run television station. (The attack on the station was justified by the fact that it was broadcasting government propaganda.) As a result, the civilian population of Serbia incurred a substantial portion of the casualties from the U.S. bombing.

Eventually Milosevic had sustained enough losses and agreed to withdraw his forces from Kosovo. A United Nations peacekeeping force was put in place, and most of the exiled Kosovars returned. In many areas, the Kosovars took Milosevic's defeat as a chance to attack the Serb population. Close to half of the Serbian population of Kosovo fled the province into Serbia proper. As of 2005, there was still no final resolution regarding the status of Kosovo or the exiled Serbs.

The 2000 Election

A great deal was at stake in the 2000 election. There was no incumbent in the presidential race, which meant that neither party had a clear advantage. Furthermore, both the House and Senate were relatively evenly divided, so control of both chambers could easily shift, depending on the outcome of the election.

The Republicans had a much more hotly contested primary, with many prominent figures initially entering the race, including Elizabeth Dole, a former cabinet secretary and the wife of Robert Dole (the 1996 Republican candidate), and Dan Quayle, the vice president during the

Milosevic from terrorizing the Balkans ("Lessons of the Balkan War," *New York Times*, June 17, 1999, A30). Most other reporting in major media outlets similarly reversed the chain of events. The reporting at the time leaves little ambiguity about the sequence of events. The bombing began on March 24 (see "NATO Authorizes Bomb Strikes: Primakov, in Air Skips U.S. Visit," *New York Times*, March 24, 1999, A1). The first reports on mass expulsions appeared three days later, on March 27 ("Conflict in the Balkans: The Refugees; White House Tells of Reports of a Forced March in Kosovo," *New York Times*, March 27, 1999, A1).

Bush administration. However, the other candidates quickly fell by the wayside, as the contest developed into a two-person race between Arizona Senator John McCain and Texas Governor George W. Bush, the son of the former president.

Bush was the early favorite. He had a massive advantage in fundraising, and he could count on the support of most of the party's establishment as a result of his family's connections. He also had the support of many of the party's hard-line conservatives. He made tax cuts a key part of his platform and also explicitly appealed to the religious right, both through his account of a personal religious conversion after problems with alcohol abuse as a young man and his plans to promote "faith-based initiatives."

However, McCain was a formidable candidate. He had the status of a war hero, having been captured in Vietnam and held prisoner for almost six years. McCain had served in the Senate since 1986, during which time he developed a reputation as a conservative who would occasionally refuse to go along with the party line. For example, he was one of the leading proponents of campaign finance reform, a goal not shared by most Republican leaders. He was an articulate speaker who could effectively address a wide range of issues. McCain appealed to many of the more moderate voters in the Republican Party as well as independents, who could vote in some of the primaries.

McCain did far better in the early Republican primaries than had generally been expected, winning several important contests, most notably New Hampshire and Michigan. However, Bush had a determined and effective political operation. They were prepared to do whatever was necessary to gain the nomination. Before the South Carolina primary, Bush spoke at a college that had gained nationwide notoriety for its ban on interracial dating. This sent a clear message in a state where many still resented the federally imposed desegregation of the sixties. (He apologized for this appearance later in the campaign.) There were also mysterious groups (presumably tied to the Bush campaign) that sought to raise questions about McCain's patriotism and military service.

These tactics, together with Bush's political connections and money advantage, eventually won out. Soon after Bush's win in the South Carolina primary, McCain dropped out and Bush had the nomination locked up.

There was a relatively short contest on the Democratic side. Bill Bradley, a former New Jersey senator and NBA basketball star, challenged Al Gore for the nomination. However, Gore effectively used his advantages as a two-term vice president to quickly sew up the nomination. Bradley could not match Gore's political base of support within the Democratic Party.

The fall campaign was hotly contested, and the polls consistently showed the race to be very close. Gore ran an ambiguous campaign. While he could point to a country that was at peace and still in the midst of an economic boom, Gore chose to distance himself from the record of the Clinton administration. He picked as his vice-presidential candidate Joe Lieberman, a senator from Connecticut who had distinguished himself by being the first prominent Democrat to publicly criticize Clinton's conduct in the Lewinsky affair. In his convention acceptance speech, Gore appealed to populist themes, speaking to the people who were still experiencing hard times in spite of the boom, but then he largely dropped these themes for the rest of the campaign. Bush placed his tax cut front and center in the fall campaign. He also implicitly campaigned against Clinton's sexual conduct, repeatedly pledging to restore honor to the presidency.

There were also two third-party candidates of some notoriety in the campaign. Ralph Nader, the anticorporate crusader, ran as the candidate of the Green Party, challenging Gore from the left. Nader had first made a national reputation back in the sixties when he exposed the dangers of U.S. automobiles at the time, eventually forcing the manufacturers to install seat belts as standard equipment. He had spearheaded numerous anticorporate drives in the intervening years on a wide range of issues. The other prominent third-party candidate was Patrick Buchanan, the conservative Republican television commentator who had effectively challenged President Bush in the 1992 primaries. Buchanan ran at the head of the ticket of Ross Perot's Reform Party. Nader ended up with 2.7 percent of the vote nationwide. Buchanan's campaign largely collapsed, netting him just 0.4 percent of the popular vote.

The Long Florida Count

Going into the final weekend before the election, most polls gave Bush a very small edge. But in the election itself, Gore managed to win the popular vote, beating Bush by more than 500,000 votes, or 0.5 percentage points. However, presidential races are not decided by the popular vote. The electoral vote was extremely close, with the winner to be determined by the outcome of the election in Florida. The vote in Florida was incredibly close, with Gore and Bush getting almost the exact same portion of the 6 million votes cast in the state.

On the night of the election itself, Gore at one point phoned Bush to concede after several news stations had called Florida for Bush. A short time later, he called back to retract his concession, when additional precinct results indicated that the state was still up for grabs. The country woke up the day after the election still not knowing who the president would be.

What followed was a series of conflicts and court battles over recounts. At the onset, many Democrats were concerned about the fact that the governor of Florida was Jeb Bush, George W. Bush's brother, and the secretary of state – the official responsible for overseeing the election – was the head of Bush's election committee in Florida.

It was clear that a certain number of votes had not been properly counted, especially in the areas where punch ballots had been used, primarily because the scan machines would occasionally fail to record a vote if the card had not been completely punched.[18] In these cases, a hand count, by picking up these missed votes, might be more accurate than the machine count. The Gore campaign picked four large, predominantly Democratic counties and requested that hand recounts be held.

The county election officials originally complied with this request, beginning a hand recount, but the process soon got shut down. The main factor preventing the count was a court action initiated by the Bush campaign, but the proximate cause in one county was a group of Republican congressional staffers who had been shipped down to Florida. They made enough noise in a public room where the votes were being hand counted that they were able to disrupt the counting process before the court issued its order. While the Gore campaign also had people who would have been willing to take matters into their own hands to press their case, the Democrats kept their supporters out of any

---

[18] There was also the bizarre "butterfly ballot" incident. Due to a confusing ballot design in one Florida county, more than 5,000 voters mistakenly cast ballots for both Gore and Patrick Buchanan, who had run on a third-party ticket. Since ballots with marks for more than one candidate are automatically discarded, Gore lost more than 5,000 votes because of this poorly designed ballot. This number is far more than Bush's official margin of 930 votes in Florida.

confrontations. If the Republicans were willing to have the presidential election decided by a street fight, the Democrats clearly were not.

The court cases went through several steps. In an initial round, the case went to the Florida Supreme Court (entirely composed of judges appointed by Democrats), which ruled unanimously that the count should proceed largely along the lines requested by the Gore campaign. Later, the case was brought to the U.S. Supreme Court (where seven of the nine justices were appointed by Republicans). On December 12, the day that the state was supposed to certify its electors under Florida statute, the Supreme Court handed down its ruling. By a five to four majority, the justices ruled that the recount should stop. Essentially, they said that time had run out. The majority argued that nothing in the facts of the case justified overturning the Florida statute providing a deadline for certifying electors.

The outcome outraged millions of Gore supporters. It was quite evident that the most conservative justices had all lined up in support of Bush. Many questioned whether their decision reflected an assessment of the evidence and the law or their desire to see a political ally in the White House.

As a final episode of this long battle, Al Gore, as the sitting vice president, had to preside over the joint session of Congress that certified the final vote of the Electoral College. He stood as chair as twenty members of the House (almost all of whom were African American) rose one after the other to challenge the electoral votes from Florida. Each time he asked whether a member of the Senate had joined the challenge, as required by the rules of a rare joint session. Each time the member said no, and Gore gaveled them down and continued with the business of the day.

The Florida battle had many lessons to teach about the state of U.S. elections. First, the number of uncounted ballots was not unusual. It is common for 2–3 percent of the ballots cast not to be counted.[19] The undercounting is highest in minority communities. What was unusual about the Florida race was not the undercount but the closeness of the election, which made the undercount matter.[20]

---

[19] For a discussion of some of the mechanical problems of the voting system in place at the time of the 2000 election, see M. Alvarez and T. Hall, *Point, Click and Vote: The Future of Internet Voting* (Washington, DC: Brookings Institution, 2004).

[20] Many Gore supporters were outraged over the fact that Ralph Nader's 97,000 vote total in Florida was far larger than Bush's official margin of victory, implying that Gore would have won the race had Nader not run on a third-party ticket.

A second fact that received more attention because of the Florida race was the number of people who have been disenfranchised because of felony convictions. Most states disenfranchise felons for some period of time after a conviction or prison term. Florida disenfranchises felons for life. More than 55,000 people in the state of Florida have lost the right to vote for this reason. This is an especially serious concern since these people are overwhelmingly African American. Since African Americans vote overwhelmingly Democratic, Republican politicians have been anxious to press for strong rules disenfranchising ex-felons. Given the closeness of the Florida vote, if even a small portion of the rehabilitated felon population had been allowed to vote, the outcome of the election would almost certainly have been reversed.

Finally, there was an ironic twist to the recount originally sought by Gore – he still would have lost if the courts had given him what he asked for. While the Gore campaign used the slogan "count every vote" to press their case, they actually only wanted to count the votes in the counties where they thought it would help them. Later analysis of these ballots by several news organizations showed that Bush still would have won the state if all the undercounted ballots had been counted in the four counties where Gore requested a hand count. On the other hand, had there been a statewide hand count of all the ballots not counted by machine, Gore would have won the state (assuming a consistent standard had been applied to the counting of votes everywhere).[21]

---

[21] An account of the recounts conducted by news organizations can be found in the introduction to A. Jacobsen and M. Rosenfeld, eds., *The Longest Night: Perspective on Election 2000* (Berkeley, CA: University of California Press, 2002).

6

The Bush Administration and
the War on Terrorism

Given the outcome of the 2000 election, there was an expectation that when President Bush took office he would try to govern in a bipartisan way, putting aside the more divisive issues on his agenda. Not only could he not claim much of a mandate, he was the first president in more than a hundred years to come in second in the popular vote. But Bush did not let the circumstances surrounding the election affect his agenda. He proceeded to push ahead as if he had won by a landslide.

At the top of the list was his plan for tax cuts. President Bush made a simple argument; because the government was running a large surplus at the time, people were paying too much in taxes. As he put it during his first address to Congress, he was there to ask for a refund. The tax cuts he proposed would reduce the income tax on average by approximately 15 percent. He also proposed ending the estate tax, which applied only to the richest 2 percent of households, along with numerous other provisions, such as an increase in the tax credit for children.

The main beneficiaries of his proposed tax cuts would be the country's wealthiest families, as they paid the most in taxes. Counting the cuts in the estate tax, the richest 1 percent of taxpayers would receive approximately 40 percent of the tax cuts in Bush's proposal.[1] Whether or not tax cuts were the best use of the funds, the official budget projections at the time made the cuts appear affordable. The Congressional

---

[1] The distributional effects of the tax cut are analyzed in W. Gale and S. Porter, *An Economic Evaluation of the Economic Growth and Tax Reconciliation Act of 2001* (Washington, DC: Brookings Institution, 2002), http://www.brookings.edu/views/articles/gale/200203.pdf.

Budget Office's numbers showed that the government could pay for the tax cuts without even dipping into the surplus from Social Security. In other words, even after the tax cuts, the projections showed that there would still be large surpluses in the unified budget, which is the most widely reported budget measure.

The approval of the tax cuts was not a foregone conclusion. The Democrats were a minority in both the House and Senate, but the Republican majority was small. And there were many Republicans who had serious reservations about such large tax cuts, especially after Congress had worked for so many years to get the Reagan-era deficits down to a manageable size.

In this context, Federal Reserve Board Chairman Alan Greenspan gave President Bush a big helping hand. When asked about the tax cuts in testimony before Congress, Greenspan argued for the cuts. He said that he was concerned that the government budget surpluses at the time were too large. Initially, the government could use its surplus to pay down the debt that it had accumulated in the years when it had run deficits. But Greenspan pointed to projections that showed the surpluses were sufficiently large to enable the government to pay off its outstanding debt in less than a decade. At that point, if the government was still running budget surpluses, it would be forced to buy up private assets, such as corporate bonds or shares of stock. Greenspan claimed that he was so frightened by the prospect of the government holding the assets of private corporations that he thought it would be better to simply reduce the surplus by having large tax cuts.[2]

As it turned out, the debate on the tax cuts extended well into the spring, and economic conditions had already begun to change. The

---

[2] Alan Greenspan's testimony can be found on the Federal Reserve Board's website at http://www.federalreserve.gov/boarddocs/testimony/2001/20010125/default. htm. It is questionable how sincere he was in his concern over paying off the debt too quickly. One of the main factors behind the large surpluses of the time was an extraordinary increase in capital gains tax revenue. This increase was largely attributable to the stock market bubble, which led people to pay substantial capital gains taxes on their stock gains. Greenspan has claimed (and is supported by transcripts of Federal Reserve Board meetings) that he had recognized there was a bubble at the time but thought it best to let the bubble run its course. However, if he recognized that there was a stock bubble, then he knew that its bursting was inevitable. The bursting of the bubble meant that tax revenue would be much lower than projected and that the huge surpluses being projected at the time would never materialize. Therefore, Greenspan should have known that there was no reason to worry that the government would pay off its debt anytime soon.

decline in the stock market, which had peaked in March 2000, had caused investment to plunge, pushing the economy into a recession. Although the full extent of the economy's weakness was not recognized at the time, President Bush was flexible enough to reformulate the rationale for his tax cuts as a form of insurance against economic weakness rather than simply a rebate of excess revenue. Congress eventually passed the tax cuts in early June. Ironically, this meant that a provision put in by the Democrats – a $300 income tax rebate to all people who had paid income tax – kicked in exactly at the point when the economy needed a boost.

Tax cuts were not the only area in which President Bush pursued a strong conservative agenda. Many of his key appointees were figures who were considered to be on the far right of the political spectrum. At the top of this list was his attorney general, John Ashcroft. Ashcroft was a senator from Missouri who had just lost a hotly contested reelection campaign. He had close ties to the evangelical Christian movement and was viewed as a reliable ally for them on issues such as abortion and gay-lesbian rights. There was a major national campaign by liberal groups to stop Ashcroft's confirmation by getting forty senators to filibuster on the vote. The campaign ultimately proved unsuccessful, as several Democrats refused to go along with a filibuster of a presidential nominee to a cabinet post, which is a rare event.

President Bush also angered many moderates and liberals by his executive actions in a wide variety of areas. These actions included the abandonment of any effort to reach an accord on the Kyoto agreement on global warming. The position of the Clinton administration had been that the treaty needed to be changed to make it acceptable to the United States. Bush's position was that the treaty was fatally flawed and that the United States was not interested in the process. Bush adopted similar positions with respect to an international treaty on prosecuting war crimes and prohibiting land mines. He also reversed a number of regulatory rulings put in place under the Clinton administration, most notably a measure on workplace safety that sought to limit health problems from repetitive motion.[3] This measure had been the result of years of study by occupational health experts.

---

[3] Some of the measures reversed by Bush were part of a last-minute burst of presidential activism by Clinton, who implemented a large number of regulations in the brief period after it became clear that Bush would be president and before Clinton left office.

One last area in which President Bush showed little interest in reaching a bipartisan compromise was Social Security. During the campaign, he had explicitly advocated privatizing a portion of the program, a position that was strongly opposed by most Democrats. In March, he appointed a commission to examine options for the program. Unlike the Social Security commission chaired by Alan Greenspan in 1982, Bush did not ask for any input from the Democratic congressional leadership on the composition of the commission. He appointed fifteen people to the commission, including several Democrats, but all the members of the commission had already been on record as supporting Social Security privatization.

The pursuit of a strong conservative agenda was not winning President Bush many political points. While his approval ratings had been reasonably high at the time of his inauguration, as many people had been willing to give the new president the benefit of a doubt despite the circumstances surrounding his election, his approval ratings were fading by the late summer. A weakening economy and policies that many viewed as extreme did not add up to a winning combination.

The September 11 Attack

There have been few single events that have had as much impact on American politics and peoples' lives as the September 11 attack on the United States. Hijackers seized four commercial jets and used them as missiles, crashing two planes into the World Trade Center in New York City, causing both towers to collapse, and one plane into the Pentagon. The fourth plane was apparently destined for another target in Washington but crashed in a field in Pennsylvania after passengers battled with the hijackers for control of the plane. Almost 3,000 people were killed in the attack. The vast majority were office workers in the World Trade Center and the police and firefighters who rushed to the towers between the time when the planes hit and the buildings collapsed.

The country responded with a combination of anger, shock, and fear. The attack was completely unexpected. Very few people in the United States had any notion that there were terrorists plotting attacks on the United States. The fact that the attacks had been so effective – four successful hijackings in a single day – and caused so much death and destruction hugely undermined the public's sense of security. To make matters worse, the hijackings coincided with an anthrax scare in which several letters containing anthrax spores were mailed to various news organizations and two U.S. senators. Five of the people exposed to the anthrax died, and several more became seriously ill.[4] Suddenly people were scared to fly, they were worried about their safety in other high-profile buildings, and they were even scared to open the mail.[5]

It was not long before investigators were able to link the hijackings to Osama bin Laden, the leader of Al Qaeda, an Islamic fundamentalist terrorist organization that was headquartered in Afghanistan. Bin Laden was from one of the wealthiest families in Saudi Arabia. He had been one of the international fighters attracted to Afghanistan in the eighties to fight against the Soviet-backed government. Working in conjunction with the CIA, he had recruited Islamic fighters from around the world to join the guerilla forces.

After the Soviets left Afghanistan, bin Laden returned briefly to Saudi Arabia but was expelled in 1991 because of antigovernment activities. After leaving Saudi Arabia, he spent several years in Sudan before returning to Afghanistan, which had fallen under the control of the Taliban, a group of strict fundamentalists. Following the removal of Soviet troops from Afghanistan, bin Laden had come to view the United States as the main enemy of Islam. He was outraged by the stationing of U.S. troops in Saudi Arabia, which had become a permanent presence after the first U.S.-Iraq war.

He also attacked U.S. support for Israel. Ever since the Six-Day War in 1967, the United States had been the main defender of Israel in the world. It supplied Israel with billions of dollars in aid and arms every year and prevented the isolation of Israel in the United Nations and other international forums. For many Arabs and Moslems who championed the Palestinian cause, the battle against Israel meant also fighting against the United States.

Bin Laden had used his international network of contacts to stage several dramatic and deadly attacks against the United States. In 1993,

---

[4] Two of the fatalities were black employees at the Washington postal facility that had processed the letters sent to the Senate. These deaths prompted considerable anger among the postal workers. While federal authorities had immediately tested the mostly upper-middle-class staffers at the Senate and gave them antibiotics as a precaution, no steps were taken to protect the health of the postal workers who could have been exposed to the letter (many of whom were African American).

[5] All commercial flights were grounded for several days following the attack, until investigators were confident that no more hijackings were imminent.

he was linked to a bombing of the World Trade Center that killed six and injured dozens more. He was also tied to the bombing of a U.S. Marine barracks in Saudi Arabia in 1996, the bombing of U.S. embassies in Kenya and Tanzania in 1998, and the bombing of the *USS Cole*, a navy destroyer that was visiting a port in Yemen. But even with this track record, very few people outside of intelligence circles had ever heard of Osama bin Laden.

When evidence first began to indicate that Islamic terrorists were behind the attack, many U.S. citizens were anxious to take vengeance.[6] There were a number of attacks on Arabs or Moslems, or people who were mistaken for Arabs or Moslems. In the months immediately following September 11, a huge amount of suspicion and hostility was directed toward foreigners. Many dark-skinned people began hanging American flags on their businesses or cars as a form of self-defense.

President Bush laid the framework for the official response to the attack in a speech on September 20, in which he declared a "war on terrorism." The immediate target was to be Osama bin Laden and his network of followers, and Bush warned the Taliban that they would face attack if they did not turn over bin Laden. Yet Bush claimed as his ultimate goal a far broader objective: the elimination of terrorism. Since terrorism is a tactic, not a specific entity or enemy, Bush was essentially declaring an open-ended war that could be pursued indefinitely. It is impossible to eliminate terrorism, since any individual or group may at any time opt to pursue terrorist tactics. Given the revulsion against the mass killings from the September 11 attack and the pressure to unite against an enemy, few people publicly questioned the logic behind the president's war at the time. His approval ratings immediately following his speech approached 90 percent, as any criticism of the president and his plans was virtually banished from public debate.

The war on terrorism proceeded on two tracks. On the international side, the main focus was capturing or killing bin Laden. On

---

[6] On the day of the attack itself, some experts were willing to blame Islamic terrorists on national television even before any evidence was available. This was an extraordinary jump, since the most deadly terrorist attack in the United States prior to September 11 was the bombing of the federal building in Oklahoma City in 1995. This attack, which killed 160 people, was carried out entirely by domestic terrorists.

the domestic side, there was an effort by law enforcement agencies to crack down on whatever elements of the terrorist network might still be in the United States. In addition, the Bush administration sought to increase protections against terrorist attacks by creating a Department of Homeland Security.

The Federal Bureau of Investigation (FBI) rounded up hundreds of Arabs and Moslems across the country in the weeks immediately following September 11 in an effort to shut down any remnants of bin Laden's network in the United States. In this roundup, the FBI did not follow normal legal procedures, claiming the right to hold people without charges for an indefinite period of time. In some cases, people were taken into custody without even being allowed to inform friends or family members. The Bush administration later got congressional authorization for such detentions when Congress passed the PATRIOT Act, a bill that vastly extended the government's police powers.

The other major thrust of domestic efforts to improve homeland security consisted of attempts to make terrorist attacks more difficult. At the top of this list was making air travel more secure. The September 11 hijackers were all able to slip their weapons past airport security. This was partly due to the fact that airport security had been handled in an extremely haphazard manner, often being contracted out to firms that hired workers who were given little training and paid very low wages. In order to upgrade the quality of airport security, the federal government took over this function, making airport security workers part of a new Transportation Security Authority.

The drive for greater security against terrorist attacks also involved efforts to warn the public about the potential for attacks. Through the fall of 2001, the Bush administration gave frequent public warnings about the possibility of new attacks. In some cases, these warnings appeared almost comical, since the officials giving the warning could not indicate whether the prior warnings were still in effect (the administration did not always inform the public when a warning ended) and it was not clear what the public was supposed to do with this information. (Bush administration officials did not encourage people to stay home from work or alter their daily routines in other ways in response to warnings of terrorist attacks.) In one instance, Tom Ridge, the head of the Department of Homeland Security, set off a run on duct tape after suggesting that it could be used effectively with plastic to protect homes against a chemical weapon attack.

Eventually, the system of alerts was formalized in a system of color coding that is supposed to indicate the degree of danger. However, the basis for determining the degree of danger has always been shrouded in secrecy, and there have been concerns that the Bush administration has used warnings of attacks for political purposes. For example, in May 2002, when the Bush administration was facing questions as to whether it had ignored warnings that might have prevented the September 11 attack, Vice President Dick Cheney suggested that it was an inappropriate time to publicly discuss such issues because another terrorist attack could be imminent.[7]

On the international side, the Bush administration prepared for its attack on Osama bin Laden and on the Taliban government in Afghanistan after they refused to turn him over to the United States. The Bush administration quickly sought and gained the assistance of other governments in the region, most importantly neighboring Pakistan, for an invasion of Afghanistan. The role of Pakistan in the war was noteworthy because it is an Islamic country with a strong fundamentalist faction. Further, it was ruled by a military dictator who had a poor human rights record. In other words, it was not a country that would have appeared to be a natural ally with the United States. But the Bush administration was willing to overlook such issues in Pakistan, as well in other countries in the region, while it planned its attack on Afghanistan.

The war began October 7, and most of the fighting was over in just more than two months. The military strategy relied primarily on U.S. airpower, with the ground forces provided by some of the remaining warlords who had been fighting for control of Afghanistan since the departure of the Soviet troops. This kept U.S. casualties to minimum, since there was very little chance that the Taliban and Al Qaeda forces would be able to shoot down U.S. planes.

Removing the Taliban from power proved to be relatively easy, but the mission failed in its primary purpose, capturing or killing Osama bin Laden. While there are varying accounts of how he eluded the U.S. military and its allied Afghan forces, most have him fleeing through the mountainous area in the southeast of the country into Pakistan, where he was believed to have been given shelter by sympathizers. Immediately following the war, the Bush administration held out the possibility that bin Laden had been killed by bombing raids, but an

---

[7] "Cheney Expects More Terror for U.S.," *New York Times*, May 20, 2002, A12.

intermittent stream of videotapes circulated by his network proved that he had survived the conflict.

One factor that likely increased the probability that bin Laden could escape was the decision to rely on Afghan troops to lead the pursuit into the hills instead of using special forces from the U.S. military. The U.S. forces were better trained and could be trusted to be loyal – if they found bin Laden, they would be determined to capture and/or kill him. However, following bin Laden through hills and caves would have exposed U.S. soldiers to guerrilla attacks. Leaving this dangerous mission to the Afghans was a way to minimize U.S. casualties.

Clearly minimizing U.S. casualties was a pressing concern in the conduct of the war in general. As was the case with the Kosovo war, U.S. planes flew at very high altitudes to make them virtually immune to antiaircraft fire from the ground. Although this protected U.S. military personnel, it vastly increased the risks to Afghan civilians from inaccurately targeted bombs. No U.S. soldiers were killed by hostile fire until January, after most of the fighting had ended. The U.S. military made a decision not to keep track of civilian casualties in the war, but those who did try to monitor the deaths of Afghan civilians arrived at counts of between 1,000 and 4,000 in the initial period of the U.S. attack.[8]

The Bush administration's conduct of the invasion of Afghanistan raised an important set of questions concerning the treatment of prisoners that continues today. The Bush administration labeled the prisoners it captured in Afghanistan "enemy combatants" and insisted that they were not entitled to be treated as prisoners of war. This meant that they could be detained indefinitely without any effort at informing family members or friends. The Bush administration also claimed that it could use physical and psychological pressure to force prisoners to provide information. Furthermore, it maintained that the classification of prisoners as enemy combatants was not subject to review either by the U.S. judiciary or by international tribunals.

These claims were still contested at the end of 2005. Many of the prisoners captured in Afghanistan were later brought to the U.S. military base at Guantanamo Bay in Cuba. U.S. courts have subsequently held that these prisoners are subject to at least a military tribunal that evaluates their designation as enemy combatants, although the rules

---

[8] "Uncertain Toll in the Fog of War: Civilian Deaths in Afghanistan," *New York Times*, February 10, 2002, A1.

under which such tribunals are to be conducted have not been clearly laid out. The Bush administration has also allowed the Red Cross to examine the conditions under which these prisoners are being held, but it has not allowed the free access that is required under the Geneva Convention for prisoners of war. The Bush administration maintains that it is not restricted in any way in the treatment of prisoners held in foreign countries. It has claimed that the United States has always treated prisoners humanely and that it has not engaged in torture, but there have been numerous incidents in which young and otherwise healthy men have died in the custody of the U.S. military.

If the invasion of Afghanistan failed in its goal of capturing or killing Osama bin Laden, it did succeed in removing his allies, the Taliban, from power. In the years since the invasion, the U.S. military has overseen elections for a president and parliament, the first democratic elections in Afghanistan's history, even if the conditions were far from ideal. U.S. forces remain in Afghanistan. The U.S. force in Afghanistan is officially part of a NATO force that includes soldiers from Germany, France, and several other U.S. allies. This force continues to protect the Afghan government, which is still the target of attacks by remnants of the Taliban.

The War in Iraq

The Buildup

After the defeat of the Taliban in Afghanistan, the Bush administration turned its attention toward Iraq. In its public statements, the main issue with Iraq was Saddam Hussein's pursuit of weapons of mass destruction and his refusal to cooperate with United Nations arms control inspectors. In reality, the Bush administration wanted to overthrow the Iraqi government. Any concerns about weapons of mass destruction were at best secondary, as the evidence available indicated that Iraq had already destroyed most or all of its weapons of mass destruction. Hussein also largely agreed (with considerable hesitation) to the inspection conditions demanded by the Bush administration.[9] In fact, United Nations

---

[9] See H. Blix, *Disarming Iraq: The Search for Weapons of Mass Destruction* (London: Reed Elsevier, 2004). In the spring of 2005, the *London Times* printed a memo that reportedly comprised the minutes of a meeting between British Prime Minister Tony Blair and his top national security officials in July 2002, eight months before

weapons inspectors were carrying out their inspections in Iraq when President Bush publicly announced his decision to go to war. They had to be evacuated to ensure their safety prior to the first attacks.

At this point, it is only possible to speculate on President Bush's actual motives for overthrowing Hussein. Perhaps the most likely explanation is that the overthrow was part of larger plan for redrawing the political map of the Middle East that several top Bush administration officials had been associated with before they had joined the administration. Vice President Dick Cheney, Secretary of Defense Donald Rumsfeld, Undersecretary of Defense Paul Wolfowitz, and several other top foreign policy officials had been associated with the Project for a New American Century, a conservative think tank that in the late nineties openly called for using military force to overthrow Hussein.[10] It is certainly plausible that President Bush sought to carry out the program that had been advocated by his top advisors before they joined his administration. Clearly their interest in overthrowing Hussein preceded the events of September 11 and even the beginning of President Bush's term of office.

If the purpose of the war was to reshape the Middle East, as had been advocated by the policy experts associated with the Project for a New American Century, President Bush might easily have sought some other rationale for the war, since the U.S. public was not likely to have supported military action in pursuit of a grand geostrategic agenda. However, determining with certainty what President Bush's motives really were will not be possible until some of his top officials become willing to provide information about the factors leading to the decision to go to war.

The lead-up to the war involved a drumbeat of statements about the potential threat posed by Saddam Hussein and the possibility that he might use weapons of mass destruction. The Bush administration

the Iraq war began. This memo presents the assessment of Britain's head of intelligence, after he had attended a meeting with top Bush administration officials, that the decision to overthrow Saddam Hussein had already been made and that intelligence reports would be adjusted to support this policy. No British official has ever denied the authenticity of this memo ("The Secret Downing Street Memo," *London Times*, May 1, 2005, A1, http://www.timesonline.co.uk/article/0,,2087-1593607,00.html).

[10] "How to Attack Iraq," *Weekly Standard*, 1998, available on the website of the Project for the New American Century, http://newamericancentury.org/AttackIraq-Nov16,98.pdf.

was assisted in its efforts to raise fears about Hussein's weapons of mass destruction by the willingness of the country's major news outlets to pass along material from administration sources without any effort at independent verification. The *New York Times*, the country's most respected newspaper, played the most prominent role in this process, printing several front page articles on Hussein's programs for biological, chemical, and nuclear weapons that were based on inaccurate information from sources associated with the Bush administration.[11] Following the *Times* lead, and often using its reports as the basis of their own reporting, other news outlets circulated the reports about Iraq's weapons of mass destruction. Little or no attention was given to the inconsistencies in these reports or to the experts who disputed the claims made in them.

President Bush also sought to link the Iraqi government with the September 11 attack in the public mind even though there was no real evidence of any link. Hussein's ruling Baath Party had championed secular nationalism and was staunchly opposed to the sort of Islamic fundamentalism promoted by bin Laden. The evidence that proponents of a link between Hussein and bin Laden put forward hinged largely on an alleged meeting between Mohammed Atta, the leader of the September 11 hijackers, and Iraqi intelligence agents in the Czech Republic. Most intelligence experts believe that such a meeting never took place.[12]

In addition to the specific claims of Iraqi involvement in the September 11 attack, President Bush and his subordinates regularly laced their public speeches with references to September 11. President Bush was so successful in this effort that, by the time of the invasion in March 2003, public opinion polls showed that most of the public actually thought that Hussein had been involved in the September 11 attack.

The Democratic Party leadership largely went along with President Bush on his path to war. Congress approved a resolution in October 2002 that essentially gave President Bush a green light to attack Iraq. Dick Gephardt, who was still the minority leader in the House at the

---

[11] The editors at the *Times* apologized for its lapses in reporting in an editor's note published a year after the war began ("The Times and Iraq," *New York Times*, May 26, 2002, A10).

[12] See "Iraqi Agent Denies He Met 9/11 Hijacker in Prague Before Attacks on the U.S.," *New York Times*, December 13, 2003, A10.

time, lent his full support to the measure, although a majority of the Democrats in the House did vote against authorizing the war.

The last major obstacle to the invasion of Iraq was the United Nations. There was considerable public pressure to seek the support of the United Nations Security Council for an attack against Iraq. Bush eventually yielded to this pressure and sent his secretary of state, Colin Powell, to the Security Council to argue the case that Saddam Hussein was stockpiling weapons of mass destruction in defiance of prior Security Council resolutions.

Powell's testimony to the Security Council was obviously intended for the U.S. public. While it was billed as a conclusive case developed by U.S. intelligence agencies, any serious analyst could see that the substance fell far short of this mark. For example, one of the pictures Powell presented by way of evidence purportedly showed vats of poisonous chemicals that could be used in weapons. Whatever was in the vats, the chemicals had nothing to do with Hussein, since the vats were located at the headquarters of a terrorist group that was operating in the Kurdish region of Iraq. This area had been outside of Hussein's control since just after the first U.S.-Iraq war. Another piece of evidence turned out not to be an intelligence report but a class paper by a British graduate student examining Iraq's ability to process weapons of mass destruction.

Most of the permanent members of the Security Council refused to buy Powell's story, with only the British going along with the U.S. position. However, the presentation did have the intended effect on U.S. public opinion. Powell's testimony was presented as serious and compelling evidence by the media, sealing the case against Iraq. Although much of the world opposed the invasion, including traditional U.S. allies such as France, Germany, and Canada, President Bush now had the support he needed to overthrow Saddam Hussein.

The War

Once the process of building support had been completed, the war itself was relatively brief. As in the case of other recent conflicts, the United States relied overwhelmingly on its airpower in order to minimize its casualties. Iraq's air defenses posed little threat to U.S. planes. They had been eroded by years of sanctions and were quite dated by 2003 in any case.

On April 9, just three weeks after the first bombing strikes at the start of the war, U.S. troops entered Baghdad. There had been few major battles with Iraqi forces, as most units either melted away or quickly surrendered to the vastly superior U.S. forces. However, as was the case with Osama bin Laden, Saddam Hussein managed to escape capture. Most of the top officials in his regime also went into hiding rather than surrender to the U.S. forces.

The initial response of the Iraqi people to Hussein's overthrow was unclear. Although it seemed that most were anxious to be rid of a ruthless dictator, they did not welcome the U.S. troops as liberators, as some top Bush administration officials had predicted. In order to produce an event that symbolized the end of the Saddam Hussein era, the military staged the tearing down of a massive statute of Hussein in the center of Baghdad. This event was presented to the world as the spontaneous actions of an overjoyed crowd, but in reality the U.S. military had sealed off the circle that housed the statue and had allowed a chosen group of Iraqis in for the event. The destruction of the statue was intended to be comparable to the tearing down of the Berlin Wall, but the celebration of the German people at the destruction of that symbol of repression really was spontaneous.

The U.S. forces seemed ill prepared for the occupation that followed their military victory. They apparently had made no plans to maintain order as the security forces of Hussein's regime crumbled. As a result, in the first days following the collapse of the regime, there was a massive wave of looting in much of the country. Public buildings, including schools and hospitals, were stripped of much of their furniture and equipment. Museums were also pillaged, and many priceless antiquities were seized by looters. The U.S. forces eventually did restore order, but this initial period of lawlessness did not get the occupation off to good start.

Before long, it became clear that the United States faced an organized guerilla resistance. The two main components of the resistance appear to be elements of the Sunni Moslem population and Islamic fundamentalists, many of them foreign, who are loosely allied with Osama bin Laden. The Sunni Moslems make up approximately one-fifth of the Iraqi population. They had enjoyed a relatively privileged status under Hussein, who was also a Sunni Moslem. They currently fear that they will lose this position under a new regime, since the majority of Iraqis are Shiite Moslems. There is also concern that the new regime may be fundamentalist in orientation, since there is much support among the Shiites for a more fundamentalist regime.

Whatever the objectives of the Bush administration in invading Iraq, the occupation following the invasion does not appear to be winning the United States many friends. In addition to the ongoing Sunni insurgency and the conflict with bin Laden followers, the United States has also had repeated clashes with Moktada al-Sadr, a young radical cleric with a substantial following among low-income Shiites in Iraq. Al-Sadr has demanded that the United States withdraw its troops from Iraq, and he has used his clashes with the occupation forces to enhance his stature in large parts of the country.

The Iraqi parties that have been most closely identified with the United States have done poorly in both parliamentary elections held since the overthrow of Hussein. The party that controlled the government in Iraq at the end of 2005 is a Shiite faction with close to ties to Iran, an explicit enemy of the Bush administration. Based on its performance in the elections in December 2005, this party appears poised to continue to play a leading role in the Iraqi government.

In the predominantly Shiite area in the south, where relatively few attacks against the occupation forces have occurred, women's rights have been severely rolled back. Under Saddam Hussein, Iraq had been a relatively secular country. The new government in the south requires women to cover themselves when they go out in public, and vigilantes have frequently attacked women whose faces are not completely covered. Steven Vincent, a U.S. reporter who spent several months in southern Iraq, was killed (possibly by local security forces) after his account of this situation appeared in the *New York Times* in the summer of 2005. Presumably, the Bush administration did not expect to see a government of this sort take power after the overthrow of Saddam Hussein.

The conduct of U.S. forces has also aroused hostility among segments of the population that may not have originally opposed the occupation. There have been many incidents in which U.S. forces have shot and killed unarmed people at checkpoints or when on patrol. Whether or not such accidents could have been prevented, the friends and family members of the victims are still likely to be angry over such killings.

In addition, the U.S. forces on several occasions have abused and tortured people taken prisoner. This was first widely publicized in the spring of 2004 when photographs of sessions in which prisoners were stripped and forced to perform various tasks appeared in magazines and on television. Numerous other accounts of abuse, humiliation, and torture have since come to light. (Similar accounts have come from the U.S.-operated prison in Guantanamo Bay, where many of the prisoners captured in Afghanistan were taken.)

It was very difficult at the end of 2005 to see how the situation in Iraq will be resolved. The U.S. military is fighting an insurgency, ostensibly to protect a fundamentalist government that seems to enjoy substantial support from the country's predominant ethnic group. This government is also closely allied with Iran, a country that the Bush administration has put on the top of its enemy list.

As of December 2005, more than 2,100 U.S. soldiers had been killed in the war, making it by far the most deadly conflict for the United States since Vietnam. The number of Iraqi deaths is in the tens of thousands, although the accounting is much less precise. In addition to the casualties, the war is costing the U.S. government close to $6 billion a month. Public opinion polls show that support for the war has fallen sharply since the quick victory over Saddam Hussein's forces.

The Economy in the Bush Years

The performance of the economy during a president's term in office can be partly attributed to the president's economic policies, but it is also largely influenced the exact timing of the transition into office. President Bush had the worst timing of any president since Herbert Hoover, coming into office just as the collapse of the stock bubble was about to the throw the economy into a recession.

It was inevitable that the stock bubble, which was such an important force propelling the economy in the late nineties, would eventually collapse. There was no obvious factor responsible for the implosion. The market continued to show strong gains through 1998 and 1999 and into 2000, with the most rapid run-ups in the high-technology sector and more narrowly in the stock of Internet retailers. The bubble finally ran out of steam in March 2000, with the NASDAQ, which specializes in high-tech stocks, losing 15 percent of its value in a single day. The broader market indexes fell also and continued down throughout the year.

When the bubble finally burst, there were a number of unanticipated secondary effects, many of which were still being felt at the end of 2005. At the top of the list was a wave of corporate fraud that had been concealed underneath the exuberance of the stock bubble. It turned out that some of the big corporate success stories of the boom were actually just inventions of creative accounting. Enron, an energy conglomerate that had been a poster child of the new economy, turned out to be a bankrupt shell of a company. Its top executives had hidden billions of dollars of debt from shareholders. This revelation destroyed not only Enron but also Arthur Andersen, one of the country's oldest and most respected accounting firms. Arthur Andersen had been the company's auditor and regularly certified Enron's books. While several other huge corporations turned out to have been equally corrupt, Enron was the symbol of this corporate accounting scandal. It had been regularly cited in the business press as one of the country's most outstanding corporations. It was also extremely well connected politically. Kenneth Lay, Enron's CEO, was on a first-name basis with President Bush. It turned out that Enron's success was built almost entirely on phony accounting.

The bursting of the bubble also left many of the country's largest pension plans severely underfunded. Pensions held much of their assets in stock. The run-up in the market made these pensions appear overfunded in the nineties. This meant that the large corporations that sponsored the funds (e.g., General Electric, General Motors, and United Airlines) did not have to make any contributions for their workers' pensions for several years. This changed with the collapse of the bubble, as the value of pension assets plummeted. As a result, corporations were suddenly required to make large contributions to bring funding to the level required under the law. Hard-pressed companies in several industries were unable to meet funding requirements and were forced into bankruptcy. Their pension obligations were turned over to the Pension Benefit Guarantee Corporation (PBGC), the government agency that insures pension funds. As a result of the large number of corporations that have turned over their pension obligations to the PBGC, it is now facing a serious deficit itself.

The bursting of the bubble also deflated the value of the defined contribution pensions, such as 401(k) accounts, of tens of millions of workers. Many workers had been eagerly accumulating wealth in these accounts during the run-up in the stock market. In many cases, they saw much of this wealth disappear with the crash. While younger workers have the opportunity to make up for these losses, many older workers found that they had to change their plans for retirement, since they had much smaller savings than they were expecting.

In the same vein, many of the workers at the high-flying high-tech companies of the period were especially hard hit because they often received much of their pay in the form of stock options. In a rising stock market, options are valuable because they allow people to buy stock at prices below their market value. With the crash of the stock bubble, these options gave people the right to buy stock at prices far above the market value. In other words, they were worthless. As a result, some workers had in effect put in years of long hours at high-tech start-ups for virtually no money.

The plunge in the stock market also affected tax revenues by drastically reducing the money obtained from taxing capital gains. This had a large impact on the federal budget and was one of the main factors, along with the tax cuts and the cost of the war, behind the shift from large surpluses to large deficits. It also had a large impact on many state budgets, most notably California's. The state's revenue projections assumed that the capital gains tax windfall experienced as a result of the bubble in Silicon Valley would continue. When this money did not come in, the state suddenly faced a huge budget shortfall. Other states were equally pressed by the combination of the loss of capital gains tax revenue and the onset of the recession.

The decline in the market began to have a clear economic impact by the fall of 2000 as investment began to drop. Employment growth also sputtered, and by March 2001 employment was actually falling. The September 11 attack was a further blow to the economy, hitting the airline and tourism sectors especially hard. However, it is important to recognize that the economy was already in a recession for six months prior to September 11; the private sector had lost 1.3 million jobs between February and September of 2001. The September 11 attack certainly affected the economy, but the recession had begun six months earlier.

Officially, the recession ended in November 2001, making it the shortest and mildest of the postwar recessions, but the recovery from the recession was extraordinarily weak. Instead of adding jobs, the economy continued to shed jobs through 2002 and into 2003; employment did not bottom out until May 2003. Job growth very gradually accelerated over the next year and a half, but by November 2004 the economy still had not added back the jobs it had lost in the downturn. This made George W. Bush the first president to run for reelection with a net loss of jobs since Herbert Hoover. (Bush is the only president to have lost jobs during his first term and still gotten reelected.)

Other labor market statistics were consistent with the data on weak growth. The percentage of the adult population employed in 2004 was down a full 2 percentage points from its 2000 level, the equivalent of 4 million fewer people with jobs. The decline in employment among young people and prime-age workers (ages twenty-five to fifty-five) was even larger, as the crash of the stock bubble pushed many early retirees back into the labor market. Even as employment rates for most age groups were plummeting, employment for workers older than fifty-five increased by more than 15 percent from January 2001 to January 2005, as older workers felt the need to make up for the loss of retirement savings.[13]

Wage growth fell off in response to the growing weakness in the labor market. Real wage growth decelerated from 1.5 percent a year in the late nineties to zero percent by 2003. From the middle of 2003 to the middle of 2005, the median hourly wage fell by more than 1 percent. This drop is especially striking because productivity continued to grow at a very rapid pace throughout this period. The gains from higher productivity growth went entirely to profits or as compensation to higher-paid workers.

The labor market picture went in exactly the opposite direction from its usual course during a recovery. Typically, as the economy starts to grow at the end of the recession, it starts adding jobs, employment growth leads to consumption growth, and increased consumption promotes further economic growth. As the economy grows, additional employment gains lead to a tighter labor market, and workers are then better positioned to demand higher wages. Wage gains increase income growth, which then allows further employment growth and additional consumption.

With few jobs generated and wages actually declining, consumption was not being supported by rising labor income. Rather, consumption growth was boosted in part by tax cuts, which did put more money in

---

[13] For a breakdown of employment trends by gender and age group, see H. Boushey, D. Rosnick, and D. Baker, *Gender Bias in the Recovery? Declining Employment Rates for Women in the 21st Century* (Washington, DC: Center for Economic and Policy Research, 2005), http://www.cepr.net/publications/labor_markets_2005_08_29.pdf.

people's pockets, and also by borrowing. Household borrowing soared between 2000 and 2005, with consumer indebtedness increasing by 4 trillion dollars, the bulk of which was mortgage debt.[14]

The recession of 2001 was caused by the collapse of the stock market bubble. The recovery from the recession has been driven by the growth of a housing bubble. In response to the economy's weakness following the collapse of the stock bubble, the Federal Reserve Board lowered interest rates to the lowest levels in fifty years. This made it easier for people to buy homes, and it also made it cheaper for people to borrow money against their homes. The low interest rates allowed a modest bubble in the housing market to continue to expand. In the postwar period up until 1997, house prices had just kept pace with the overall rate of inflation. In the period from 1997 to 2005, home prices increased by more than 45 percent after adjusting for inflation. The excess growth in housing prices over this period created more than $5 trillion of additional housing wealth. This excess wealth spurred the economy from the 2001 to 2005, both through borrowing and by promoting a boom in home construction. But just as the collapse of a stock bubble is inevitable, so is a collapse of a housing bubble. The timing and the exact set of events that will cause the deflation of the bubble remain to be seen.[15]

Inflated housing prices were not the only looming problem for the economy in 2005. The United States was also running a current account deficit of more than $700 billion, the equivalent of 6 percent of GDP. The current account deficit is the amount of money that the United States must borrow from foreigners to cover its deficit on trade in goods and services. No advanced industrialized economy had ever run a current account deficit this large relative to the size of its economy. Typically, only a developing country would every run a deficit this large, either during a period of extraordinarily rapid growth or during

---

[14] This is taken from the Federal Reserve Board, *Flow of Funds Accounts*, table L.2, line 18, http://www.federalreserve.gov/releases/z1/current/default.htm.

[15] For an account of the housing bubble, see the R. Shiller, *Irrational Exuberance*, 2nd ed. (Princeton, NJ: Princeton University Press, 2005); see also D. Baker, *The Run-up in Home Prices: Is It Real, or Is It Another Bubble?* (Washington, DC: Center for Economic and Policy Research, 2002), http://www.cepr.net/publications/housing_2002_08.pdf, and D. Baker and D. Rosnick, *Will a Bursting Bubble Bother Bernanke?* (Washington, DC: Center for Economic and Policy Research, 2005), http://www.cepr.net/publications/housing_bubble_2005_11.pdf.

a period of economic collapse. In the latter case, the deficit is soon corrected by the unwillingness of foreigners to make further loans.

The United States was able to run current account deficits of this size because foreign central banks, primarily the central banks of Japan and China, were supporting the U.S. dollar to sustain exports from their countries to the United States. The United States can continue to run deficits of this magnitude as long as these foreign central banks continue to support the dollar. At some point, presumably, these central banks will decide that they no longer need to have U.S. consumers buy exports from their countries (as an alternative, Japanese and Chinese consumers can buy their own products), and they will then stop supporting the dollar. This will lead to a sharp fall in the dollar, which will in turn lead to rising import prices. The immediate effect of a falling dollar is higher import prices, which usually leads to higher interest rates. A sharp rise in interest rates would almost certainly collapse the housing bubble, if it has not already collapsed for other reasons. The longer-term effect will be a more balanced current account.

The Buildup to the 2004 Election

Following the bitterness of the 2000 presidential election, many Democrats were anxious to have another shot at the Republicans. Their prospects originally looked promising going into the 2002 midterm elections. While the Republicans controlled the House (the Democrats controlled the Senate by a single vote), their margin was very small, and the party in control of the White House typically loses seats in an off-year election. After benefiting from a spirit of national unity following in the wake of the September 11 attack, President Bush's popularity ratings had fallen sharply by the summer of 2002. The continuing economic weakness, coupled with the wave of corporate accounting scandals, was damaging Bush's standing with the public.

However, this downward trend had turned by election day. The main factor was growing concern about Iraq. The Bush administration had made Saddam Hussein and his potential use of weapons of mass destruction a major political theme by constantly talking about the risk he posed. In October, Bush managed to get Congress to approve the resolution authorizing war against Iraq. With the national security theme dominating political debate, the Republicans actually managed to increase their majority in the House by picking up eight seats. They also won two seats in the Senate, allowing them to retake control.

The contest for the Democratic presidential nomination began to pick up steam not long after the 2002 election. It soon became intertwined with the expanding protest movement opposed to going to war in Iraq. This antiwar movement grew with remarkable speed, driven in large part by the spread of information over the Internet. In the months just before the war began, there were major protests involving hundreds of thousands of people in New York, San Francisco, and Washington, along with hundreds of smaller protests in other cities across the country. The growth of the antiwar movement was especially striking since it was almost entirely a grassroots phenomenon. At that point, most prominent political figures, including those who had opposed the congressional resolution authorizing the war, were keeping their distance from the antiwar movement.

When the war began in March, the effort to prevent the war had come to an end, but the antiwar movement created a fertile organizing base for ambitious politicians. The one who most effectively took advantage of this base was Howard Dean, former governor of Vermont, who had declared his candidacy the prior year. In a field that included several prominent national politicians, Dean was viewed as a real long shot. He was little known outside of Vermont, one of the country's smallest states.

Dean had a reputation as a moderate when he was governor, but he quickly became the favorite of liberal Democrats by taking a strong stand against the war and by having spoken up against the congressional resolution authorizing the war. While there were other candidates in the race who had also opposed the war, most notably Ohio Congressman Dennis Kucinich, Dean managed to largely corner this position in the media. Through the summer of 2003, he attracted large crowds and considerable media attention and, perhaps most importantly, raised vast sums of money by being the antiwar candidate.

Dean's ability to raise money from this grassroots movement was a new phenomenon. Political campaigns had been getting ever more expensive. This led politicians to focus their energies increasingly on lobbyists and well-connected fundraisers who could raise the money needed to run a successful campaign. Naturally, political platforms had to be adjusted to meet the interests of these donors, which meant that business interests and the wealthy were getting an ever larger voice in U.S. politics.

However, Dean's campaign found a way around this network. He used the Internet as an organizing tool. His campaign was able to mobilize tens of thousands of people to make phone calls, write letters, hold meetings, or come to campaign rallies. It also was able to use the Internet to raise funds for the campaign. Dean raised more than $40 million for his presidential race by January 2004, far more than any of the other candidates for the nomination. Although his campaign quickly flared out for a variety of reasons, he opened a new door in American politics. Dean showed that a candidate could be competitive in a race even for the highest office without going to the traditional powerbrokers. The Internet had vastly increased the range of political possibilities.

When Dean's candidacy crashed in the first primaries, John Kerry, a four-term senator from Massachusetts, stepped forward as the front-runner. Kerry was a decorated Vietnam War veteran who had joined the antiwar movement after finishing his tour of duty in Vietnam. Kerry was a moderate liberal who was very much in the center of the party. He had supported the resolution authorizing the Iraq war. Kerry had been the early favorite of many party insiders, in large part because his status as a veteran seemed to be a big advantage in an election where national security issues were likely to figure prominently.

After Dean's candidacy collapsed, Kerry was able to lock up the nomination relatively quickly. This meant that the general election campaign began somewhat earlier than had typically been the case. Kerry tried to emphasize both domestic and foreign policy issues in his campaign. On the domestic side, he criticized Bush for the failure of the economy to produce jobs. He focused on the massive shift from large budget surpluses under the Clinton administration to large government deficits in the Bush years. Kerry also criticized Bush for the conduct of the war in Iraq, arguing that he should have gotten more support from U.S. allies before making the decision to go to war. However, Kerry was quite explicitly not running on an antiwar platform. He promised to send more troops to Iraq, arguing that this would be necessary to secure a peaceful outcome.

Bush emphasized national security themes in his campaign. He argued that Kerry could not be counted on to stand up to U.S. enemies. In particular, Bush noted a Senate vote in which Kerry had opposed a specific funding measure to support the U.S. forces in Iraq.[16] Bush attributed the country's economic problems to the stock crash and the impact of the September 11 attack. He argued that his tax cuts had helped to boost the economy out of recession.

Bush's campaign also managed to pull less obviously relevant issues into the campaign. The Massachusetts Supreme Court struck down the state's prohibition on same-sex marriage in the spring of 2004, thereby allowing same-sex couples to get married in the state. Groups allied with the Bush campaign raised this as an issue among conservative Christians, even though Kerry himself had indicated his opposition to same-sex marriage.

The Bush campaign also raised questions about Kerry's war record. It sponsored a group of Vietnam War veterans who claimed that Kerry had lied about his Vietnam record in order to get his medals. They succeeded in putting Kerry on the defensive over his war record, even though President Bush had never gone to Vietnam in spite of having supported the war. Bush had spent the war years in the Texas National Guard. At the time, many politically connected young men, like the president, used their family connections to get into the National Guard in order to avoid being drafted and sent to Vietnam. The fact that Kerry's war record became an issue and President Bush's record generally did not testifies to the effectiveness of the Bush campaign.

The race ended up being very close, as the polling indicated throughout most of the fall. However, it did not produce the same sort of deadlock as the 2000 election. Bush won the popular vote by almost 3 full percentage points. His victory in the electoral college depended on an extremely close race in Ohio. While there were irregularities in this vote (many predominantly African American precincts had too few voting machines, leading to waits of more than five hours in some cases), they did not produce the same sort of outrage as the long count in Florida in 2000. For his second term, President Bush also had a slightly more Republican Congress to work with, as the party picked up seats in both the House and the Senate.

---

[16] Kerry had objected to the fact that the bill in question placed few restrictions on the way in which the money would be spent. He had voted for a version of the bill that more explicitly designated the funds for specific purposes. In describing the issues involved, Kerry managed to give the Republicans a line they used with great relish, explaining that he had actually voted for the bill before he had voted against it.

President Bush's Second Term

The Drive to Privatize Social Security

In both the 2000 and 2004 campaigns, President Bush had raised the issue of Social Security. He had proposed a partial privatization of the program that would allow workers to put a portion of their taxes into an individual account in exchange for a cut in benefits. In 2001, he had taken the step of appointing a commission to determine how best this could be done. But before the commission issued its report, the stock market crashed, reducing the interest in private accounts. The commission ended up issuing its report on the Friday evening just before Christmas, guaranteeing that it would receive almost no attention. However, Bush decided it was time to return to Social Security after he was reelected. Two days after the election, he held a press conference in which he said that he had gained political capital as a result of the election and that he intended to expend some of this capital on restructuring the Social Security system.

President Bush was not the first person to want to overhaul Social Security. There has been an ongoing effort by ideological conservatives to privatize the program since the early Reagan years. Because they recognized that Social Security was a hugely popular program and that no major changes would be implemented overnight, they crafted a long-term strategy. One of the tactics was to convince the public that the system was going broke. The proponents of Social Security privatization could also count on the support of the financial industry, which stood to gain tens of billions in fees and commissions each year if Social Security funds were deposited in private institutions.

Another group that stood to gain from privatizing Social Security consisted of higher-income workers. The program has a progressive payback structure, which means that it provides a better rate of return to low-income workers than high-income workers. In many cases, high-income workers would be better off with a privatized system, which could give them a higher rate of return on the money they pay as payroll taxes to Social Security.

These groups were joined in the privatization effort by fiscal conservatives who wanted to roll back the welfare state in the United States, including Social Security. The fiscal conservatives promoted a theme of generational equity, arguing that the cost of paying for a growing elderly population will impose a devastating burden on the children and grandchildren of those currently in the workforce. The most prominent group in this effort was the Concord Coalition, a bipartisan organization started by Pete Peterson, a wealthy investment banker and former secretary of commerce under Richard Nixon.[17]

While the increased costs resulting from the aging of the population will not present a qualitatively new problem for the United States, Peterson was able to use his wealth and political connections to get his views taken seriously in the national debate on the issue of privatization.[18] As a result, much of the public came to believe that Social Security was on the edge of bankruptcy and that future generations would face a crushing tax burden as a result of the benefits provided to the elderly. Against this backdrop, President Bush proposed an alternative system that would allow workers to take their money out of the Social Security system and place it instead in individual accounts.

There also had been many examples of social security privatization elsewhere, although the record was not especially good. Prodded by the World Bank, most of the countries in Latin America had partially privatized their social security systems in the nineties. Among the wealthy countries, England had privatized its social security system under Margaret Thatcher. Sweden had also added private accounts to its social security system, although the government-guaranteed benefit in the reformed Swedish system was still close to one-third larger than the benefit in the unreformed U.S. system.[19]

---

[17] Peterson's books warning of a demographic disaster include *Will America Grow Up Before It Grows Old: How the Coming Social Security Crisis Threatens You, Your Family and Your Country* (New York: Random House, 1996); *Gray Dawn: How the Coming Age Wave Will Transform American and the World* (New York: Crown, 1999); *Running on Empty: How the Democratic and Republican Parties Are Bankrupting Our Future and What Americans Can Do About It* (New York: Farrar, Straus and Giroux, 2004).

[18] Projections show that the cost of providing health care for the elderly will be a serious burden, but this is due to the fact that these projections assume that health care costs in the private sector will continue to rise at a rate that will leave large segments of the country unable to afford health care. The issue raised by these projections is the cost of the health care system, not the problem of paying for an aging population. This point can be seen clearly in the Congressional Budget Office's long-term budget projections, which show Medicare and Medicaid costs rising by far more than Social Security costs (Congressional Budget Office, *The Long-Term Budget Outlook* [Washington, DC: Congressional Budget Office, 2005], http://www.cbo.gov/ftpdocs/69xx/doc6982/12-15-LongTermOutlook.pdf).

[19] For a discussion of the social security reforms in Latin America, see I. Gill, T. Packard, and J. Yermo, *Keeping the Promise of Social Security in Latin America* (Washington, DC: Stanford University Press and the World Bank, 2005). For an account of the reform of the United Kingdom's pension system, see *Challenges and Choices: The First Report of the Pensions Commission* (Pensions Commission, 2004), http://www.pensionscommission.org.uk/publications/2004/annrep/index.asp.

Much groundwork had been laid over the past two decades for privatizing and/or cutting back Social Security, but the base of support for the program proved much deeper than President Bush had anticipated. The Democrats managed to keep the party united in support of the existing Social Security system. This was crucial, since Social Security is an issue where the Democrats were prepared to stage a filibuster in the Senate. Overcoming such a filibuster required at least four Democratic votes, assuming that the Republicans voted as a block in support of the president.

A variety of liberal organizations, including unions and civil rights and women's organizations, along with the American Association of Retired Persons (AARP), staged a nationwide grassroots campaign in opposition to President Bush's proposal. This led to hundreds of protests, meetings, and debates across the country. The campaign was successful enough that many Republican members of Congress refused to support President Bush's privatization plan, and some Republicans actually spoke out against it. Having made the privatization of Social Security the centerpiece of his second-term agenda, President Bush appeared to be stuck on a rock six months into his second term.

By the summer of 2005, most Republicans had accepted that President Bush's plan for privatizing Social Security was not going to be approved. While the Republican leadership could possibly muster enough votes to have a privatization bill approved in the House, they had no chance of getting the necessary votes to shut off a filibuster in the Senate. In fact, since several moderate Republicans sat on the Senate Finance Committee, it was not clear that they even had the votes to get a privatization plan out of the committee to be voted on by the Senate as a whole.

The Rest of the Second-Term Agenda

Social Security privatization was not the only area in which the Bush administration faced serious obstacles in 2005. As a result of policy mistakes and bad luck, the Bush administration faced a series of crises over the course of the year. The net effect was to badly erode Bush's personal popularity as well as the popularity of the Republican congress. Without a sharp reversal in this course, President Bush will not be able to accomplish very much of his second-term agenda.

The most visible and ongoing source of bad news for President Bush was the persistence of the insurgency in Iraq. This led to a regular stream of casualties among U.S. soldiers. At the beginning of the war, the administration had sought to highlight some of the casualties, making heroes out of the dead or wounded, even if this required bending some of the facts.[20] As the number of casualties increased, the administration and its supporters moved in the other direction, trying to minimize the attention given to casualties. In fact, reporting on casualties became somewhat of a political issue. The administration prohibited the filming of coffins of dead soldiers, ostensibly out of respect for the dead. Similarly, when a national television news show devoted an hour to reading the list of soldiers killed in Iraq, many supporters of the war attacked the network for what they claimed was criticism of the Bush administration's policy.

In addition to being bad for public relations, the ongoing stream of casualties also created problems for the military in recruiting new soldiers. The active-duty army and the Army National Guard both missed their recruitment targets in 2004 and 2005, in spite of lowering qualification standards.

The rising cost of the war has also been a public embarrassment for the Bush administration. The administration refused to provide estimates of the cost of an invasion prior to the attack, claiming that the costs were easily manageable and not large enough to be a major consideration in the decision to go to war. Administration officials assured the country that the reconstruction of Iraq following the war would not be expensive and that Iraq would be able to pay the costs itself from its oil revenue. By the end of 2005, the cumulative cost of the war and reconstruction approached $250 billion, an amount equal to 2 percent of annual GDP, or almost 10 percent of the annual

---

[20] Two prominent examples where the government misrepresented facts to promote heroes were the death of Pat Tillman, a former NFL football player, in the Afghan war, and the capture and eventual freeing of Jessica Lynch in the first weeks of the Iraq war. In the case of Pat Tillman, the military constructed an elaborate story about how he held a position under heavy fire in order to protect his fellow soldiers. Subsequent evidence indicated that he had been killed accidentally by friendly fire. The military initially circulated stories of how Jessica Lynch had heroically fired her gun at Iraqi soldiers until she ran out of ammunition and then was captured and beaten. Subsequent reports indicated that she was knocked unconscious when the military vehicle in which she was traveling was attacked. Her subsequent freeing was a staged incident. She was being held in a hospital in an area where Hussein had already lost control. The hospital staff would have brought her to the door. There was no need to stage a military assault on her hospital room, which was filmed for national television.

federal budget. Initially the cost of the war had been met by running larger deficits than would otherwise have been the case through 2005. However, in the fall of 2005, Congress approved a series of cuts in various categories of social spending in order to reduce the size of the deficit, implying that spending in areas such as Medicaid and student loans was being cut in order to pay for the cost of the war. With the projected deficits expected to be quite large for the foreseeable future, the continuation of Iraq war spending at the same pace as in 2005 will impose a serious strain on the budget.

In addition to the bad news over the course of the war itself, the Bush administration also faced ongoing controversy around the circumstances leading up to the war. Having been forced to acknowledge that much of the information presented to the public to justify the war was wrong (most importantly, the claims about weapons of mass destruction), the Bush administration faced the awkward situation of walking a line between saying that it went to war based on faulty intelligence reports and saying that it deliberately misled the public. If the situation in Iraq were more positive, there would probably be little public interest in the circumstances leading up to the war (at least there would be little media attention to the issue), but the ongoing stream of bad news has kept this topic in the media.[21]

In the same vein, an investigation of a White House leak of the identity of an undercover CIA agent also kept the events leading up to the war in the news. This leak was apparently part of an effort to discredit a Bush administration critic who had disputed the accuracy of claims about Iraq's nuclear weapons program. In the fall of 2005, an independent prosecutor indicted a top White House official in connection with this leak, calling attention again to the use of inaccurate information to justify the war. The investigation also called attention to the fact that an administration that had publicly committed itself to protecting national security as its top priority was willing to expose an undercover operative to advance its political agenda.

---

[21] Presumably, President Bush believed that Saddam Hussein still had at least some weapons of mass destruction (WMDs), even if they might be only old weapons that had not been properly destroyed. Given the uncritical media coverage prior to the invasion, it was likely that the bulk of the media would accept almost anything as proof of Hussein's WMD program. The remarkable discovery following the invasion is that Hussein had apparently been quite thorough in complying with his commitment to dismantle his WMD program.

The weather – in particular, several powerful and destructive storms – caused serious political difficulties for the Bush administration in 2005. The country faced one of the worst hurricane seasons ever, in both the number and severity of storms.[22] This proved to be a political problem for the Bush administration for two reasons. First, it was yet one more piece of evidence that weather patterns were changing in unusual ways and thus evidence that global warming was already having noticeable climatic effects. Since the Bush administration had minimized any potential negative consequences of global warming (and denied that it was human caused in any case), the storms of 2005 seemed to provide a clear example of how global warming could cause serious damage. The other reason that the hurricanes presented a serious political problem is that the Bush administration, along with the state and local governments in the most affected areas, showed themselves to be unprepared for a serious storm.

The most severe damage was caused by Hurricane Katrina, which struck land just east of New Orleans at the end of August. The path of the hurricane was well charted, and there were several days of advance notice before it actually reached land. Nonetheless, adequate precautions were not taken to protect the population of the region and especially the city of New Orleans. The mayor of New Orleans gave an evacuation order two days before the hurricane reached shore, but tens of thousands of people who did not have cars were left stranded. The city dealt with the situation by urging people to go the Superdome, the stadium for the city's football team, which was set up as an emergency storm shelter.

The initial damage to the city when the storm hit shore on the morning of August 29 was not unduly heavy, but the storm surge from the hurricane weakened the levees that protected New Orleans from Lake Pontchartrain on the city's north side. The levees broke later in the day, and virtually the whole city was flooded as water streamed out of the lake. This left the people in the Superdome (as many as 60,000 by some estimates) stranded with limited amounts of food, water, and medical supplies. Another group of 10,000 to 20,000 were similarly stranded in the city's convention center.

---

[22] For the first time since the modern system of naming hurricanes was instituted in 1933, the National Weather Service ran out of letters in the Roman alphabet for picking names. The last six named tropical storms of the season were given letters from the Greek alphabet.

Remarkably, these people were left largely to fend for themselves for three days until an evacuation began on September 2. During this time, there were shortages of basic necessities, with some people dying because they could not get medicine or other items. Both the Superdome and convention center lost electric power soon after the storm, so it was dark at night, with no ventilation. The sanitation facilities were also grossly inadequate for the number of people seeking shelter. In addition, there was a breakdown of order, as there were very few law enforcement officers present to protect public safety in a situation where many people were getting desperate. Although the extent of lawlessness was almost certainly exaggerated by the media (unsubstantiated rumors of rapes and killings were quickly broadcast around the world), there clearly was considerable fear among the tens of thousands of people left behind in New Orleans.

The responsibility for this tragedy remains in dispute, as local, state, and federal officials have each sought to blame the others for the failure to protect the public.[23] But the fact that the government (at whatever level) was completely unprepared for a totally foreseeable set of events was apparent for the whole world to see.[24] Television camera crews were able to get into the city and film hundreds of desperate people looking for help. For three days, the various levels of government were unable to arrange for adequate supplies of food, water, and medicine to be brought to the people stranded in the city or for the people to be evacuated to a safer location.

There was also an important racial dimension to this tragedy. The vast majority of the people left stranded in New Orleans were African American. Undoubtedly this was a factor in the willingness of news reporters to pass along unsubstantiated rumors of violence in the Superdome and the convention center. But it also led to an obvious question: would the government have been as incapable of helping tens of thousands of white people if they had been trapped in similar

---

[23] One reason that the government may have been poorly prepared to deal with the hurricane is that much of the Louisiana National Guard was stationed in Iraq, along with its equipment.

[24] The fact that the levees could break because of a storm of Katrina's magnitude was well known among disaster relief planners. The levees were designed to withstand a category 3 hurricane. Katrina had approached shore as a category 5 hurricane, weakening to a category 4 just before hitting land. Therefore, it was reasonable to expect that the levees might break.

circumstances. Many poor developing countries have been far more effective in protecting their people from natural disasters.

The federal agency that had the immediate responsibility for over-seeing the disaster relief effort was the Federal Emergency Management Administration (FEMA). FEMA had been led by highly regarded professionals during the Clinton administration, but Bush had appointed a political supporter, Michael Brown, to head the agency. Brown had no prior experience in disaster management. His most recent job before taking charge of FEMA was working as a commissioner of the International Arabian Horse Association.

FEMA was clearly unprepared for dealing with the hurricane, and it showed. Bush originally had stayed at his Texas ranch, where he had been in the middle of a long vacation. On the third day after the hurricane hit, he finally went back to the White House to begin to oversee the relief effort. At that point, he publicly commended Brown for his performance, even though tens of thousands of people remained stranded in New Orleans at the time. Eventually, FEMA was able to bring in supplies and evacuate the people stranded in the city, but there were more than a thousand deaths and much suffering that could have been prevented had the relief effort been better planned.

There was a third source of bad political news that was directly of the administration's own making. This was the Medicare prescription drug benefit that the administration got passed into law in 2003 and that was slated to come into effect in 2006. In the 2000 election, both Bush and Gore had promised to add a prescription drug benefit to the Medicare program to help seniors cope with the rapidly increasing expense of purchasing medications. Drugs had not originally been included under Medicare because their cost was inconsequential, but by 2000 the average senior household was spending more than $1,000 a year on prescription drugs, and the cost was rising at the rate of 10 percent a year.

President Bush did little to advance legislation on a prescription drug benefit in his first two years in office, as the administration's attention was tied up elsewhere. However, he did not want to run for reelection without carrying through on his pledge. In the fall of 2003, he managed to push through a drug benefit on almost a straight party-line vote. On the one hand, this bill marked the largest expansion of the welfare state since the passage of Medicare. On the other hand, many Democrats and liberals objected to the bill on the grounds that it would still leave many seniors facing substantial drug expenses and that it was extraordinarily complex in its design.

The Republican drug benefit was designed to allow private insurers a role in the new program. The bill also included a set of subsidies to provide private insurers with a better opportunity to compete with the core government-run Medicare plan. The bill prohibited Medicare from directly negotiating drug prices with the pharmaceutical companies to get a lower price for drugs. Including private insurers and prohibiting direct negotiations substantially raised the cost of the bill, while also adding to its complexity. The Republicans claimed to prefer this approach because of their commitment to market mechanisms. The other possible explanation was that the insurance industry and the pharmaceutical industry were both major contributors to Republican campaigns, and this design ensured that the bill would protect their interests.

Regardless of the motivations of the bill's supporters, the reaction of seniors when they actually began to sign up for their drug insurance at the end of 2005 was overwhelmingly negative. The design of the benefit requires seniors to decide among a number of competing drug insurance plans (sometimes as many as fifty). The plans differ by the drugs they cover, the discounts they provide, the copayments they require, and the deductibles they charge. Deciding among these plans would likely be complicated for anyone, but the task is especially difficult for seniors, who are not generally accustomed to using computers, often have bad eyesight, and may have difficulty maintaining attention. Instead of being thankful for this new benefit, many seniors were angry at being forced to jump through hoops for what could have been designed as a simple add-on to Medicare.[25]

A final problem facing the Bush administration at the end of 2005 was the evidence of corruption surrounding many of the leaders of the Republican Party. At the top of this list was the indictment of House majority leader Tom DeLay on the charge that he had laundered money for political campaigns. Bill Frist, the Senate majority leader, was facing an investigation by the Securities and Exchange Commission over suspicions that he had engaged in insider trading.

---

[25] A *Wall Street Journal* poll in December 2005 found that seniors, by a margin of 40 percent to 23 percent, had a negative opinion of the Medicare drug benefit ("Senior Citizens' Unhappiness with Issues Has Implications for Midterm Elections," *Wall Street Journal*, December 15, 2005, A4).

Frist's family was the biggest stockholder in one of the country largest health maintenance organizations. Frist had dumped millions of dollars of his own holdings of the company's stock just before it issued negative earnings projections. In addition, a lobbyist with close ties to the Republican leadership was indicted on charges of fraud.

These events, together with other questionable actions by high-level Republicans, led many people to distrust the Republican Party, according to a number of polls in the second half of 2005. The small consolation for the Bush administration was that the polls showed that the public did not think much better of the Democrats. Nonetheless, at the end of 2005, President Bush faced approval ratings of less than 40 percent, extraordinarily low for a second-term president.

7

The United States in 2005: The Impact of the Last Quarter Century

The United States was a very different country in 2005 than it was in 1980. It had changed politically, socially, and demographically. Its economy was structured very differently, with workers facing vastly different job options and life prospects. The position the United States held in the world order had also changed a great deal over this quarter century. This chapter outlines some of the key features of the changes that have occurred since 1980.

Demographics

The United States was a considerably older, more ethnically diverse country in 2005 than it was in 1980. The share of the population that was older than age sixty-five had risen by 10 percent (from 11.1 percent in 1980 to 12.2 percent in 2005), while the share of the population that was younger than age twenty had fallen by more than 12 percent (from 31.7 percent in 1980 to 27.8 percent in 2005).[1]

However, this demographic shift is relatively minor compared to the aging of the baby boom generation, the massive group of 79 million people born between 1946 and 1964. In 1980, the baby boomers, ranging in age from sixteen to thirty-four, were the young people just entering the labor force and forming their own families. In 2005, the baby boom cohort had matured, and some of its oldest members, at fifty-nine years old, had already reached retirement age. The aging of this huge cohort has changed the character of the country. Not

---

[1] These data are taken from the *2005 Annual Report of the Board of Trustees of the Federal Old-Age and Survivors Insurance and Disability Insurance Trust Funds* (Washington, DC: U.S. Government Printing Office, 2005), table V.A.2.

only will there be more elderly, but they will also live longer. The life expectancy of a person aged sixty-five had already risen from 16.2 years in 1980 to 17.6 years by 2005. It is projected to rise further, to 18.4 years, by 2020.[2] While this increase in the relative size of the elderly population will not produce the economic disaster that some have claimed (the impact of gains in productivity on living standards dwarf any negative demographic effects), the concerns of the elderly and retirees will loom as far more important in political, cultural, and economic matters than they ever have before.[3]

Although there was a large increase in the share of older people in the population in the period from 1980 to 2005, there also were important changes in the situation of children. In 1980, more than 80 percent of the families with children were married couples. This percentage had fallen to 72 percent by 2003.[4] Part of the decline is explained by a rise in the number of single mothers. Single mothers accounted for 22.6 percent of families with children in 2003, compared to 17.6 percent in 1980. In 2003, single mothers accounted for 52.3 percent of African American families with children, while married couples accounted for just 42 percent. The fastest percentage growth occurred among families headed by single fathers. In 1980, 2 percent of families with children were headed by a single father. This figure had more than doubled by 2003 and stood at 5.3 percent.

The last quarter century has also seen a large growth in the share of the U.S. population that is not of European ancestry, as there have been several large waves of immigration from other regions in the world. The most important of these immigration flows has been from Latin America. The share of people of Hispanic origin in the U.S. population more than doubled, rising from 6.4 percent in 1980 to 14.1 percent in 2005. The vast majority of the Latin American immigrants came from Mexico and Central America.[5] These people were attracted by

---

[2] Ibid., table V.A.3.

[3] The economic impact of a growing population of seniors is discussed in D. Baker and M. Weisbrot, *Social Security: The Phony Crisis* (Chicago: University of Chicago Press, 1999), chap. 2.

[4] These data are taken from the U.S. Census Bureau, *Statistical Abstract of the United States 2005* (Washington, DC: U.S. Government Printing Office, 2005), tables 56 and 60.

[5] Data on the composition of the U.S. population are taken from the U.S. Census Bureau estimates of the U.S. population. The data for 2005 are projections. These data are available at http://www.census.gov/population/www/.

opportunities in relatively low paying sectors of the U.S. economy, working in restaurants and hotels, as custodians in office buildings, in the apparel industry, as domestic workers in affluent households, and increasingly in construction and food processing. The latter two sectors had not previously been low-wage industries, but wages in these sectors fell substantially as firms were able to weaken unions and take advantage of the availability of relatively cheap immigrant labor. There was another important factor pushing immigrants from Latin America to move north. Many could no longer support themselves on the small farms they owned because of competition from low-cost imported food from the United States. In the case of Central America, the wars of the eighties further encouraged immigration to the United States.

Wars also played a major role in other waves of immigration. With the collapse of the U.S.-backed government in South Vietnam, there was a major wave of immigrants from Southeast Asia in the mid-seventies. This led to a continuing flow of immigrants from the region, as recent arrivals sought to bring over friends and family members. More than half a million people from Indochina immigrated to the United States from 1980 to 2005.[6] There was also a continuing inflow of people from China and other Asian countries. By 2005, people who identified themselves as being of Asian ancestry comprised 4.2 percent of the U.S. population, nearly triple the 1.5 percent share in 1980.

Since the Asian population is highly concentrated, the share is much higher in some states, most notably California, where 10.9 percent of the population identify themselves as having Asian ancestry.[7] There were also substantial flows of immigrants from other regions, including India and some sub-Saharan African nations, such as Ethiopia, which was the victim of a long civil war.

Table 7–1 shows the distribution of the population in 1980 and 2005 by race and Hispanic origin.

The United States was not alone in seeing a large influx of immigrants during this period. Most of the rich countries experienced

---

[6] Data taken from the Department of Justice, Immigration and Naturalization Service, *Statistical Yearbook of the Immigration and Naturalization Service* (Washington, DC: U.S. Government Printing Office, 1981–2001).

[7] U.S. Census Bureau, *Profile of General Demographic Characteristics for California* (Washington, DC: U.S. Government Printing Office, 2001), table DP-1, http://www.census.gov/Press-Release/www/2001/tables/dp_ca_2000.PDF.

Table 7–1. *Distribution of the population by race and Hispanic origin*

	1980	2005
White	83.2%	80.4%
Black (only)	11.7%	12.9%
Hispanic (all races)	6.4%	14.1%
Asian	1.5%	4.2%

Source: U.S. Census Bureau, *Statistical Abstract of the United States 2006*, tables 12–13, and *Statistical Abstract of the United States 1982*, table 6. Data for 2005 are projections. The percentages sum to more than 100 because people can report more than one category.

substantial waves of immigration over this quarter century. The percentage of foreign-born among the total population in some European countries, such as Germany and Austria, is not very different from the percentage of foreign-born in the United States, although the Europe-wide average is considerably lower.[8] The integration of migrants from developing world into the larger society has posed problems in all of the developed countries. In all countries, these populations experience higher unemployment and have substantially worse living standards than the native-born population.

In some ways, the experience of immigrants in the United States has been better than in the majority of European countries; most important, the children of immigrants have full rights of citizenship, which is not generally true in European countries. However, immigrant populations in Europe have access to health care coverage and other benefits of the welfare state, which even U.S. citizens are not guaranteed.

The geographic distribution of the population of the United States also shifted substantially over the last quarter century. The flow of people and jobs from the Frostbelt (the Northeast and Midwest) to the Sunbelt that had been going on throughout the postwar period accelerated rapidly during this quarter century. Both economics and aging were key forces. On the economic side, the Midwest and Northeast

---

[8] For data on the immigration into wealthy countries, see *Trends in International Migration: 2001* (Paris: Organisation for Economic Co-operation and Development, 2001), http://www.oecd.org/dataoecd/23/41/2508596.pdf.

Table 7–2. *Distribution of the population
by region*

	1980	2004
Northeast	21.7%	18.6%
Midwest	26.0%	22.3%
South	33.3%	36.1%
West	19.1%	23.0%

Source: U.S. Census Bureau, *Statistical Abstract of the United States 2006*, table 24, and
Statistical Abstract of the United States 1982,
table 9.

were badly hit by the loss of manufacturing jobs, which had been the
basis of the economy for many cities in the region. Midwest industrial
centers such as Cleveland and St. Louis, among the biggest cities in the
country at midcentury, had fallen to the rank of a midsize California
city by 2005. Cleveland's 2005 population of 458,000 would rank it
sixth in the state of California, while St. Louis, with a population
of 340,000, would barely be big enough to scrape into California's
top ten.

   The growth of the Sunbelt was fueled first by the defense buildup
of the eighties, with much of the spending concentrated in Sunbelt
states. There was also a drift of manufacturing jobs to the South,
as corporations sought to take advantage of low-cost and generally
nonunion labor. The high-tech boom of the nineties was a major fuel
for the economies of California and the Pacific Northwest. The aging
of the population also tended to favor the Sunbelt, as many retirees
chose to escape northern winters and took advantage of the relatively
cheap real estate available in the South.

   Table 7–2 shows the regional composition of the country in 1980
and 2004. In 1980, the Northeast and Midwest together comprised
47.7 percent of the country's population. In 2004, the share of these
regions had fallen to 40.9 percent. This shift in population is reflected
in the political power of the regions. Before the redistricting based on
the 1980 census, the Northeast and Midwest together had a majority
of the seats in the House of Representatives (52 percent). After the
redistricting based on the 2000 census, their combined share of the
representatives was down by more than 20 percent (they had 42 percent

of the seats in 2002). After the Republican takeover in 1995, the House had a speaker from Georgia, a majority leader from Texas, and a majority whip from Texas. The following year the newly elected Senate majority leader was from Mississippi. This reflected the vastly increased importance of the South in the country's politics.

The Status of Women

There have been enormous changes in the economic and social status of women over the last quarter century. The rapid flow of women into the labor force continued throughout this period. By 2005, the gap in the labor force participation rates (the percentage of adults who hold a job or are looking for work) for men and women had been cut to half of its 1980 level. Women had also entered most of the highest-paying professions in large numbers, even though substantial barriers still existed. In addition, there were substantial shifts in social attitudes and law enforcement, so that crimes largely directly against women, such as rape and spousal abuse, were treated far more seriously than twenty-five years previously. At the same time, the situation of some women suffered. Poor women had less access to abortion in many states than they did in 1980. Similarly, the 1996 welfare reform law took away a crucial form of support for many low-income mothers. In short, there was progress toward equality, but setbacks as well.

The trend toward the increasing participation of women in the labor market continued the earlier postwar pattern. From 1960 to 1980, the rate of labor force participation among women increased from 37.6 percent to 51.3 percent. Women's labor force participation rate increased further until 1999, when it peaked at 60.8 percent. Women's labor force participation dipped slightly between 2000 and 2005, but this is most likely due to the weakness of the labor market rather than any change in women's attitudes toward the labor market.[9]

The rise in women's labor force participation in the United States paralleled developments in other wealthy countries. Women's labor force participation rates rose everywhere in this period, and in many countries these rates rose more than in the United States. By 2005, its

---

[9] See H. Boushey, *Are Women Opting Out: Debunking the Myth* (Washington, DC: Center for Economic and Policy Research, 2005), http://www.cepr.net/publications/opt_out_2005_11.pdf

Table 7–3. *Average hourly wages by gender and education level*

	Less than high school	High school	Some college	College	Advanced degree
1979					
Men	$14.81	$17.35	$18.05	$23.69	$23.96
Women	$9.50	$11.27	$12.10	$15.32	$19.62
W/M	64.2%	65.0%	67.0%	64.6%	81.9%
2003					
Men	$11.74	$16.02	$18.10	$28.31	$35.41
Women	$9.11	$12.62	$14.46	$21.46	$27.07
W/M	77.6%	78.8%	79.9%	75.8%	76.5%

Note: Amounts are in 2005 dollars.

Source: L. Mishel, J. Bernstein, and S. Allegretto, *The State of Working America 2004/2005* (Ithaca, NY: Cornell University Press, 2005), tables 2.18 and 2.19.

rate placed the United States in the middle of the wealthy countries. Several countries that had started the period with considerable lower rates, such as France, Germany, and Portugal, had higher rates by the end of the period.[10]

There was also a substantial reduction in the gender pay gap over this period. Table 7–3 shows average hourly earnings for men and women at various levels of educational attainment in 1979 and 2003. At every educational level, women substantially reduced the size of the gap, but even in 2003, women with a college degree still earned on average only three-quarters as much as men with a college degree.

The top occupations were also far more open to women than had previously been the case. While women are still rare among the CEOs of major companies, there were no women CEOs of major corporations in 1980. In politics, five of sixteen of President Clinton's cabinet appointees were women, including a secretary of state and his attorney general for his full two terms in office. Five of twenty-six of George W. Bush's cabinet appointees were women, including the secretary of state for his second term. By contrast, only three of President Reagan's thirty-three cabinet appointees were women, and all were appointed

[10] For data on women's labor force participation, see *Female Labor Force Participation: Past Trends and Main Determinants in OECD Countries* (Paris: Organisation for Economic Co-operation and Development, 2004), http://www.oecd.org/dataoecd/25/5/31743836.pdf.

to relatively minor cabinet posts. His first cabinet included no women. The number of women senators went from one in 1980 to fourteen in 2005, while the number of women in the House of Representatives rose from seventeen to fifty-nine in the same period. Also, women were appointed to the U.S. Supreme Court for the first time ever (two women were appointed during this period).

In high-paying professions, such as medicine and law, women are now approaching parity in numbers with men, even if men still dominate the top positions in these fields. In the 1979–80 academic year, 27.8 percent of the students enrolling in medical school in the United States were women. This figure had risen to 49.2 percent in the 2002–3 academic year.[11] Fifty-one percent of the recipients of law degrees in 2005 were women.[12] By comparison, just 31 percent of the students enrolled in law school were women in the 1979–80 academic year.[13] There were comparable increases in most other professions, although some occupations, such as engineering, continue to be overwhelmingly male.

The changing status of women is perhaps best exemplified by their role in sports. While men's sports continue to feature far more prominently in the news and attract much more money, the top women stars in tennis, golf, and soccer are household names and can command endorsement fees that are exceeded by few male athletes. Women's sports have also advanced enormously at the college and high school level, in large part due to federal legislation mandating equal treatment. In sports, as in other areas, there are still very large gender-based inequities, but there has also been enormous progress toward equality during this quarter century.

Part of this progress has been the increased seriousness with which crimes against women are now regarded, most importantly rape and domestic violence. Michigan passed the first state rape shield law in 1974. These laws make most questions about a rape victim's prior sexual conduct inadmissible in a rape case. Prior to the passage of such laws, it was a common practice for defense lawyers in rape cases to use

[11] American Association of Medical Colleges, *Women in U.S. Academic Medicine Statistics, 2002–2003* (Washington, DC: American Association of Medical Colleges, 2005), http://www.aamc.org/members/wim/statistics/stats03/table1.pdf.

[12] American Bar Association, Commission on Women in the Profession, *A Current Glance at Women in the Law* (Washington, DC: American Bar Association, 2005), http://www.abanet.org/women/ataglance.pdf.

[13] C. Epstein, *Women in Law* (Champaign, IL: University of Illinois, 1993), 53.

such questioning as a form of harassment in the hope of getting a rape victim to drop charges or to discourage them from filing charges. A federal rape shield law was passed in 1978, and by the early eighties nearly every state had passed a rape shield statute. Legal concepts of rape were also broadened during this period, as courts came to recognize the possibility of "date rape" and "spousal rape," crimes that would have almost certainly gone unprosecuted prior to 1980.[14]

Domestic violence also came to be treated increasingly as a crime. It had been a common practice for law enforcement officers to view even violent disputes between a married couple or domestic partners as a private matter. This began to change in the seventies in response to the feminist movement. Recognition of domestic violence as a crime became more commonplace throughout the period. For the most part, it fell on local government to implement laws and procedures to protect women against domestic violence, but the Family Protection and Domestic Violence Prevention Act, passed by Congress in 1994, helped to establish national standards. This law required that hospitals report, and police departments record, incidents in which they suspected domestic violence. It also set out procedures designed to ensure that domestic violence victims have the opportunity to leave a home where they face an ongoing threat of abuse. While police will still often ignore violent acts committed against women within the home, the laws and practices have changed enormously in this area over the last quarter century.[15]

There were several important court decisions during this period that provided workers for the first time with serious legal protections against sexual harassment in the workplace. A 1986 Supreme Court decision held that a sexual relationship between an employee and a supervisor who has the authority to fire or promote the worker cannot be viewed as consensual. This ruling gave workers (most often women) who faced sexually abusive bosses the opportunity to turn to the courts for help. A 1993 ruling vastly broadened the definition of a "hostile work environment," holding that open displays of pornography and

---

[14] For a useful discussion of some of the issues in this section, see M. Ferree and B. Hess, *Controversy and Coalition: The New Feminist Movement Across Four Decades of Change* (New York: Routledge and Kegan Paul, 2000).

[15] See E. Buzawa and C. Buzawa, *Domestic Violence: The Criminal Justice Response* (Thousand Oaks, CA: Sage Publications, 2003).

sexual jokes can be seen as creating a work environment hostile toward women and therefore can be forms of discrimination.[16]

However, the single most important event in altering public attitudes toward sexual harassment in the workplace during this period was the testimony of Anita Hill during the confirmation hearings for the nomination of Clarence Thomas to the Supreme Court. Hill made her allegations in nationally broadcast hearings that topped the news for several days. Although many people disputed the truthfulness of her testimony, no public figures were prepared to trivialize the seriousness of the charges. While Thomas's appointment was narrowly approved by the Senate, the hearing effectively established as a public norm that sexual harassment was unacceptable in the workplace.

One last area in which women made substantial progress over this period was in the laws on nonpayment of child support. Although it has become more common for men to become the custodial parent or to have joint custody following a family breakup, women still generally end up being the sole custodial parent in most cases of separation and divorce. For this reason, the enforcement of child support rulings is a very important issue for millions of women. Most states made substantial efforts to increase their enforcement of child support during this period, as did the federal government. Congress passed the Child Support Recovery Act of 1992, which made nonpayment of child support to a child living in another state a criminal offense, punishable by jail time. (It is important to note that efforts to increase child support collection were often motivated in large part by a desire to reduce public expenditures on welfare and other forms of assistance to low-income families rather than a desire to ensure that women were treated fairly.)[17]

On the other side, there are areas in which the situation of women deteriorated over this period. At the top of this list for lower-income women is the quality of the safety net provided by the welfare system. The 1996 welfare reform act seriously weakened an important source of support for tens of millions of low- and moderate-income women. Although the number of women receiving welfare at any point in time was only about 4 million prior to the passage of the bill, the number

---

[16] See A. Conte, *Sexual Harassment in the Workplace: Law and Practice* (New York: Panel Publishers, 2000).

[17] J. Crowley, *The Politics of Child Support in America* (Cambridge: Cambridge University Press, 2003).

who passed through the system over a ten-year period was far larger – close to 40 percent of the families in the bottom four income deciles.[18] This is due to the fact that the vast majority of beneficiaries passed through the system relatively quickly. For the most part, even prior to the 1996 reform, the welfare system provided a temporary system of support for families during an illness or after losing a job or a family breakup.

The 1996 reform act, which renamed the core welfare program "Temporary Assistance to Needy Families," imposed much harsher conditions on welfare beneficiaries. Most immediately, it imposed substantial work requirements, which meant that many mothers would not have the opportunity to attend school or receive other training that could allow them to obtain a better-paying job. It also put a two-year limit on continuous welfare stints and a lifetime limit of five years for receiving cash assistance. The law gives states the discretion to provide more generous assistance. For example, they could extend the period over which they would pay for benefits, but under the new law additional spending would come entirely out of state budgets, without any federal match. Most states followed the lead of the federal government and substantially reduced benefits, weakening this safety net program.

The other important source of deterioration in the situation of women is the added limitations on access to abortion. In 1977, the federal government stopped paying for abortions for low-income women through Medicaid except when a woman's life is endangered. (In 1993, this exception was broadened to include cases of rape and incest.) In several state Medicaid programs, including those in California and New York, abortion is treated as a covered medical procedure subject to few limitations. In most states, Medicaid coverage of abortion is restricted to exceptional cases, with the vast majority of abortions going uncovered. In addition to the difficulty that many low-income women may face in paying for an abortion, in many parts of the country they also have considerable problems finding a doctor to perform the procedure.

Doctors who perform abortions have faced serious harassment in many states as a result of organized activity by groups opposed to abortion. This harassment has included everything from protests and blockades at clinics that perform abortion to death threats, bombings,

---

[18] H. Chernick, *Wide Cast for Safety Net: Over Time Middle Class, as Well as Poor, Rely on Entitlement Help* (Washington, DC: Economic Policy Institute, 1995).

and even assassinations. As a result, there are many counties, mostly in the South and rural Midwest, where there are no doctors willing to perform abortions on a regular basis. In these cases, women often must travel long distances to obtain an abortion. Most middle-income women would be able to afford the travel, even if it does impose a serious hardship. For lower-income women, the lack of an abortion provider in the area may present an insurmountable obstacle to obtaining an abortion.[19]

The Status of Racial and Ethnic Minorities

If this quarter century can be seen as a period in which there was important progress toward the achievement of gender equality, the record on racial equality is far more mixed. There clearly have been some important gains. For example, the percentage of African Americans living below the poverty line fell by a fifth, from 31 percent in 1979 to 24.7 percent in 2004. The presence of African Americans in higher-paying professions and political office has grown substantially, but most of the racial gap in socioeconomic status that existed in 1980 is still present in 2005 and in some ways has increased. It would be difficult to say that in 2005 the United States was on a path toward racial equality.

The clearest source of gains for African Americans over the quarter century was the substantial opening of positions in high-paying professions, corporate boardrooms, and politics. African Americans continue to be underrepresented in these areas relative to their share of the larger population, but at the start of this period, they were rarely found in these positions at all. In 1982, blacks accounted for 2.9 percent of lawyers, 2.3 percent of doctors, and 5 percent of accountants. By 2003, these figures had risen to 3.6 percent, 5 percent, and 9.6 percent, respectively.[20] African Americans comprised 12.9 percent of the population as a whole in 2003. Clearly, they are still underrepresented in these professions, but their share of the jobs in these high-paying fields

[19] See R. Solinger, ed., *Abortion Wars: A Half Century of Struggle 1950–2000* (Berkeley, CA: University of California Press, 1998).

[20] These data are taken from U.S. Census Bureau, *Statistical Abstract of the United States 1984*, table 696, and *Statistical Abstract of the United States 2005*, table 597. The year 1982 is used in this comparison because in earlier years, the table provides data for "black and other."

increased substantially over this quarter century. The growth in the number of African Americans in these fields led to a substantial increase in the size of black upper middle class – people who were relatively comfortable financially and more easily able to exert political power.

The number of African Americans holding political office increased enormously during this period at all levels of government. In 1980, there were seventeen African American members of the House of Representatives and none in the Senate. In 2005, the number of African American members of the House had more than doubled, to forty-two, with one African American serving in the Senate. Although Reagan had appointed only one African American to his cabinet during his term in office, Clinton appointed four to his cabinet. George W. Bush has also appointed four to his cabinet, including the first two African Americans to serve as secretary of state.

Beyond these clear gains achieved by the relatively prosperous segments of the African American community, the picture was very mixed. Overall, the ratio of black family income to white family income rose, but not by much. In 1980, the ratio of the median family income of blacks to the median family income of whites was 57.9 percent. This had risen to 64.5 percent by 2004.[21] The percentage of black children in poverty stood at 42.1 percent in 1980. In 2004, 33.3 percent of black children were living below the poverty line. (The poverty rate among non-Hispanic white children in 2004 was 9.9 percent.) Income equality between the races, or anything close to it, was still very far off in 2005.

In some important ways, the situation of African Americans deteriorated over this period, most notably the increase in the number of African Americans in prison or jail or subject to court supervision through parole or probation. Efforts to get tough on crime during this period lead to more punitive laws and longer sentences. African Americans were disproportionately affected by these measures. In 2004, 1,235,000 African Americans were on probation and another 314,000 were on parole.[22] The combined total of 1,550,000 is equal

---

[21] These numbers are taken from the U.S. Census Bureau, *Historical Income Tables–Families* (Washington, DC: U.S. Government Printing Office, 2005), table F-6, http://www.census.gov/hhes/www/income/histinc/f06w.html.

[22] Data on the number of people on probation or parole are taken from L. Glaze and S. Palla, "Probation and Parole in the United States, 2004," *Bureau of Justice Statistics Bulletin*, November 2005, http://www.ojp.usdoj.gov/bjs/pub/pdf/ppus04.pdf.

to 5.9 percent of the adult African American population. Another 869,000 African Americans were in state and federal prisons or jails, equal to 3.3 percent of the adult population.[23] Thus, 9.2 percent of African American adults were either incarcerated or under court supervision in 2004. For young men, the percentage was well over 20 percent.

By contrast, in 1980 approximately 195,000 African Americans were incarcerated, less than one-quarter the 2004 figure. The numbers who were subject to probation or parole supervision in 1980 were presumably proportionately less than the 2004 numbers as well.[24] In effect, the toughening of attitudes toward crime during this period made dealing with the criminal justice system a normal part of life for a large segment of the African American population. It is important to recognize that in addition to harsher treatment of violent offenders, the rise in incarceration and probation and parole over this period has been partly due to increased prosecution for property crimes and drug-related offenses. Just over half of the inmates of state prisons in 2003 were convicted of violent crimes, while just 11 percent of the much smaller number of federal prisoners were convicted of violent crimes.[25]

Insofar as African Americans lost ground economically, part of the explanation is that the economic trends that worked to the disadvantage of less-educated workers in the this period hit them especially hard. For example, blacks are more likely than whites to be employed in manufacturing or to be union members. (The wage premium for union membership is also larger for blacks than for whites.) Therefore the loss of manufacturing employment and the decline in unionization rates was especially hard on the African American population.

Some of the limited gains for African Americans in this period were undoubtedly attributable to affirmative action policies. These

[23] This is taken from P. Harrison and A. Beck, "Prisoners in 2004," *Bureau of Justice Statistics Bulletin*, October 2005, http://www.ojp.usdoj.gov/bjs/pub/pdf/p04.pdf. This article gives a breakdown of the prison population by race. The calculation in the text assumes that the racial breakdown of the jail population is the same as the prison population.

[24] Reliable data on incarceration rates by race are not available for 1980. The estimate in the text is obtained by assuming that the share of African Americans in the total incarcerated population in 1980 (473,000) is equal to the share of African Americans in the state jail population in 1978 (41.1 percent). The latter number is taken from table 334 in the 1981 Statistical Abstract. The total prison population is taken from table 330.

[25] Harrison and Beck, "Prisoners in 2004."

policies opened doors to African Americans who might have lacked the formal credentials or the connections to otherwise get accepted into a school or to get a job. There was a strong political reaction to race-based affirmative action toward the end of this period, with many states, including California, outlawing the use of race as a criterion in universities or other public institutions. This trend raises the possibility that further growth in the share of African Americans in higher-paying professions may be limited in the future.

However one evaluates the gains made by blacks in this period, there clearly were enormous differences between whites and blacks in their assessment of racial progress. This was perhaps best evidenced by their differing attitudes toward the murder trial of O. J. Simpson, a former football star and widely recognized sports commentator and actor. Simpson was placed on trial for the murder of his ex-wife and a friend of hers. While Simpson is black, both his ex-wife and her friend were white.

In the course of the trial, it came out that one of the police officers responsible for the investigation of the crime had been involved with an openly racist group.[26] In addition, there were some holes in parts of the prosecution's case, although perhaps no more than would have been typical of any trial. Simpson had the money to hire a top-rate defense team that effectively exploited the holes in the evidence and managed to win an acquittal from the jury. While the vast majority of whites in the United States saw a murderer being set free, the vast majority of blacks applauded Simpson's success in defeating a racist prosecution. It would be hard to imagine a more diametrically opposed reaction to a single event.

The picture for Hispanic Americans during this period was also mixed, albeit somewhat more positive than for African Americans. Their labor market picture showed some gains, but the gaps between Hispanic Americans and non-Hispanic whites remained large. The average unemployment rate for Hispanic Americans was 7 percent in 2004, compared to 4.8 percent for whites (including Hispanics). This was somewhat lower than the 10.2 percent unemployment rate for Hispanic Americans in 1980, a year when the unemployment rate for whites was 6.4 percent. The average per capita income of Hispanics

---

[26] For an account of public attitudes toward the Simpson trial, see D. Hunt, *O. J. Simpson Facts and Fictions: News Rituals in the Construction of Reality* (New York: Cambridge University Press, 1999).

relative to whites actually fell over this period, from 59.1 percent in 1980 to 54.8 percent in 2003.[27] This reflected a decline in the median hourly wage of both Hispanic men and women relative to their white counterparts over much of this period.[28] The socioeconomic status of Hispanics has lagged in other ways as well. For example, 32.7 percent of Hispanics lacked health insurance overage in 2004, compared to 19.7 percent of African Americans and 14.9 percent of non-Hispanic whites.

However, this picture may understate the gains made by Hispanic Americans over this period. There was a huge inflow of people from Latin America over this quarter century, many of them very recent arrivals. The 2000 census found that more than 40 percent of the people of Hispanic ancestry were foreign born, and more than half of this group had arrived in the prior decade.[29] There is a substantial gap between the economic status of new immigrants, on the one hand, and the native-born population and immigrants who have been in a country for a long time, on the other. (This gap expanded during this period.) The large increase in the number of recent immigrants over this period had the effect of lowering the average wage and increasing unemployment rates for the Hispanic population as a whole, offsetting gains by those who had been in the country at the beginning of the period. In short, the economic situation of Hispanics who were in the country in 1980 looks considerably better when viewed without including recent Hispanic immigrants in the picture.

As was the case for African Americans, there were important advances for Hispanic Americans in obtaining top positions of power. The number of Hispanic American members of the House of Representatives rose from just five in 1980 to twenty-two in 2005. The number of Hispanics in the Senate rose from zero in 1980 to two in 2005. Only one of President Reagan's thirty-three cabinet appointees was Hispanic, President Clinton appointed two Hispanic cabinet members, and President George W. Bush appointed three, including the first Hispanic attorney general. As with African Americans, it is possible to find Hispanic Americans among the top executives at most major companies, which would not have been true a quarter of a

[27] U.S. Census Bureau, *Historical Income Tables–Families*, table P-1.
[28] L. Mishel, J. Bernstein, and S. Allegretto, *The State of Working America 2004/2005* (Ithaca, NY: Cornell University Press, 2005), table 2.24.
[29] U.S. Census Bureau, *Statistical Abstract 2004–2005*, table 41.

century ago, even though Hispanic Americans continue to be seriously underrepresented among CEOs and in other top positions.

The Hispanic population currently faces a somewhat different prospect than the African American population. Hispanic Americans have never been as tied into the unionized manufacturing sectors of the economy. While the decline of this sector has been a serious setback to African Americans, it has been of less consequence to Hispanic Americans. Geographically, the Hispanic American population is concentrated more in the Sunbelt states, which are growing rapidly (in part because of the influx of Hispanic immigrants), than the African American population. It remains to be seen whether this will be a net benefit. While a more rapidly growing economy in the Sunbelt should in principle provide more opportunities, schools and infrastructure are also much more stressed. If these states do not provide the public infrastructure to support the population growth they are experiencing, the least advantaged among the population are likely to suffer the most.

The data for other ethnic groups, such as people descended from various Asian nationalities, are more difficult to evaluate, since there are not consistent series through time and the experiences of different national groups vary substantially (as is also the case with people of Hispanic ancestry). People of Asian ancestry have on average fared relatively well over this period. The most recent data on household income show that the median income of Asian households is 17.3 percent higher than the median income of white households.[30] The number of people of Asian ancestry in most of the higher-paying occupations exceeds their share of the population, suggesting that they been relatively successful in overcoming the obstacles they have faced.

The Status of Gay-Lesbian Rights

In 1980, millions of nonheterosexuals kept their sexual orientation a tightly guarded secret, fearing ridicule, harassment, job loss, and even loss of the custody of their children if their sexual orientation became more widely known. Outside of New York City, San Francisco, and a few other liberal enclaves, politicians were scared to be associated

---

[30] U.S. Census Bureau, *Income, Poverty and Health Insurance Coverage in the United States, 2004* (Washington, DC: U.S. Census Bureau, 2005), table 1, http://www.census. gov/prod/2005pubs/p60–229.pdf.

with any legislation that protected the legal rights of gays and lesbians. In fact, they were generally scared to be seen even associating with the people who advocated such legislation. It was still common to see people ridiculed for their sexual orientation in movies, television shows, and public discussions. There were serious public debates as to whether gays and lesbians should be allowed to teach school or hold other positions of responsibility. There were no openly gay members of Congress, and if a politician was identified as not being heterosexual, it almost certainly meant the end of his or her career. In fact, in 1980 homosexual activity was illegal, even if rarely prosecuted, in many states.[31]

There has been a remarkable change of attitudes toward nonhetero-sexuals over the last quarter century. In 2005, there were few main-stream national political figures who openly defended discrimination based on sexual orientation in most areas of employment (the mili-tary continues to explicitly discriminate based on sexual orientation). The lines of national public debate are now drawn around the issue of same-sex marriage, an issue that would have been almost unthinkable in most policy circles in 1980. In fact, even some conservative Republicans have now endorsed the concept of a civil union for same-sex couples – a bond that would provide couples with most of the same legal protections as marriage. This constitutes an enormous shift in public attitudes over a relatively short period of time.

The advance in the rights of nonheterosexuals was the result of numerous political battles at all levels of government.[32] Gay-lesbian activists were first able to score political victories at the local level in more liberal cities, where there was already a substantial presence of openly gay and lesbian individuals. San Francisco, in 1972, passed the first ordinance banning employment discrimination based on sex-ual orientation. Several other cities followed suit over the next two decades, with New York City approving an antidiscrimination statute in 1979. Wisconsin, in 1982, became the first state to pass a law prohibiting employment discrimination based on sexual orientation, followed by Massachusetts in 1989. By 2003, eleven states, including

---

[31] It was not until 2003 that the Supreme Court ruled that laws prohibiting homo-sexual activity by consenting adults were unconstitutional.

[32] For a discussion of the legal status of prohibitions of discrimination based on sexual orientation and other legal issues affecting nonheterosexuals, see L. Keen and S. Goldberg, *Strangers to the Law: Gay People on Trial* (Ann Arbor: MI: University of Michigan Press, 2003).

California and New York, had laws that prohibited discrimination based on sexual orientation by both public and private employers. An additional ten states had either laws or executive orders in effect that prohibited such discrimination in the public sector.[33]

Gay-lesbian activists also sought to extend to same-sex couples the rights enjoyed by married heterosexual couples. As of 2002, seven states, including New York and California, along with eighty-three municipal governments offered employment benefits to domestic partners.[34] (This category includes couples who live together and opt for this status regardless of their sexual orientation.) In the summer of 1997, Hawaii became the first state to recognize civil unions for same-sex couples and in so doing offered these couples most of the legal protections provided by marriage. Vermont approved similar legislation in 1999. While these measures were considered pathbreaking at the time, in a 2000 debate, Dick Cheney, the Republican candidate for vice president, announced his support for the principle of civil unions for same-sex couples.

In 2004, the state supreme court in Massachusetts held that the state's marriage law violated the Massachusetts state constitution by not allowing same-sex marriage. In effect, this legalized same-sex marriage in Massachusetts, making it the first state in the country to take this step.

The advancement in the rights of nonheterosexual individuals goes far beyond the legal gains achieved during this quarter century. While many people of same-sex orientation still choose to keep their orientation private – for example, by not bringing a same-sex partner to workplace social events – there has been an enormous change in the public acceptance of homosexuality. There are prominent people who are openly gay or lesbian in most prestigious occupations. In most major cities, there are restaurants, bars, and other businesses that openly cater to gays or lesbians. And most colleges and universities have organizations of students who are openly gay, lesbian, or bisexual. Major political battles over the rights of nonheterosexual individuals continue to be fought, but there can be little doubt that major advances occurred in this area from 1980 to 2005.

---

[33] A. Wilkinson and M. Belli, *Everybody's Guide to the Law* (New York: Harper Collins, 2003), 238.

[34] M. Riccucci, *Managing Diversity in Public Sector Workforces* (Boulder, CO: Westview Press, 2002), 144.

Of course the United States was not alone in recognizing rights for nonheterosexuals. By 2005, most Western European countries allowed legal recognition of same-sex couples that provided most of the benefits of marriage. Several countries, such as the Netherlands and Belgium, allowed same-sex marriage. In this area, the United States was neither a laggard nor a leader.[35]

Trends in Religious Practices

The role of religion in public life is an area that continued to separate the United States from most other wealthy countries in 2005. In particular, debates over issues such as stem cell research and the teaching of evolution in school, which were very heated in the United States in 2005, were largely nonexistent elsewhere.

The United States is a far more religious country than other rich nations. In a recent survey, nearly 60 percent of Americans reported that religion plays a "very important" role in their daily lives.[36] By comparison, 21 percent of the respondents in Germany gave this answer, and just 11 percent in France. In Canada, the second most religious wealthy country in the survey, 30 percent of the people answered that religion plays a very important role in their daily lives. The greater religiosity of people in the United States is not new, although the difference between the United States and other wealthy countries is likely growing through time. Whereas other wealthy countries have grown more secular, there does not appear to be any comparable trend in the United States. Religion continues to be an important force in people's lives and in shaping their worldviews.

There were some shifts in religious commitments in this quarter century. Most important, there was substantial growth in evangelical Christian denominations at the expense of establishment Protestant denominations. The membership of the Southern Baptist Convention rose by 15 percent between 1980 and 2002, the membership of

---

[35] For the laws on the status of same-sex couples across Europe, see *Same-Sex Marriage and Partnership, Country-by-Country* (Brussels: International Lesbian and Gay Association-Europe, 2005), http://www.ilga-europe.org/europe/issues/marriage_and_partnership/same_sex_marriage_and_partnership_country_by_country.

[36] Pew Research Center for the People and the Press, *Among Wealthy Nations . . . U.S. Stands Alone in Its Embrace of Religion* (Washington, DC: Pew Research Center, 2002), http://pewglobal.org/reports/pdf/167.pdf.

the Assemblies of God rose by 56 percent, and the membership of the
Church of Latter-Day Saints (Mormons) doubled.[37] By contrast, the
membership of the largest Lutheran Church fell by 5 percent, and
the membership of the Episcopal Church fell by 16 percent. The membership of the Catholic Church rose by 32 percent over this period,
driven in large part by the flow of immigrants from Latin America.

While the growing strength of evangelical denominations has had
a substantial political impact over this period, the effects are sometimes not always entirely straightforward. Evangelical white Protestants
are disproportionately Republican, but they do not always share the
agenda of the leadership of the Republican Party. For example, Gary
Bauer, who headed the socially conservative Family Research Council, opposed the privatization of Social Security because he felt that
the current system provides important security to families, especially
to families with stay-at-home moms.

The Catholic Church has fit even less well into the partisan politics
of the last quarter century. It has stood at the forefront in opposing
legalized abortion and has often been active in efforts to restrict the
rights of nonheterosexuals as well. At the same time, many of the
leaders of the Catholic Church have been very visible in efforts to
protect programs for the poor, have opposed the death penalty, and
have protested against U.S. foreign policy in Central America and
elsewhere during this period.

By 2005, the moral of standing of the Catholic Church and its
ability to influence the debate on political issues had been severely
damaged by a series of scandals involving pedophile priests. These
scandals first began to receive substantial attention in the late nineties.
The scandals revealed not only that a substantial number of priests
had used their position to sexually abuse young boys but that this
behavior was apparently tolerated by much of the church leadership,
which sought to cover up the crimes. In December 2002, Cardinal
Bernard Law, who was the archbishop of Boston and one of the most
prominent members of the Catholic hierarchy in the United States,
was forced to resign his position after it was revealed that he had long
protected priests accused of child molestation.

It is also important to note the role that the African American
church continues to play in politics in the United States. The civil

---

[37] Data on religious affiliation is taken from the U.S. Census Bureau Statistical
Abstracts, 1982, table 80; 2005, table 68.

rights movement of the fifties and sixties was very deeply rooted in the African American church. Many of the most prominent leaders in the movement, including Martin Luther King Jr., were ministers. Although the African American community has grown more diverse in many respects, the church continues to play an important role in the lives of most African Americans. The Republican Party leadership has sought to reach out to the African American church, claiming that their views on many social issues are closer to the views of the Republican Party than those of the Democratic Party. To date, this effort has not been very successful, and close to 90 percent of African Americans regularly vote Democratic.

The Media in the Internet Age

The quarter century from 1980 to 2005 was a period of enormous change in the media and access to news. The importance of the traditional sources of news – evening news shows and newspapers – declined sharply during these years. There also was a huge increase in the degree of concentration in the traditional media, as weakened regulation, technological change, and globalization produced a wave of mergers and takeovers that continued right through the end of the period. At the same time, the development of digital technology and the Internet has led to the growth of new and alternative media. The new media are still in their infancy but could eventually have a major impact on politics and culture.

In 1980, nearly 40 percent of households watched the network news broadcasts each night, and more than two-thirds of adults reported reading a daily newspaper.[38] By 2005, viewership of network evening news shows had been cut in half, to 20 percent of households, while

---

[38] Data on historical newspaper readership is taken from the Newspaper Association of America, *Daily Newspaper Readership Trend: Total Adults (1964–1997)* (Vienna, VA: Newspaper Association of America, 2006), http://www.naa.org/marketscope/pdfs/Daily_National_Top50_64–97.pdf. The discussion of more recent trends in news viewership relies on data from the "Network TV" section of the publication *The State of the News Media 2004* (Washington, DC: Project for Excellence in Journalism, 2004), http://www.stateofthenewsmedia.org/narrative_networktv_intro.asp?media=4. Data on newspaper readership at the end of the period is taken from the "Newspapers" section of the same publication, http://www.stateofthenewsmedia.org/narrative_newspapers_intro.asp?cat= 1&media=2.

the readership of daily newspaper had fallen by more than one-third, to 40 percent of adults. There is an important generational dimension to this falloff – younger people are the ones least likely to be regular viewers of network news or readers of daily newspapers, with the ongoing decline showing up most clearly among people younger than age forty. The decrease in the audience for traditional news outlets has been at least in part offset by an increase in the audience for new media, most importantly cable news and the Internet. Neither of these news sources even existed in 1980. By 2003, more than twice as many people reported getting their knowledge of breaking news events from cable news stations as from the major television news networks. In addition, close to 100 million people reported going online at some point in the year to get news. While the traditional national evening news broadcasts and daily newspapers remained important sources of news in 2005, their impact was far less than in 1980, and alternative sources were increasingly available.

Although the decline of the traditional news outlets stems partly from the greater convenience of the new media, it also reflects a loss of confidence in the credibility of the news presented on television and in daily newspapers. The percentage of people giving the network news shows the highest marks for believability fell from 35 percent in 1985 to 23 percent in 2002. Similarly, the share of the public that gave top marks to newspapers for believability fell from 28 percent in 1985 to 20 percent in 2003. It is important to note that this survey preceded several important media scandals, such as the public acknowledgement by the *New York Times* that it had presented articles purporting to show evidence of weapons of mass destruction in Iraq without adequate investigation of the sources and the presentation on *CBS News* of fraudulent documents that supposedly showed that President Bush had not fulfilled his commitment to the Texas National Guard. These highly publicized lapses in editorial judgment (or instances of bias) almost certainly further eroded public confidence in traditional news sources.

The extent to which cable news and Internet news will provide effective alternative outlets remains to be seen. Two of the four leading cable news networks are directly tied to existing broadcast networks. However, the growth of cable outlets and the opportunities for virtually unlimited channels through satellite television allow viewers more options, whether they include new news networks in the United States or just news shows broadcast in Canada, England, or other countries. In 2005, the vast majority of the people obtaining news over the Internet did so by visiting one of the websites of the traditional news outlets. But the low costs of establishing a website mean that a much larger pool of information is readily available to the public. Furthermore, bloggers – individuals presenting their own analysis and commentary on the Web – have already had a large impact on public debate in many areas, often calling attention to events that were originally ignored by the mainstream news outlets.

The development of the new media has coincided with an enormous consolidation within the traditional media.[39] During this period, corporations both got larger within sectors in which they were already operating and expanded into new sectors. For example, in 1990, the Time-Life Corporation, which was one of the country's largest publishers of magazines, merged with Warner Brothers, one of the largest movie and music production companies. In 1996, the combined company bought up CNN, the country's largest cable news network. This company in turn merged with AOL, at the time the country's biggest Internet service provider. In addition, to magazines, movies, Internet access, and cable news, the Time-Warner Company also owned cable television providers and several major publishers.

There were similar consolidations throughout the media. Newspaper chains grew larger by adding more newspapers and/or buying into television and radio markets. For example, the New York Times Corporation bought the *Boston Globe*, one of the country's oldest and most respected newspapers, along with many other smaller papers across the country. The Tribune Corporation, which publishes the *Chicago Tribune*, the *Los Angeles Times*, and many smaller papers, increased its holdings of television stations to the extent that its broadcast outlets reached more than 80 percent of the population in 2005. The radio market was transformed by the growth of nationwide networks of radio stations, such as Clear Channel Communications, which owned more than 1,200 radio stations across the country in 2005. These networks benefited from the enormous economies of scale that result from broadcasting the same material over dozens of local stations. In a further shakeup of the radio market, by 2005 satellite radio networks were broadcasting to millions of paying subscribers

---

[39] On media concentration, see B. Bagdikian, *The New Media Monopoly* (Boston: Beacon Press, 2004), and R. McChesney, *The Problem of the Media: U.S. Communication Politics in the Twenty-First Century* (New York: Monthly Review Press, 2004).

across the country. This fast-growing market has already pulled many of the wealthiest (and therefore most valued) listeners out of the broadcast radio market.

This consolidation also led to a degree of cross-marketing and commercialization that would have been unimaginable in 1980. For example, with many movies (especially those intended primarily for children), companies make as much profit from toys or video games that are designed around the movie's characters as from the movie itself. It has also become increasingly common to sell "product placements" in movies, television shows, or even books. With a product placement, the advertisement is effectively inserted directly into the artistic work. For example, a specific car is highlighted in a movie scene, with the brand name clearly visible, before the hero drives away into the sunset. This sort of mixing of content and advertising was virtually nonexistent in 1980.

As with news reporting, the development of new media has been an important potential force allowing for the decentralization of control over the distribution of creative and artistic work. In principle, the development of satellite broadcast systems that can allow hundreds of digital television signals to be transmitted simultaneously should vastly increase the ability of independent developers of creative material to reach a wide audience. The Internet should also serve this purpose, especially as high-speed connections become more common and as the carrying capacity of these systems allows for visual material to be transferred more quickly. It was partly in recognition of the potential impact of these new media that regulatory agencies (primarily the Federal Communications Commission) relaxed restrictions on concentration in the traditional media.

It is still too early to determine the full impact of these new media. The large corporations that dominate the traditional media have moved aggressively to ensure that they have a strong presence in the new media. However, these new media have the potential to carry an almost limitless amount of content. Furthermore, the costs of producing and distributing material through satellite television or the Internet are low enough that many more people should be able to harness these outlets than could ever effectively take advantage of the traditional media. While the major media corporations may come to dominate the new media as effectively as they did the traditional media, it is also reasonable to believe that satellite television and the Internet will lead to a vastly increased array of creative and artistic work that goes well beyond the items offered up by the current collection of media conglomerates.

Major Trends in Health

The quarter century from 1980 to 2005 saw important developments in health care, due to technology and to changes in lifestyle. A wide range of medical advances led to substantial increases in life expectancy and improvements in the quality of life for large segments of the population. At the same time, there were important ways in which public health deteriorated over this period, most notably through a rise in obesity. For large segments of the population, trends toward less active lifestyles and poorer dietary habits had a negative effect on health outcomes.

Probably the largest single cause of improved health for people in the United States over this period was the sharp decline in smoking. In 1980, 32.8 percent of adults reported being regular smokers. This figure had fallen by almost one-third, to 22.4 percent, in 2002.[40] Among men, the percentage reporting to be regular smokers fell from 36.5 percent in 1980 to 24.8 percent in 2002, a drop of 14.1 percentage points. For women, the percentage of regular smokers fell from 29.1 percent to 20.1 percent.

This decline in smoking was attributable to both public education about the dangers of smoking and an enormous expansion of regulations surrounding smoking. In 1980, people were to free to smoke in most public places, including restaurants, office buildings, and airplanes. Insofar as regulations existed, they usually involved a requirement that a nonsmoking section be provided to the public. This often meant setting aside a few tables in one corner of a restaurant or a few rows of seats at the front of a plane.

Over the course of this period, restrictions on smoking became progressively stricter, as locations where smoking was permitted became increasingly limited. By 2005, smoking was banned by federal or state laws on planes, in millions of workplaces, and in many public buildings. The price of tobacco had also been pushed up by more than 200 percent, after adjusting for inflation, due to higher tobacco taxes and fees

---

[40] These data are taken from the U.S. Census Bureau Statistical Abstracts for 1984 (table 198) and 2004 (table 188).

imposed on the tobacco industry after it lost a series of major liability suits.[41] There were also substantial restrictions imposed on the marketing of cigarettes, including the prohibition of television advertising as well as any efforts aimed at children.

There was a similar, if less dramatic, decline in alcohol consumption over this period, with per capita consumption falling by 11.3 percent between 1980 and 2002.[42] The sharpest decline was in the consumption of hard liquor, with a falloff of 35 percent during the period. This decline was also due in part to greater public awareness of the health problems associated with alcohol consumption in addition to harsher sanctions for abusing alcohol. The group Mothers Against Drunk Driving (MADD) played a key role in the latter effort. MADD was formed in 1980. It led a successful drive to raise the drinking age to 21 across the country. It also pushed for harsher penalties for drunk driving. In addition, laws in most states now hold restaurants and bars liable for the consequences if they knowingly serve alcohol to an inebriated customer.

On the negative side, obesity had become a much more serious problem by 2005 than it had been at the start of the period, with almost a quarter of the population qualifying as obese in 2002 and another 35 percent being heavier than their healthy weight.[43] This rise in weight problems can be attributed to increasingly unhealthy diets, with average daily calorie consumption rising by 22 percent between 1980 and 2000.[44] Average daily consumption of fat rose by 14 percent in the period.

There was an important class dimension to this deterioration in public health. In 2002, only 17.4 percent of people with college degrees were classified as obese, while 29.7 percent of people with less than a high school degree fell into this category. This gap reflected a substantial and growing disparity in health outcomes by income. Many college-educated people consciously tried to pursue healthier lifestyles and to eat healthier (and more expensive) foods, whereas the quality of the diets of most low- and middle-income people deteriorated over this period. Coupled with less access to health care, more exposure

---

[41] This calculation is based on the Bureau of Labor Statistics' consumer price index for tobacco products.

[42] U.S. Census Bureau, *Statistical Abstract of the United States 2005*, table 201.

[43] Ibid., table 194.

[44] Ibid., table 197.

to environmental hazards, and often more stress in their lives due to financial circumstances, the poorer diet of the less affluent led to a growing gap in health outcomes that paralleled the growing income gap.[45]

America and the World

In 1980, the United States was the undisputed leader of a cold war alliance that included the countries of Western Europe, Japan, Australia, South Korea, and almost the whole Western Hemisphere. In 2005, the United States continues to be the leading military, economic, and political force in the world, but there are far larger and more open divisions between the United States and its allies. In particular, the United States now often finds itself at odds with several of the major European countries in international disputes.

The most obvious example of such a dispute was the refusal of France and Germany to support the U.S. invasion of Iraq in 2003. At the time, the invasion was justified internationally by the Iraqi government's refusal to destroy its weapons of mass destruction, which had been a condition of the ending of the first Iraq war in 1991. The French and German governments argued that United Nations weapons inspectors should be allowed to carry through with their work and determine if in fact Saddam Hussein possessed weapons that violated the conditions imposed in 1991. The refusal by these governments, as well as several other formerly reliable U.S. allies, to support the war was a major embarrassment for the Bush administration. It gave added credibility to the opponents of the war both within the United States and around the world.

The decision by France and Germany to refuse to join the U.S. invasion of Iraq may have stemmed more from calculations of narrow political interests than from any concerns about the morality of the war, but the outcome from the standpoint of the United States was the same. It now cannot count on the support of its European allies in its military actions around the world. While such support would have mattered little in the initial invasion, if the war in Iraq turns into a lengthy guerilla war, the United States will miss the help that could

---

[45] M. Marmot, *The Status Syndrome: How Social Standing Affects Our Health and Longevity* (New York: Times Books, 2004).

have been provided by these allies in shouldering the burden of the occupation, both in terms of troops on the ground and funds to cover the cost of the war. In addition, if participation in the occupation makes countries a target for terrorist attack, there will be an important divergence of interests between the U.S. allies that remain part of the occupation force and those that refuse to participate.[46]

It is also important to note that the ability of the United States to project force elsewhere in the world will be seriously limited as long as it remains bogged down in the occupation of Iraq. The Iraq war is a substantial strain on country's military resources. Given the current size of the military, a second engagement of comparable magnitude would almost certainly require a draft to ensure enough personnel. Reinstalling the military draft would be extremely unpopular, and any administration would be very reluctant to do it.

Although there are important divisions within Europe that limit the ability of the European Union to act as an independent political force in the world, there are clearly substantial pressures in this direction. The decision of European governments to embrace the Kyoto agreement, which caps greenhouse gas emissions, was a response to powerful domestic environmental movements. When the Bush administration unambiguously declared a lack of interest in such an agreement, the European governments were effectively forced to move ahead on their own. There have been similar pressures in Europe to pursue other international arrangements that have excluded the United States. European governments have signed treaties on a wide range issues – treaties prohibiting discrimination against women, banning land mines, and enabling the prosecution of war crimes – to which the United States has opted not to be a party. European governments, along with the governments of other wealthy countries, have been far more willing to contribute to development aid than the United States. In fact, the European Union set a target of contributing 0.7 percent of their GDP annually to foreign aid for the world's poorest countries by 2015. Current U.S. spending on aid is just over 0.1 percent.

---

[46] In March 2004, there was a terrorist attack against Spain that killed 191 people in a Madrid subway. This was generally believed to be a response to Spain's participation in the occupation of Iraq. Three days later, the Spanish electorate voted in a government that pledged to remove Spain's troops, although part of the motivation for this vote was the fact that the government in power had not been truthful in reporting about the perpetrators of the bombing.

In all of these cases, there is probably much more agreement between the U.S. government and the governments of other wealthy countries than is indicated by their stands on these issues. For example, the European governments that signed the Kyoto agreement do not take their commitments to this treaty as seriously as they do their commitments on tariff reductions under the World Trade Organization or restrictions from other agreements governing business commitments. However, the European governments that have made commitments on environmental regulations, foreign aid, and other issues have done so because of public pressure. Popular pressure could force European governments to break more sharply with the United States in the future, even if the heads of these governments would prefer to defer to the leadership of the United States.

The loss of U.S. influence in the world is perhaps nowhere more striking than in Latin America. Ever since its rise as an industrial power at the beginning of the twentieth century, the United States has played an enormous role in steering events in Latin America. This has been primarily due to its economic importance as the main consumer of raw material exports from the region and the main supplier of capital and manufactured goods. In addition, the United States has frequently been willing to intervene militarily on behalf of its interests, either directly, as when it occupied Haiti and Nicaragua in the early decades of the last century, or indirectly, as when it supported coups in countries such as Guatemala and Chile.

In the period since 1980, the United States has publicly supported the transition of most countries in the region from military dictatorships to democracies. However, it has also supported the "Washington Consensus" economic policies that have proved disastrous for the region. Per capita income in Latin America grew by 80 percent in the years from 1960 to 1979. By comparison, per capita income grew by just 15 percent in the last quarter century. This growth failure has meant that these countries have made very little progress in alleviating poverty and increasing living standards since 1980, in contrast to the prior twenty years, during which there were substantial gains for large segments of the population in many Latin American countries.

One result of this growth failure has been that democratically elected governments across the region are increasingly rejecting the direction being given them either directly by the United States or indirectly through its control of the International Monetary Fund (IMF) and the World Bank. Among the most visible symbols of this rejection is the lack of interest that many countries of the region have for the Free Trade of the Americas Agreement under which the United States seeks to extend the conditions imposed on Mexico through NAFTA. In the same vein, Argentina openly flouted long-established rules of international finance when it defaulted on its debt in 2001 and then offered creditors repayment of just twenty-five cents on the dollar more than three years later. Although the IMF objected strenuously to this treatment of creditors, it was not able to force a settlement on Argentina that would be more generous to its creditors.

Political leaders throughout the region have gained popularity by taking strong positions against the United States. This has been most apparent in the case of Venezuela, whose president, Hugo Chavez, was the target of coup attempt in 2002 that clearly had the sympathy (if not active support) of the Bush administration.[47] Governments have also come to power in Brazil, Argentina, Uruguay, and most recently Bolivia by explicitly campaigning against the model of development promoted by the United States. Even in Mexico, there has been a strong backlash due to the economic hardships that followed in the wake of the NAFTA agreement. The runner-up in Mexico's 2006 presidential race was a strong critic of NAFTA and the neo-liberal path of development advocated by the United States. He lost by less than 0.5 percentage points according to an official count that was widely questioned.

In 2004 and 2005, several Latin American countries actively sought to deepen their political and economic ties with China, and improved relations will presumably imply a reduction in U.S. influence in the region. Given the projected growth path of China's economy, this switch is understandable. While the U.S. import market is virtually certain to shrink over the next decade, the volume of China's annual imports is likely to increase by at least $200 billion in the same period.[48] Given China's growing need for a wide variety of agricultural products and raw materials, it is virtually certain that a much larger share of Latin America's trade will be directed toward Asia. In addition, China

[47] The Bush administration issued false public statements about the set of events surrounding the military coup at the time it took place. Documents later revealed that it had been in contact with groups plotting the coup and knew of their plans.

[48] D. Baker and M. Weisbrot, *Fool's Gold: Projections of the U.S. Import Market* (Washington, DC: Center for Economic and Policy Research, 2004), http://www.cepr.net/publications/trade_2004_01_08.pdf.

in 2005 was a major supplier of capital to the world, in contrast to the United States, which was a huge net borrower.

The position of the United States as a net borrower of capital is likely to leave it vulnerable to the actions of other economic powers in the years ahead. Foreign investors have accumulated more than $12.5 trillion worth of U.S. financial assets – land, buildings, shares of stock, and corporate and government bonds.[49] This amount is larger than the GDP of the United States. Most of this wealth is held by private investors because they anticipate a good return. However, at the end of 2004, foreign central banks already held $1.9 trillion of U.S. financial assets. The Japanese and Chinese central banks (including Hong Kong) together held almost $1 trillion in U.S. assets. These central banks purchased U.S. financial assets either to hold dollars as foreign reserves or out of a desire to prop up the value of the dollar relative to their own currencies.

Foreign central banks will not discard their dollar assets for frivolous reasons, but it is possible to imagine economic or political situations in which it would prove desirable for them to dump their dollars, or at least gradually cut back their holdings. This could have serious consequences for the U.S. economy. A sharp reduction in foreign holdings of U.S. financial assets could lead to large fall in the value of the dollar against other major currencies. This in turn would lead to large increases in import prices, as it will take more dollars to buy the same amount of imported goods. Higher import prices imply higher inflation in the United States and almost certainly an increase in interest rates. The net effect of this chain of events would almost certainly be a recession and quite likely a very severe one. It is not necessary to work through all the economic implications of a decision by foreign central banks to reduce their dollar holdings in order to see that their vast holdings of dollar assets have given these countries an important potential source of leverage with the United States.

Remarkably, U.S. foreign policy continues to be designed with little appreciation of the country's changed role in the world. While foreign policy analysts routinely weigh the potential military responses of

---

[49] These figures refer to gross holdings by foreigners of U.S. assets at the end of 2004. The net number, which subtracts the value of U.S. holdings of foreign assets, was $2.5 trillion. E. Nguyen, "The International Investment Position of the United States at Yearend: 2004," *Survey of Current Business*, July 2005, 30–9. http://bea.gov/bea/ARTICLES/2005/07July/0705_IIP_WEB.pdf.

various countries to U.S. actions, there is almost no recognition of the fact that many countries also have the potential to inflict substantial economic damage on the United States in the event that relations turn hostile.

There also is very little awareness of the extent to which the relative economic standing of the United States has changed in the world over the last quarter century. Based on purchasing power parity measures of GDP (the measures that most economists view as the best basis for cross-country comparisons of economic output), the size of India's economy in 2005 was 30 percent of the size of the U.S. economy,[50] and the size of China's economy was approximately 65 percent of the size of the U.S. economy.[51] Given the projected growth paths of the economies of these three countries, the size of China's economy will exceed the size of the U.S. economy in little more than a decade, and the size of India's economy will be approximately 40 percent of the size of the U.S. economy in 2015. As the economies of China and India catch up to and surpass the U.S. economy, it is virtually inevitable that the political power of these countries in international affairs will rise relative to that of the United States, as will their military power. Yet, foreign policy planners largely assume that the United States will be the preeminent world power for the indefinite future.

This misperception of the future standing of the United States in the world was perhaps best demonstrated by an article that appeared in *Foreign Affairs*, the nation's most influential foreign policy journal, in the summer of 2004. This article, "A Global Power Shift in the

---

[50] The GDP data for India and China use the 2000 estimate for purchasing power parity GDP (combining China and Hong Kong) from the Penn World Tables version 6.1 (available at http://datacentre.chass.utoronto.ca/pwt/) and project forward the growth rate of GDP from Goldman Sachs ("Dreaming with the BRICS: The Path to 2050" [New York: Goldman Sachs, 2004], http://www.gs.com/insight/research/reports/report6.html). The estimates for growth for the U.S. GDP are taken from the Congressional Budget Office, *The Budget and Economic Outlook 2006–2015* (2005). Purchasing power parity GDP evaluates the goods and services produced in different countries at a common set of prices.

[51] China's government released new data at the end of 2005 indicating that its economy was 17 percent larger than previously reported ("That Blur, It's China Moving Up in the Pack," *New York Times*, December 21, 2005, C1). While there is clearly a great deal of uncertainty about the size of China's economy, this revision indicates that the size of China's economy could already have been close to 80 percent of the size of the U.S. economy by the end of 2005. If it grows at its projected 7 percent annual rate, China's economy could equal the U.S. economy in size by 2012.

Making," noted that China's size and rapid pace of economic growth implied that its economy would soon be larger than Germany's economy and that by 2020 China's economy would be larger than Japan's.[52] The author, as well as the editors, apparently failed to realize that the article was using the wrong measure of GDP for the sort of comparisons it was making. At the time the article was written, China's economy was already twice the size of Germany's economy and considerably larger than Japan's economy as well. While the article was right to call attention to the imminent shift of power to China (and India), the shift was far more advanced than the author or subsequent commentators realized.

[52] J. Hoge, "A Global Power Shift in the Making," *Foreign Affairs*, July–August 2004, http://www.foreignaffairs.org/20040701facomment83401-p0/james-f-hoge-jr/a-global-power-shift-in-the-making.html.

Epilogue: Different Directions, Missed Opportunities

History does not offer second chances, but it can nonetheless be informative to ask whether over the last quarter century the United States could have chosen a different path than the one it actually pursued. The election of 1980 was a major turning point for the United States, as the Reagan presidency reversed many of the key trends of the postwar period. Reagan administration policies substantially weakened union power and undermined the bargaining position of less-educated workers. They also limited and partially reversed the growth of the welfare state.

Internationally, the Reagan administration pushed the United States in a more unilateralist direction. Rather than trying to construct an international institutional framework that might constrain U.S. power in some ways but could ultimately protect U.S. interests, the Reagan administration largely pursued a go-it-alone strategy. This is perhaps best exemplified by its determination to overthrow the Nicaraguan government, an enterprise in which it was unable to enlist the open support of any major ally. The United States has moved further along this unilateralist path in the years since Reagan left office.

The question is whether a different direction was possible. Most immediately, it was not inconceivable that Carter would have been reelected. The polls indicated that it would be a close race until the final few weeks before the election. Certainly if President Carter had managed to arrange for an October celebration on the White House lawn with the newly freed hostages from Iran, there would have been a very good chance that he would have been reelected. In this sense, it is easy to imagine an alternative scenario in which the Reagan presidency never took place.

At the same time, Reagan was responding to real pressures in the economy and the political structure. There was certainly strong political support for much of Reagan's agenda, in both domestic and international affairs, before he took office. For example, the push to deregulate many major industries, such as airlines and trucking, began under Carter. Labor unions complained about hostility from employers and the difficulty it created for organizing drives before Reagan came into office. In the same vein, the percentage of capital gains income that was subject to taxation was reduced from 50 percent to 40 percent in 1978, a tax cut that almost exclusively benefited the wealthy. And Paul Volcker was appointed as Federal Reserve Board chairman by Jimmy Carter explicitly because he was expected to take a hard line on inflation.

Internationally, Carter had already begun a military buildup in his last two years in office. He was very displeased with the Nicaraguan revolution and went to considerable lengths to keep the Sandinistas from coming to power. If it had been possible to sustain the shah in Iran without a large-scale U.S. military commitment, it is likely that Carter would have done so, even though the shah's rule was clearly opposed by the vast majority of Iranians.

These are important points to keep in mind – it would be wrong to imagine that Reagan's policies had no antecedents in the prior administration. At the same time, he clearly took these policies much further than President Carter would have, or than any other Republican who might plausibly have been elected president at the time. Reagan was willing to be confrontational in ways that his predecessors had not been – perhaps the most visible example of this was his firing of the air traffic controllers in his first months in office. As a result, his policies had a large and lasting impact on the country in a wide variety of areas.

Again, although recognizing that the past cannot be changed, we can ask how the quarter century has prepared the United States to confront the problems it will face in the future. On this score, the answer is not very positive. The path pursued by the United States over this quarter century is not sustainable on economic, political, and environmental grounds. The political system in the United States is largely structured so that it can be oblivious to the long-term costs of public policies. Those who try to raise such concerns are systematically excluded from public debate.

The logic of exclusion is essentially this: the media opts to ignore any long-term problems, and those who control the media justify their neglect by saying that there is little public interest in them. Since most of the public is almost completely ignorant of these problems (because they are not often mentioned in news reports), it is in fact true that there is little public interest. As a result, many of the most important problems facing the country are almost never discussed.

On the economic front, the United States faces two unsustainable trends, the cost of its health care system and its trade deficit. There has been virtually no discussion of either in national political debates. In the case of the U.S. health care system, the per person cost is already more than twice the average for other rich countries, yet the United States ranks at the bottom in terms of life expectancy and other health care outcomes. These simple facts would probably come as a great surprise to even most highly educated people in the United States.

Furthermore, the gap in health care costs continues to grow, as costs in the United States are rising more rapidly than in other wealthy countries. This gap in costs will have greater consequences as the country ages. Since people older than age sixty-five have far higher health care costs than younger people, the costs of the health care system will impose a much greater burden on the country when the baby boom cohort reaches its retirement years.

Most politicians have been reluctant to say anything about the cost of the health care system, and those who have tried to bring the issue to the fore have been almost completely shut out of national debate.[1] There are very powerful interests, specifically the insurance industry, the pharmaceutical industry, and the doctors' organizations, that have worked actively to oppose any major overhaul of the U.S. health care system. Thus far, they have been successful.

---

[1] For example, in the 2004 presidential campaign, there were three Democratic contenders who did advocate a plan for a universal Medicare system, which could have gone far toward containing health care costs. In rare articles, the *New York Times* and the *Washington Post* discussed the substance of the health care proposals put forward by the presidential candidates after a forum devoted to the topic ("Other Candidates Again Target Dean," *Washington Post*, October 16, 2003, A4, and "Democrats Focus on Health Plans at Iowa Forum," *New York Times*, October 16, 2003, A25). Neither article included any discussion of the merits of a universal Medicare system. While the candidates who put forward these proposals were regarded as "minor" candidates, this was the judgment of the media, not the voters, since no votes had yet been cast at the time of this forum.

A similar story can be told about the trade deficit. The basic story of the trade deficit is relatively simple; it is taught in most introductory economics courses. A trade deficit is financed by borrowing money from abroad. The deficit allows the country to enjoy a higher living standard for a period of time, but at the cost of a lower standard of living at some point in the future, when it is necessary to start paying interest on the money borrowed. In this sense, the trade deficit is similar to a budget deficit – the country can spend more than it taxes for a period of time, but at some point it will eventually have to bring spending and taxes more closely in line. In the case of a trade deficit, the country will have to face the interest burden on the money it borrowed when it was running a deficit.

The cause of a trade deficit is also fairly straightforward: a high dollar makes imports cheap to people in the United States, leading U.S. consumers to buy imported goods rather than domestic goods. At the same time, a high dollar makes U.S. exports expensive for people in other countries, causing them to buy less of them.

Whereas the budget deficit has been an issue in political debates, the much larger trade deficit has been almost invisible. (The Congressional Budget Office projected a budget deficit for fiscal 2006 of $337 billion for the unified deficit and $518 billion for the on-budget deficit, which includes borrowing from Social Security.[2] By comparison, the trade deficit was running at a $784 billion annual rate in the fourth quarter of 2005 and was rising rapidly.) Virtually all economists agree that at some point in the not very distant future the United States will have to move its trade deficit close to zero. Given the current size of the trade deficit, moving to balanced trade would have roughly the same impact on living standards as a $784 billion increase in annual tax collections (approximately 6 percent of GDP).

The adjustment from large trade deficits to near balanced trade will not be easy under any circumstances. It is likely to be associated with higher inflation, higher interest rates, and quite possibly a steep recession. The fact that the country has taken no steps toward preparing for this adjustment – or, more importantly, did little to prevent the deficit from getting this large in the first place – was a major failing of the political system.

---

[2] Congressional Budget Office, *Economic and Budget Outlook: 2007–2016* (Washington, DC: U.S. Government Printing Office, 2006), summary table 1, http://www.cbo.gov/ftpdocs/70xx/doc7027/01-26-BudgetOutlook.pdf.

The second major area where the political system has failed is in building an international structure in which the interests of the United States can be protected when it is not the world's preeminent economic and military power. There had been efforts dating back before the end of World War II to create institutional structures, such as the United Nations, that would ensure that the interests of all countries were protected regardless of their economic or military power. While the United States was originally at the forefront in promoting the development of these structures, it become much less supportive when it became clear that these international structures could not always be counted on to support U.S. interests. In the last quarter century in particular, the United States has backed away from its commitment to the United Nations and other international institutions, preferring to act unilaterally, pulling along whatever allies it could on ad hoc basis. The invasion of Iraq, accomplished with the support of the "Coalition of the Willing," provides the clearest example of such unilateralism.

Regardless of the desirability of this manner of conduct, it is only feasible as long as the United States is the preeminent military and economic power in the world. The leadership of both major parties has conducted the debate over foreign policy issues as though U.S. pre-eminence can be assumed for the indefinite future. This assumption reflects a failure to properly read basic economic data. Using a purchasing power parity measure of GDP (the measure that economists usually apply to international comparisons), China's economy was already close to two-thirds as big as the U.S. economy in 2005.[3]

Furthermore, China's economy had been growing at the rate of more than 7 percent annually for two decades, and in recent years it has grown at more than a 9 percent annual rate. This growth path implies that China's economy may first pass the U.S. economy in size in less than a decade. The time in which the United States enjoys unchallenged economic preeminence is clearly very limited. Furthermore, it is reasonable to believe that military power will follow economic power. If it so chooses, China will be able to support a military that is comparable in size and strength to the U.S. military in the not very distant future.

---

[3] Large upward revisions to Chinese economic data at the end of 2005 indicate that the size of its economy actually may be close to 80 percent of the size of the U.S. economy ("That Blur, It's China Moving Up in the Pack," *New York Times*, December 21, 2005, C1).

Along the same lines, India's economy is currently close to one-third as big as the U.S. economy measured on a purchasing power parity basis. It is projected to equal the U.S. economy in size by 2038.[4] In the not very distant future, India will also be a serious economic and possibly military rival to the United States.

Whether these ascendant countries will accommodate the interests of the United States remains to be seen. The likelihood that they would respect the interests of the United States might have been greater if the United States had sought to create genuine international structures that had some real autonomy and legitimacy. Given its unrivaled strength in the years following the collapse of the Soviet Union, it was uniquely positioned to try to erect such a system. It may regret not having gone this route in the decades ahead.

The third area in which the United States political leadership has largely failed to address pressing problems is climate change. There is little serious dispute among scientists that climate change is taking place at a rapid pace and that human emissions are an important cause. The consequences of climate change will include not only the destruction of habitats for thousands of species but very concrete weather-related damage, like the devastation that Hurricane Katrina inflicted on the Gulf Coast in the summer of 2005.

A serious debate on this topic would include concrete efforts to try to quantify all the forms of weather-related damage that could be caused by climate change, compared with the costs of measures designed to limit the impact of climate change by reducing emissions of greenhouse gases. Although there have been some studies that have attempted preliminary assessments of these costs and benefits, they have been virtually invisible in the policy debate on the issue.

The Kyoto agreement was ostensibly deadlocked (from the U.S. vantage point) over the noninvolvement of the developing countries. Here, too, the discussion never proceeded along a serious path. The stated position of both the Clinton and the Bush administrations was that developing countries should also be subject to emission ceilings.

---

[4] The growth projections for China's and India's GDP use the 2000 estimate for purchasing power parity GDP (combing China and Hong Kong) from the Penn World Tables (table 6.1) and project forward the GDP for both countries using the growth projections from Goldman Sachs ("Dreaming with the BRICS: The Path to 2050" [New York: Goldman Sachs, 2004], http://www.gs.com/insight/research/reports/report6.html).

The agreement that was approved in 2001 only placed ceilings on the emissions of the wealthy countries.

Obviously, the developing countries never would agree to rules that held them to per capita emissions levels that were a small fraction of the emissions levels of the rich countries. This would seriously impede, if not actually prevent, economic development. Such constraints were especially hard to justify because the emissions of the rich countries are the primary cause of climate change. Any realistic solution to the problem of climate change would require payments from rich countries to poor countries to get them to restrict their emissions growth path, while rich countries would have to achieve absolute reductions in emissions.[5]

It is possible that the public would decide that the costs of restricting emissions are simply too great and that is better to deal with the consequences of more frequent and destructive hurricanes and other implications of global warming. These consequences may include not only damage to the economies of the rich countries but also, in a world not dominated by the United States, compensation paid by the current group of rich countries to victims of global warming in the developing world. This could mean, for example, that heavily populated low-lying countries such as Bangladesh could demand compensation for weather-related damage and loss of life that is plausibly linked to climate change. Of course, any discussion of how the world might cope with the effects of climate change twenty to thirty years in the future must necessarily be highly speculative. However, climate change is an issue that demands this sort of speculation, since it can only be addressed through long-term planning. The political system in the United States, including the national media, has not made space for such long-term planning.

A reasonable assessment of any political system must take into account its ability to address the problems that it has created for itself. By this measure, it does not look like the political system of the United States performed very well in the quarter century from 1980 to 2005. Of course, we will be better positioned to assess this record when we have a few more years of hindsight on which to base an evaluation.

[5] See J. Barrett and D. Baker, *Cleaning Up the Kyoto Protocol* (Washington, DC: Economic Policy Institute, 1999).

Bibliography

Alvarez, M., and Hall, T. *Point, Click and Vote: The Future of Internet Voting.* Washington, DC: Brookings Institution, 2004.

American Association of Medical Colleges. *Women in U.S. Academic Medicine Statistics, 2002–2003.* Washington, DC: American Association of Medical Colleges, 2005. http://www.aamc.org/members/wim/statistics/stats03/table1.pdf.

American Bar Association, Commission on Women in the Profession. *A Current Glance at Women in the Law.* Washington, DC: American Bar Association, 2005. http://www.abanet.org/women/ataglance.pdf.

Andrews, R. *Managing the Environment, Managing Ourselves: A History of Environmental Policy in America.* New Haven, CT: Yale University Press, 1999.

Andriote, J. *Victory Deferred: How AIDS Changed Gay Life in America.* Chicago: University of Chicago Press, 1999.

Arnett, P. *Live from the Battlefield: From Vietnam to Baghdad, 35 Years in the World's War Zones.* New York: Touchstone, 1995.

Atkinson, R. *Crusade: The Untold Story of the Persian Gulf War.* New York: Houghton Mifflin Books, 1994.

Bagdikian, B. *The New Media Monopoly.* Boston: Beacon Press, 2004.

Baily, N., and Gordon, R. "The Productivity Slowdown, Measurement Issues, and the Explosion of Computer Power." *Brookings Papers on Economic Activity* 2 (1998): 465–521.

Baker, D. "Bull Market Keynesianism." *American Prospect*, January–February 1999.

———. *Double Bubble: The Implications of the Over-valuation of the Stock Market and the Dollar.* Washington, DC: Center for Economic and Policy Research, 2000.

———. *The Effect of Mis-measured Inflation on Wage Growth.* Washington, DC: Economic Policy Institute, 1998.

———. *The Run-up in Home Prices: Is It Real, or Is It Another Bubble?* Washington, DC: Center for Economic and Policy Research, 2002. http://www.cepr.net/publications/housing_2002_08.pdf.

Baker, D., and Rosnick, D. *Will a Bursting Bubble Bother Bernanke?* Washington, DC: Center for Economic and Policy Research, 2005. http://www.cepr.net/publications/housing_bubble_2005_11.pdf.

Baker, D., and Weisbrot, M. *Social Security: The Phony Crisis.* Chicago: University of Chicago Press, 1999.

———. *Fool's Gold: Projections of the U.S. Import Market.* Washington, DC: Center for Economic and Policy Research, 2004. http://www.cepr.net/publications/trade_2004_01_08.pdf.

Basu, S., Fernald, J., Oulton, N., and Srinivasan, S. "The Case of the Missing Productivity Growth, or Does Information Technology Explain Why Productivity Accelerated in the United States but Not in the United Kingdom?" In *NBER Macroeconomics Annual 2003*, edited by M. Getler and K. Rogoff, 9–63. Cambridge, MA: MIT Press, 2003.

Bell, C. *The Reagan Paradox: American Foreign Policy in the 1980s.* New Brunswick, NJ: Rutgers University Press, 1989.

Bennet, W., and Paletz, D., eds. *Taken by Storm: The Media, Public Opinion, and U.S. Foreign Policy in the Gulf War.* Chicago: University of Chicago Press, 1994.

Bernstein, J., and Baker, D. *The Benefits of Full Employment.* Washington, DC: Economic Policy Institute, 2004.

Bertram, E. *Drug War Politics.* Berkeley, CA: University of California Press, 1996.

Birdsall, N., Rodrick, D., and Subramaman, A. "How to Help Poor Countries?" *Foreign Affairs* 84, no. 4 (2005): 136–52.

Blank, R., Dabady, M., and Citro, C., eds. *Measuring Racial Discrimination.* Washington, DC: National Academies Press, 2004.

Blinder, A. *Economic Policy and the Great Stagflation.* New York: Academic Press, 1981.

Blinder, A., and Baumol, W. *Macroeconomics: Principles and Policies.* Mason, OH: Thomson South-Western, 2005.

Blinder, A., and Yellen, J. *The Fabulous Decade: Macroeconomic Lessons from the 1990s.* New York: Century Foundation, 2001.

———. "The Fabulous Decade: Macroeconomic Lessons from the 1990s." In *The Roaring Nineties*, edited by A. Krueger and R. Solow, 91–156. New York: Russell Sage Foundation and Century Foundation, 2002.

Blix, H. *Disarming Iraq: The Search for Weapons of Mass Destruction.* London: Reed Elsevier, 2004.

Bosworth, B., and Burtless, G. "Effects of Tax Reform on Labor Supply, Savings, and Investment." *Journal of Economic Perspectives* (Winter 1992): 3–25.

Boushey, H. *Are Women Opting Out: Debunking the Myth.* Washington, DC: Center for Economic and Policy Research, 2005. http://www.cepr. net/publications/opt_out_2005_11.pdf.

Boushey, H., Rosnick, D., and Baker, D. *Gender Bias in the Recovery? Declining Employment Rates for Women in the 21st Century.* Washington, DC: Center for Economic and Policy Research, 2005. http://www.cepr.net/ publications/labor_markets_2005_08_29.pdf.

Bowles, S., Gordon, D., Bell, D., and Kristol, I., eds. *The Crisis in Economic Theory.* New York: Basic Books, 1981.

Bronfenbrenner, K. "Employer Behavior in Certification Elections and First Contract Campaigns: Implications for Labor Law Reform." In *Restoring the Promise of American Labor Law,* edited by S. Friedman, 75–89. Ithaca, NY: ILR Press, 1994.

Brzoska, M., and Pearson, F. *Arms and Warfare: Escalation, De-escalation, and Negotiation.* Columbia, SC: University of South Carolina Press, 1994.

Buckley, K. *Panama.* New York: Touchstone, 1992.

Bureau of Economic Analysis. *2005 Annual Revision of the National Income and Product Accounts.* Washington, DC: U.S. Government Printing Office, 2005.

Buzawa, E., and Buzawa, C. *Domestic Violence: The Criminal Justice Response.* Thousand Oaks, CA: Sage Publications, 2003.

Canon, L. *President Reagan: The Role of a Lifetime.* New York: Public Affairs Press, 2000.

Chambliss, J. *Power, Politics, and Crime.* Boulder, CO: Westview Press, 2000.

Chernick, H. *Wide Cast for Safety Net: Over Time Middle Class, as Well as Poor, Rely on Entitlement Help.* Washington, DC: Economic Policy Institute, 1995.

Clinton, W. *My Life.* New York: Knopf, 2004.

Coll, S. *Ghost Wars: The Secret History of the CIA, Afghanistan, and Bin Laden, from the Soviet Invasion to September 10, 2001.* New York: Penguin Books, 2004.

Conte, A. *Sexual Harassment in the Workplace: Law and Practice.* New York: Panel Publishers, 2000.

Cooley, J. *Unholy Wars: Afghanistan, America, and International Terrorism.* London: Pluto Press, 2002.

Crowley, J. *The Politics of Child Support in America.* Cambridge: Cambridge University Press, 2003.

Currie, E. *Crime and Punishment in America.* New York: Owl Books, 1998.

D'Emillo, J. *Making Trouble: Essays on Gay History, Politics, and the University.* London: Routledge, 1992.

DeNavas-Walt, C., Proctor, B., and Lee, C. *Income, Poverty and Health Insurance Coverage in the United States: 2004.* U.S. Census Bureau Current Population

Reports P60–229. Washington, DC: U.S. Government Printing Office, 2005. http://www.census.gov/prod/2005pubs/p60–229.pdf.

Denison, E. *Accounting for Slower Economic Growth.* Washington, DC: Brookings Institution, 1979.

Donner, F. *Protectors of Privilege: Red Squads and Police Repression in Urban America.* Berkeley, CA: University of California Press, 1992.

Eekhoff, J. *Competition Policy in Europe.* Berlin: Springer-Verlag, 2004.

Ehrlich, R. *Waging Nuclear Peace: The Technology and Politics of Nuclear Weapons.* Albany, NY: SUNY Press, 1985.

Epstein, C. *Women in Law.* Champaign, IL: University of Illinois, 1993.

Epstein, S. *Impure Science: AIDS, Activism, and Politics of Knowledge.* Berkeley, CA: University of California Press, 1992.

European Union. *Activities of the European Union, Summaries of Legislation: Social Charter.* 2005. http://europa.eu.int/scadplus/leg/en/cha/c10107.htm.

Feagin, J., Vera, H., and Batur, P. *White Racism.* London: Routledge, 2001.

Federation of European Employers. *Industrial Relations Across Europe, 2004.* London: Federation of European Employers, 2004. http://www.fedee.com/condits.html.

Ferree, M., and Hess, B. *Controversy and Coalition: The New Feminist Movement Across Four Decades of Change.* New York: Routledge and Kegan Paul, 2000.

Freeman, R., Katz, L., and Borjas, G. "How Much Do Immigration and Trade Affect Labor Market Outcomes?" *Brookings Papers on Economic Activity* 1 (1997): 1–90.

Friedman, N. *Desert Victory: The War for Kuwait.* Annapolis, MD: Naval Institute Press, 1991.

Galbraith, J. *Created Unequal: The Crisis in American Pay.* Chicago: University of Chicago Press, 2000.

Gale, W., and Porter, S. *An Economic Evaluation of the Economic Growth and Tax Reconciliation Act of 2001.* Washington, DC: Brookings Institution, 2002. http://www.brookings.edu/views/articles/gale/200203.pdf.

Garthoff, R. *Detente and Confrontation: American-Soviet Relations from Nixon to Reagan.* Rev. ed. Washington, DC: Brookings Institute, 1994.

Gelbspan, R. *Break-ins, Death Threats and the FBI: The Covert War Against the Central America Movement.* Boston: South End Press, 1991.

Gill, I., Packard, T., and Yermo, J. *Keeping the Promise of Social Security in Latin America.* Washington, DC: Stanford University Press and the World Bank, 2005.

Glaze, L., and Palla, S. "Probation and Parole in the United States, 2004." *Bureau of Justice Statistics Bulletin,* November 2005. http://www.ojp.usdoj.gov/bjs/pub/pdf/ppus04.pdf.

Goldfield, M. *The Decline of Organized Labor in the United States.* Chicago: University of Chicago Press, 1989.

Goldman Sachs. "Dreaming with the BRICS: The Path to 2050." New York: Goldman Sachs, 2004. http://www.gs.com/insight/research/reports/report6.html.

Green, J., Rozell, M., and Wilcox, W. *The Christian Right in American Politics: Marching to the Millennium.* Washington, DC: Georgetown University Press, 2003.

Greenspan, A. *Outlook for the Federal Budget and Implications for Fiscal Policy.* Committee on the Budget, U.S. Senate, January 25, 2001.

Greider, W. *Secrets of the Temple: How the Federal Reserve Runs the Country.* New York: Simon and Schuster, 1987.

Guatemala's Historical Clarification Commission. *Guatemala: Memory of Silence.* New York: United Nations, 1999. http://shr.aaas.org/guatemala/ceh/report/english/.

Hacker, J. *The Great Risk Shift: The New Economic Insecurity and What Can Be Done About It.* Oxford: Oxford University Press, 2005.

Hague, R. "The United States." In *Power and Policy in Liberal Democracies,* edited by M. Harrop, 95–119. Cambridge: Cambridge University Press, 1992.

Harris, D. *The Crisis: The President, the Prophet, and the Shah – 1979 and the Coming of Militant Islam.* New York: Little, Brown and Company, 2004.

Harrison, P., and Beck, A. "Prisoners in 2004," *Bureau of Justice Statistics Bulletin,* October 2005. http://www.ojp.usdoj.gov/bjs/pub/pdf/p04.pdf.

Heston, A., Summers, R., and Aten, B. *Penn World Table Version 6.1.* Philadelphia: Center for International Comparisons at the University of Pennsylvania (CICUP), 2002.

Hill, A., and Jordon, E., eds. *Race, Gender, and Power in America: The Legacy of the Hill-Thomas Hearings.* New York: Oxford University Press, 2005.

Hoge, J. "A Global Power Shift in the Making." *Foreign Affairs* 83, no. 4 (2004):2–7. http://www.foreignaffairs.org/20040701facomment83401-p0/james-f-hoge-jr/a-global-power-shift-in-the-making.html.

Horne, G. *From the Barrel of a Gun: The United States and the War Against Zimbabwe, 1965–1980.* Chapel Hill, NC: University of North Carolina Press, 2001.

Howell, D., ed. *Fighting Unemployment: The Limits of Free Market Orthodoxy.* New York: Oxford University Press, 2004.

Hufbauer, G., and Schott, J., eds. *NAFTA Revisited: Achievements and Challenges.* Washington, DC: Institute for International Economics, 2005.

Human Rights Watch, Americas, El Salvador. *El Salvador's Decade of Terror, 1981–1991: Human Rights Since the Assassination of Archbishop Romero.* New York: Human Rights Watch, 1991.

Hunt, D. *O. J. Simpson Facts and Fictions: News Rituals in the Construction of Reality.* New York: Cambridge University Press, 1999.

Inouye, D., and Hamilton, L., eds. *Iran-Contra Affair: Report of the Congressional Committees*. New York: Three Rivers Press, 1998.

International Lesbian and Gay Association-Europe. "Same-Sex Marriage and Partnership, Country-by-Country." 2005. http://www.ilga-europe. org/europe/issues/marriage_and_partnership/same_sex_marriage_and_ partnership_country_by_country.

Jacobsen, A., and Rosenfeld, M., eds. *The Longest Night: Perspective on Election 2000*. Berkeley, CA: University of California Press, 2002.

Johnson, H. *Sleepwalking Through History: America in the Reagan Years*. New York: W. W. Norton and Company, 2003.

Judah, T. *Kosovo: War and Revenge*. New Haven, CT: Yale University Press, 2002.

Kakar, M. *Afghanistan: The Soviet Invasion and the Afghan Response 1979–82*. Berkeley, CA: University of California Press, 1997.

Keating, D., and Hertzman, C., eds. *Developmental Health and the Wealth of Nations: Social, Biological, and Educational Dynamics*. New York: Guilford Press, 1999.

Keddie, N. *Modern Iran: Roots and Results of Revolution*. New Haven, CT: Yale University Press, 1993.

Keeble, J. *Out of the Channel: The Exxon Valdez Oil Spill in Prince William Sound*. Spokane, WA: Eastern Washington University Press, 1999.

Keen, L., and Goldberg, S. *Strangers to the Law: Gay People on Trial*. Ann Arbor, MI: University of Michigan Press, 2003.

Kellner, D. *Media Culture: Cultural Studies, Identity and Politics Between the Modern and the Postmodern*. London: Routledge, 1995.

Kennickell, A., Starr-McCluer, M., and Surette, B. "Recent Changes in U.S. Family Finances: Results from the 1998 Survey of Consumer Finances." *Federal Reserve Bulletin* (January 2000): 1–29.

Kenworthy, L. *Egalitarian Capitalism: Jobs, Incomes, and Growth in Affluent Countries*. New York: Russell Sage Foundation, 2004.

Khadduri, M., and Ghareeb, E. *War in the Gulf, 1990–91: The Iraq-Kuwait Conflict and Its Implications*. Oxford: Oxford University Press, 1997.

Kirkpatrick, J. *Legitimacy and Force: National and International Dimensions*. Somerset, NJ: Transactions Publishers, 1988.

Kornbluh, P., and Byrne, M., eds. *The Iran-Contra Scandal: The Declassified History*. New York: New Press, 1993.

Kryzanek, M. "The Grenada Invasion: Approaches to Understanding." In *United States Policy in Latin America: A Decade of Crisis and Challenge*, edited by J. Martz, 58–79. Omaha, NE: University of Nebraska Press, 1995.

LaFeber, W. *Inevitable Revolutions: The United States in Central America*. New York: W. W. Norton and Company, 1993.

LaLonde, R., Meltzer, B., and Weiler, P. "Hard Times for Unions: Another Look at the Significance of Employer Illegalities." *University of Chicago Law Review* 58 (1991): 953–1014.

MacArthur, J. *Second Front: Censorship and Propaganda in the 1991 Gulf War.* Berkeley, CA: University of California Press, 2004.

_____. *The Selling of "Free Trade": NAFTA, Washington, and the Subversion of American Democracy.* Berkeley, CA: University of California Press, 2001.

Magnus, R., Naby, E., and Rather, D. *Afghanistan: Mullah, Marx, and Mujahid.* Boulder, CO: Westview Press, 2002.

Maraniss, D. *First in His Class: A Biography of Bill Clinton.* New York: Touchstone, 1996.

Marmot, M. *The Status Syndrome: How Social Standing Affects Our Health and Longevity.* New York: Times Books, 2004.

McChesney, R. *The Problem of the Media: U.S. Communication Politics in the Twenty-First Century.* New York: Monthly Review Press, 2004.

Meerepol, M. *Surrender: How the Clinton Administration Completed the Reagan Revolution.* Ann Arbor, MI: University of Michigan Press, 2000.

Mishel, L., Bernstein, J., and Allegretto, S. *The State of Working America 2004/2005.* Ithaca, NY: Cornell University Press, 2005. http://www.bls.gov/news.release/pdf/union2.pdf.

National Research Council. *Evaluating Welfare Reform in an Era of Transition.* Washington, DC: National Academies Press, 2001.

Newspaper Association of America. *Daily Newspaper Readership Trend: Total Adults (1964–1997).* Vienna, VA: Newspaper Association of America, 2006. http://www.naa.org/marketscope/pdfs/Daily_National_Top50_64–97.pdf.

Nguyen, E. "The International Investment Position of the United States at Yearend 2004." *Survey of Current Business,* July 2005, 30–9. http://bea.gov/bea/ARTICLES/2005/07July/0705_IIP_WEB.pdf.

Olmstead, K. *Challenging the Secret Government: The Post-Watergate Investigations of the CIA and FBI.* Chapel Hill, NC: University of North Carolina Press, 1996.

Organisation for Economic Co-operation and Development. *Economic Policy Reforms: Going for Growth; Annex A: Structural Policy Indicators.* Paris: OECD, 2006. http://www.oecd.org/dataoecd/40/56/36014946.pdf.

_____. *Female Labor Force Participation: Past Trends and Main Determinants in OECD Countries.* Paris: OECD, 2004. http://www.oecd.org/dataoecd/25/5/31743836.pdf.

_____. *Trends in International Migration: 2001.* Paris: OECD, 2001. http://www.oecd.org/dataoecd/23/41/2508596.pdf.

Organisation for Economic Co-operation and Development. Development Center. *OECD Health Data, 1998.* Paris: OECD, 1998.

Oxley, H., and Martin, J. *Controlling Government Spending and Deficits: Trends in the 1980s and Prospects for the 1990s.* OECD Economic Studies no. 17. Paris, OECD, 1991. http://www.oecd.org/dataoecd/33/12/34259242.pdf.

Parsa, M. *Social Origins of the Iranian Revolution.* New Brunswick, NJ: Rutgers University Press, 1989.

Pastor, R. *Exiting the Whirlpool: U.S. Foreign Policy Toward Latin America and the Caribbean.* Boulder, CO: Westview Press, 2001.

Peoples, J. "Deregulation and the Labor Market." *Journal of Economic Perspectives* (Summer 1998): 111–30.

Peterson, P. *Gray Dawn: How the Coming Age Wave Will Transform American and the World.* New York: Crown, 1999.

———. *Running on Empty: How the Democratic and Republican Parties Are Bankrupting Our Future and What Americans Can Do About It.* New York: Farrar, Straus and Giroux, 2004.

———. *Will America Grow Up Before It Grows Old: How the Coming Social Security Crisis Threatens You, Your Family and Your Country.* New York: Random House, 1996.

Pew Research Center for the People and the Press. *Among Wealthy Nations . . . U.S. Stands Alone in Its Embrace of Religion.* Washington, DC: Pew Research Center, 2002. http://pewglobal.org/reports/pdf/167.pdf.

Physicians for Human Rights. *"Operation Just Cause": The Human Cost of Military Action in Panama.* Boston: Physicians for Human Rights, 1991.

Project for Excellence in Journalism. *The State of the News Media 2004.* Washington, DC: Journalism.org, 2004. http://www.stateofthenewsmedia.org/2004/index.asp.

Project for the New American Century. "How to Attack Iraq." Editorial. *Weekly Standard*, November, 16, 1998, 17–18.

Remnick, D. *Lenin's Tomb: The Last Days of the Soviet Empire.* New York: Vintage, 1994.

Riccucci, M. *Managing Diversity in Public Sector Workforces.* Boulder, CO: Westview Press, 2002.

Rochon, T., and Meyer, D., eds. *Coalitions and Political Movements: The Lessons of the Nuclear Freeze.* Boulder, CO: Lynne Rienner Publishers, 1997.

Rubin, R., and Weisberg, J. *In an Uncertain World: Tough Choices from Wall Street to Washington.* New York: Random House, 2003.

Sawhill, I., Haskins, R., and Weaver, R., eds. *Welfare Reform and Beyond: The Future of the Safety Net.* Washington, DC: Brookings Institution, 2003.

Sayigh, Y. *Armed Struggle and the Search for State: The Palestinian National Movement, 1949–1993.* Oxford: Oxford University Press, 2000.

Schaller, M. *Reckoning with Reagan: America and Its President in the 1980s.* Oxford: Oxford University Press, 1994.

Scott, P., and Marshall, J. *Cocaine Politics: Drugs, Armies and the CIA in Central America.* Berkeley, CA: University of California Press, 1991.

Shiller, R. *Irrational Exuberance.* Princeton, NJ: Princeton University Press, 2000.

———. *Irrational Exuberance.* 2nd ed. Princeton, NJ: Princeton University Press, 2005.

Smith, D. A. *Tax Crusaders and the Politics of Direct Democracy*. London: Routledge, 1998.

Smith, J. *The Cold War 1945–1991*. 2nd ed. Oxford: Blackwell Publishers, 1997.

Social Security Administration. *2005 Annual Report of the Board of Trustees of the Federal Old-Age and Survivors Insurance and Disability Insurance Trust Funds*. Washington, DC: U.S. Government Printing Office, 2005.

Solinger, R., ed. *Abortion Wars: A Half Century of Struggle 1950–2000*. Berkeley, CA: University of California Press, 1998.

Stahl, L. *Reporting Live*. New York: Touchstone Press, 1999.

Stephanopoulos, G. *All Too Human*. Boston: Back Bay Books, 2000.

Stiglitz, J. *Globalization and Its Discontents*. New York: Norton, 1990.

Sullivan, A., Sexton, T., and Sheffrin, F. *Property Taxes and Tax Revolts: The Legacy of Proposition 13*. Cambridge: Cambridge University Press, 1995.

Suny, G. *The Revenge of the Past: Nationalism, Revolution, and the Collapse of the Soviet Union*. Stanford, CA: Stanford University Press, 1993.

United Kingdom Pensions Commission. *Challenges and Choices: The First Report of the Pensions Commission*. London: Stationary Office, 2004. http://www.pensionscommission.org.uk/publications/2004/annrep/index.asp.

United Nations Commission on the Truth for El Salvador. *The Report of the United Nations Commission on the Truth for El Salvador*. New York: United Nations, 1993. http://www.hrw.org/reports/pdfs/e/elsalvdr/elsalv938.pdf.

U.S. Bureau of Economic Analysis. *2005 Annual Revision of the National Income and Product Accounts*. Washington, DC: U.S. Government Printing Office, 2005.

U.S. Census Bureau. *Historical Income Tables–Families*. Washington, DC: U.S. Government Printing Office, 2005. http://www.census.gov/hhes/www/income/histinc/f06w.html.

————. *Profile of General Demographic Characteristics for California*. Washington, DC: U.S. Government Printing Office, 2001. http://www.census.gov/Press-Release/www/2001/tables/dp_ca_2000.PDF.

————. *Statistical Abstract of the United States 1982*. Washington, DC: U.S. Government Printing Office, 1982.

————. *Statistical Abstract of the United States 1984*. Washington, DC: U.S. Government Printing Office, 1984.

————. *Statistical Abstract of the United States 1989*. Washington, DC: U.S. Government Printing Office, 1989.

————. *Statistical Abstract of the United States 1993*. Washington, DC: U.S. Government Printing Office, 1993.

————. *Statistical Abstract of the United States 2004*. Washington, DC: U.S. Government Printing Office, 2004.

————. *Statistical Abstract of the United States 2005*. Washington, DC: U.S. Government Printing Office, 2005.

U.S. Congress. House. Committee on Education and Labor. Subcommittee on Labor-Management Relations. *Oversight Hearings on the Subject "Has Labor Law Failed."* 98th Cong., 2d sess., June 1984.

U.S. Congressional Budget Office. *The Budget and Economic Outlook 2006– 2015*. Washington, DC: U.S. Government Printing Office, 2005.

————. *The Challenges Facing Federal Rental Assistance Programs*. Washington, DC: U.S. Government Printing Office, 1994. http://www.cbo.gov/ ftpdocs/48xx/doc4850/doc54.pdf.

————. *Changes in Participation in Means-Tested Programs*. Washington, DC: U.S. Government Printing Office, 2005. http://www.cbo.gov/ showdoc.cfm?index=6302&sequence=0.

————. "Effects on the 1981 Tax Act on the Distribution of Income and Taxes Paid." Staff working paper, Congressional Budget Office, Washington, DC, 1986. http://www.cbo.gov/ftpdocs/61xx/doc6173/ doc20a-Entire.pdf.

————. *Historical Effective Federal Tax Rates: 1979 to 2002*. Washington, DC: Congressional Budget Office, 2005. http://www.cbo.gov/Spreadsheet/ 6133_Tables.xls

————. *The Long-Term Budget Outlook*. Washington, DC: Congressional Budget Office, 2005. http://www.cbo.gov/ftpdocs/69xx/doc6982/12–15– LongTermOutlook.pdf.

U.S. Council of Economic Advisors. *1994 Economic Report of the President*. Washington, DC: U.S. Government Printing Office, 1994.

————. *2005 Economic Report of the President*. Washington, DC: U.S. Government Printing Office, 2005.

U.S. Department of Commerce. *National Income and Product Accounts*. Washington, DC: U.S. Government Printing Office, 2005.

U.S. Department of Justice. Immigration and Naturalization Service. *Statistical Yearbook of the Immigration and Naturalization Service (Fiscal Years 1980– 2000)*. Washington, DC: U.S. Government Printing Office, 1981–2001.

U.S. Federal Reserve. Board of Governors. *Flow of Funds Accounts of the United States, 1995–2005*. Washington, DC: U.S. Government Printing Office, 2005.

U.S. Office of Management and Budget. *The Budget for the Fiscal Year 2006, Historical Tables*. Washington, DC: U.S. Government Printing Office, 2005.

U.S. Treasury Department. Social Security Trustees. *2005 Annual Report of the Board of Trustees of the Federal Old-Age and Survivors Insurance and Disability Insurance Trust Funds*. Washington, DC: U.S. Government Printing Office, 2005.

————. *2006 Annual Report of the Board of Trustees of the Federal Old-Age and Survivors Insurance and Disability Insurance Trust Funds*. Washington, DC: U.S. Government Printing Office, 2006.

Vanden, H., and Prevost, G. *Democracy and Socialism in Sandinista Nicaragua.* Boulder, CO: Lynne Rienner Publishers, 1992.

Vogel, D. *Fluctuating Fortunes: The Political Power of Business in America.* New York: Basic Books, 1989.

Walker, T. *Nicaragua: Living in the Shadow of the Eagle.* Boulder, CO: Westview Press, 2003.

Waller, D. *Congress and the Nuclear Freeze: An Inside Look at the Politics of a Mass Movement.* Amherst, MA: University of Massachusetts Press, 1986.

Walsh, L. *Final Report of the Independent Counsel for the Iran/Contra Matters.* Vol. 1, *Investigations and Prosecutions.* Washington, DC: United States Court of Appeals for the District of Columbia Circuit, 1993. http://www.fas.org/irp/offdocs/walsh/.

———. *Firewall: The Iran-Contra Conspiracy and Cover-up.* New York: W. W. Norton and Company, 1998.

Wanniski, J. *The Way the World Works.* Parsippany, NJ: Polyconomics, 1989.

Weil, D. "OSHA: Beyond the Politics." *Frontline,* 2003. http://www.pbs.org/wgbh/pages/frontline/shows/workplace/osha/weil.html.

Weiner, R. *Live from Baghdad: Making Journalism History Behind the Lines.* New York: St. Martin's Press, 2002.

Weisskopf, T. *Beyond the Wasteland: A Democratic Alternative to Economic Decline.* New York: Anchor Press/Doubleday, 1983.

Weisskopf, T., Bowles, S., and Gordon, D. "Hearts and Minds: A Social Model of U.S. Productivity Growth." *Brookings Papers on Economic Activity* 2 (1983):381–441.

Wilcox, C. *Onward Christian Soldiers.* Boulder, CO: Westview Press, 1995.

Wilkinson, A., and Belli, M. *Everybody's Guide to the Law.* New York: Harper Collins, 2003.

Williamson, J. "What Washington Means by Policy Reform." In *Latin American Adjustment: How Much Has Happened?*, edited by J. Williamson, 5–20. Washington, DC: Institute for International Economics, 1990.

Woodward, R. *Central America: A Nation Divided.* New York: Oxford University Press, 1999.

———. *The Agenda: Inside the Clinton White House.* New York: Simon and Schuster, 1994.

World Bank. *Global Development Finance.* Washington, DC: World Bank, 2001.

Index